SOCIAL AND POLITICAL THOUGHTS OF AMBEDKAR

SOCIAL AND POLITICAL THOUGHTS OF AMBEDKAR

Dr. Anil Kumar Singh

CENTRUM PRESS
NEW DELHI-110002 (INDIA)

CENTRUM PRESS
H.O.: 4360/4, Ansari Road, Daryaganj,
New Delhi-110002 (India)
Tel: 23278000, 23261597, 23255577, 23286875

B.O.: No. 1015, Ist Main Road, BSK IIIrd Stage,
IIIrd Phase, IIIrd Block, Bangalore-560085 (INDIA)
Tel: 080-41723429

Email: centrumpress@gmail.com
Visit us at: www.centrumpress.com

Social and Political Thoughts of Ambedkar

First Edition, 2011

ISBN 978-93-80836-43-0

PRINTED IN INDIA

Printed at Mehra Offset Press, Delhi

Contents

Preface (*vii*)

1. Ancient India on Exhumation 1

2. Reformers and Their Fate 15

3. The Decline and Fall of Buddhism 61

4. The Triumph of Brahmanism: Regicide or the Birth of Counter-Revolution 101

5. Essays on the Bhagwat Gita : Philosophic Defence of Counter-Revolution: Krishna and His Gita 205

6. Brahmins Versus Kshatriyas 244

7. Shudras and the Counter—Revolution 270

Bibliography 281

Index 285

Bibliography

Index

Preface

Ambedkar launched numerous movements for Dalits. One of the memorable struggles of the Dalits was the Vaikkom Satyagraha in Travancore in Maharashtra, which asserted the right of the Dalits to worship in Hindu temples without hindrance. Another very significant movement was Mahad March to assert the rights of Dalits to take water from public watering places. Ambedkar organized the Dalit rally to assert their legal right to take water from the Chowdar tank. The Chowdar tank of Mahad was made a public tank in 1869. In 1923, the Bombay Legislative Council passed a resolution to the effect that the Dalits be allowed to use all public watering places. The Mahad Municipality passed a resolution on 5 January 1927 to the effect that the Municipality had no objection to allowing the Dalits to use the tank. But the higher castes were hesitant in allowing the Dalits to use the tank. Soon after this resolution was passed a conference of the Dalits of the Colaba district was held for two days. Ambedkar also convened a conference on 18-20 March 1927 on this issue. On 20 March 1927, the conference exhorted the Dalits to go to the Chowdar Tank and exercise their right to take water from it. The Hindus who had exhorted them to be bold instantly realized that this was a bombshell and immediately ran away. But the electrified Dalits led by Ambedkar marched in a procession through the main streets and for the first time drank the water from Chowdar tank.

Another temple entry movement took place at the Kalaram temple at Nasik in Maharashtra State. On 13

October 1935, at a conference convened on the issue, Ambedkar recounted the experience of the depressed classes and the immense sacrifices made by them to secure minimum human rights under the aegis of Hinduism.

The book, which provides a rare opportunity to debate and discuss the contribution of Dr. Ambedkar in nation-building, will be great interest to all sections of people.

—Dr. Anil Kumar Singh

1

Ancient India on Exhumation

There are two typed copies of this Chapter. Both of them contain additions and corrections in the handwriting of Dr. Babasaheb Ambedkar. After consideration, we decided that the latter version should be included here. This essay, consisting of three pages only, seems to be an introduction to a larger subject Dr. Ambedkar probably had in his mind.—Editors.

Much of the ancient history of India is no history at all. Not that ancient India has no history. It has plenty of it. But it has lost its character. It has been made mythology to amuse women and children. This seems to have been done deliberately by the Brahminical writers. Take the word *Deva*. What does it mean? Is the word Jana Vishesh representing a member of the human family? It is made to appear superhuman agency. By this the pith of history contained in it is squeezed out.

Along with the word Deva occur the names of Yaksha, Gana, Gandharva, Kinnars. Who were they? The impression one gets on reading the Mahabharat and Ramayan is that they are imaginary beings who filled the horizon but did not exist.

But the Yaksha, Gana, Gandharva, Kinnaras were also members of the human family. They were in the service of the Devas. The Yakshas were guarding the palaces. Ganas were guarding the Devas. Gandharvas were amusing the Devas by music and dancing. The Kinnaras were also in the service of the Gods. The descendants of the Kinnaras are even now living in Himachal Pradesh.

Take the name Asura. The description of Asura given in the Mahabharat and Ramayana make out as though hey belonged to non-human world. An Asura is described to eat ten carts-load of food. They are monsters in size. They sleep for six months. They have ten mouths. Who is a Rakshas? He too is described as a non-human creature. In size, in his capacity for eating, in his habits of life he resembled the Asura.

There is a plenty of references to the Nagas. But who is a Naga ? A Naga is represented as a serpent or a snake. Can this be true ?

Whether true or not, it is so and Hindus believe it. Ancient Indian history must be exhumed. Without its exhumation Ancient India will go without history. Fortunately with the help of the Buddhist literature, Ancient Indian History can be dug out of the debris which the Brahmin writers have heaped upon in a fit of madness.

The Buddhist literature helps a great deal to remove the debris and see the underlying substance quite clearly and distinctly.

The Buddhist literature shows that the Devas were a community of human beings. There are so many Devas who come to the Buddha to have their doubts and difficulties removed. How could this be unless the Devas were human beings

Again the Buddhist canonical literature throws a food of light on the puzzling question of the Nagas. It makes a distinction between womb-born Nagas and egg-born Nagas and thereby making it clear that the word Naga has two-fold meaning. In its original sense it stood for the name of a human community.

The Asuras again are not monsters. They too are a Jan-Vishesh human beings. According to Satpatha Bramhana, the Asuras are the descendants of Prajapati the Lord of the creation. How they became evil spirits is not known. But the fact is recorded that they fought against the Devas for the possession of the earth and that they were overcome by the Devas and that they finally succumbed. The point is clear that the Asuras were members of the human family and not monsters.

With this exhumation of debris, we can see Ancient Indian History in a new light.

The Ancient Regime : The State of the Aryan Society

This essay consists of II typed foolscap pages tagged into a file. From the last sentence it appears that the Chapter is incomplete. —Editors

Buddhism was a revolution. It was as great a Revolution as the French Revolution. Though it began as a Religious revolution, it became more than Religious revolution. It became a Social and Political Revolution. To be able to realise how profound was the character of this Revolution, it is necessary to know the state of the society before the revolution began its course. To use the language of the French Revolution, it is necessary to have a picture of the ancient regime in India.

To understand the great reform, which he brought about by his teaching, it is necessary to have some idea of the degraded condition of the Aryan civilisation at the time when Buddha started on the mission of his life.

The Aryan Community of his time was steeped in the worst kind of debauchery; social, religious and spiritual.

To mention only a few of the social evils, attention may be drawn to gambling. Gambling had become as widespread among the Aryans as drinking.

Every king had a hall of gambling attached to his palace. Every king had an expert gambler in his employment as a companion to play with. King *Virat* had in his employment *Kank* as an expert gambler. Gambling was not merely a pastime with kings. They played with heavy stakes. They staked kingdoms, dependants, relatives, slaves, servants King Nala staked everything in gambling with *Paskkar* and lost everything. The only thing he did not stake was himself and his wife Damayanti. Nala had to go and live in the forest as a beggar. There were kings who went beyond Nala. The Mahabharat tells how Dharma the eldest of the Pandavas gambled and staked everything, his brothers and also his and their wife Draupadi. Gambling was a matter of honour with the Aryans and any invitation to gamble was regarded as an injury to one's honour and dignity. Dharma gambled with such disastrous consequences although he was warned beforehand. His excuse was that he was invited to gamble and that as a man of honour, he could not decline such an invitation.

This vice of gambling was not confined to kings. It had infected even the common folk. Rig-Veda contains lamentations of a poor Aryan ruined by gambling. The habit of gambling had become so common in Kautilya's time that there were gambling houses licensed by the king from which the king derived considerable revenue.

Drinking was another evil which was rampant among the Aryans. Liquors were of two sorts *Soma* and *Sura*. *Soma* was a sacrificial wine. The drinking of the Soma was in the beginning permitted only to Brahmins, Kshatriyas and Vaishyas. Subsequently it was permitted only to Brahmins and Kshatriyas. The Vaishyas were excluded from it and the Shudras were never permitted to taste it. Its manufacture was a secret known only to the Brahmins. *Sura* was open to all and was drunk by all. The Brahmins also drank Sura. Shukracharya the priest to the *Asuras* drank so heavily that in his drunken state he gave the life giving *Mantra* known to him only and with which he used to revive the *Asuras* killed by the Devas—to *Katch* the son of Brahaspati who was the priest of the Devas. The Mahabharat mentions an occasion when both Krishna and Arjuna were dead drunk. That shows that the best among the Aryan Society were not only not free from the drink habit but that they drank heavily. The most shameful part of it was that even the Aryan women were addicted to drink. For instance *Sudeshna* the wife of King Virat tells her maid *Sairandhri* to go to *Kichaka's* palace and bring Sura as she was dying to have a drink. It is not to be supposed that only queens indulged in drinking. The habit of drinking was common among women of all classes and even Brahmin women were not free from it. That liquor and dancing was indulged in by the Aryan women is clear from the *Kausitaki Grihya Sutra* 1. 11-12, which says ; "Four or eight women who are not widowed, after having been regaled with wine and food are to dance for four times on the night previous to the wedding ceremony."

That the drinking of intoxicating liquor was indulged in by Brahmin women, not to speak of women of the lower *Varnas,* as late as the seventh and eighth centuries A.D. in the Central region of Aryavarta, is clear from Kumarila Bhatta's *Tantra-Vartika* I (iii). 4, which states, "Among the people of modern days we find the Brahmin women of the countries of Ahicchatra and Mathura to be addicted to drinking". Kumarila condemned the practice in the case of Brahmins only, but not of Kshatriyas and Vaishyas men and women, if the liquor was distilled from fruits or flowers (Madhavi), and Molasses (Gaudi) and not from grains (Sura).

The sexual immorality of the Aryan Society must shock their present day descendants. The Aryans of pre-Buddhist days had no such rule of prohibited degrees as we have today to govern their sexual or matrimonial relationship.

According to the Aryan Mythology, Brahma is the creator. Brahma had three sons and a daughter. His one son Daksha married his sister. The daughters born of this marriage between brother and sister were married some to Kashyapa the son of Marichi the son of Brahma and some to Dharma the third son of Brahma.

In the Rig-Veda there is an episode related of Yama and Yami brother and sister. According to this episode Yami the sister invites her brother Yama to cohabit with her and becomes angry when he refuses to do so.

A father could marry his daughter. *Vashishta* married his own daughter *Shatrupa* when she came of age *Manu* married his daughter *Ila Janhu* married his daughter *Janhavi. Surya* married his daughter *Usha.*

There was polyandry not of the ordinary type. The polyandry prevalent among the Aryans was a polyandry when kinsmen cohabited with one woman. Dhahaprachetani and his son Soma cohabited with Marisha the daughter of Soma.

Instances of grandfather marrying his granddaughter are not wanting. Daksha gave his daughter in marriage to his father Brahma and from that marriage was born the famous Narada. Dauhitra gave his 27 daughters to his father Soma for cohabitation and procreation. The Aryans did not mind cohabiting with women in the open and within sight of people. The Rishis used to perform certain religious rites which were called *Vamdevya vrata.* These rites used to be performed on the *Yadnya bhumi.* If any woman came there and expressed a desire for sexual intercourse and asked the sage to satisfy her, the sage used to cohabit with her then and there in the open on the *Yadnya bhumi.* Instances of this may be mentioned.

The case of the sage Parashara had sexual intercourse with Satyavati and also of Dirghatapa. That such a custom was common is shown by the existence of the word Ayoni. The word Ayoni is understood to mean of immaculate conception. That is not however the original meaning of the word. The original meaning of the word Yoni is house. Ayoni means conceived out of the house i.e. in the open. That there was nothing deemed to be wrong in this is clear from the fact that both Sita and Draupadi were Ayonija. That this was very common is clear from the fact that religious injunctions had to be issued against such a practice.

There was prevalent among the Aryans the practice of renting out their women to others for a time. As an illustration may be mentioned the story of *Madhavi.* The king *Yayati* gave his daughter *Madhavi* as an offering to his Guru *Galav. Galav* rented out the girl *Madhavi* to three kings, each a period. Thereafter he gave her in marriage to *Vishwamitra.* She remained with him until a son was born to her. Thereafter *Galav* took away the girl and gave her back to her father *Yayati.*

Besides the practice of letting out women to others temporarily at a rent there was prevalent among the Aryans another practice namely allowing procreation by the best amongst them. Raising a family was treated by them as though it was a breeding or stock raising. Among the Aryas there was a class of persons called *Devas* who were Aryans but of a superior status and prowess. The Aryans allowed their women to have sexual intercourse with any one of the class of Devas in the interest of good breeding. This practice prevailed so extensively that the Devas came to regard pre libation in respect of the Aryan Women as their prescriptive right. No Aryan woman could be married unless this right of pre-libation had been redeemed and the woman released from the control of the Devas by offering what was technically called *Avadan.* The *Laja Hoame* which is performed in every Hindu marriage and the details of which are given in the *Ashwalayan Grahya Sutra* is a relic of this act of the redemption of the Aryan woman from the right of pre-libation of the Devas. The *Avadan* in the *Laja Hoama* is nothing but the price for the extinguishing of the right of the Devas over the bride. The *Saptapadi* performed in all Hindu marriages and which is regarded as the most essential ceremony without which there is no lawful marriage has an integral connection with this right of pre-libation of the Devas. Saptapadi means walking by the bridegroom seven steps with the bride. Why is this essential? The answer is that the Devas, if they were dissatisfied with the compensation, could claim the woman before the seventh step was taken. After the seventh step was taken, the right of the Devas was extinguished and the bridegroom could take away the bride and live as husband and wife without being obstructed or molested by the Devas.'"

There was no rule of chastity for maidens. A girl could have sexual intercourse with and also progeny from anybody without contracting marriage. This is evident from the root meaning of the word *Kanya* which means a girl. Kanya comes from the root *Kam* which means a girl free to offer herself to any man. That they did offer themselves to any man and had children without contracting regular marriage is illustrated by the case of *Kunti* and *Matsyagandha. Kunti* had children from different men before she was married to *Pandu* and *Matsyagandha* had sexual intercourse with the sage *Parashara* before she married to *Shantanu* the father of *Bhishma.*

Bestiality was also prevalent among the Aryans. The story of the sage Dam having sexual intercourse with a female dear, is well known. Another instance is that of Surya cohabiting with a mare. But the most hideous instance is that of the woman having sexual intercourse with the horse in the Ashvamedha *Yadna.*

A Sunken Priesthood

This essay is numbered as Chapter III in the file of the Ancient Regime and contains 16 foolscap-typed pages. This Chapter also seems to be left incomplete.—Editors.

The priestly profession in the ancient Aryan Society was monopolised by the Brahmins. None except a Brahmin could become a priest. As custodians of religion, the Brahmins were the guides of the people in moral and spiritual matters. They were to set the standard for people to follow. Did the Brahmins act up to the standard? Unfortunately, all the evidence we have, shows that the Brahmins had fallen to the utmost depth of moral degradation. A Shrotriya Brahmin was supposed not to keep with him a store of provision lasting for more than a week. But they had systematically trampled upon this rule and were addicted to the use of the things stored up ; stores, to wit, of foods, drinks, clothing, equipages, bedding, perfumes, and curry-stuffs. The Brahmins were addicted to visiting shows such as :—

(1) Nautch dances (nakkam).

(2) Singings of songs (gitam).

(3) Instrumental music (vaditam).

(4) Shows at fairs (pekham).

(5) Ballads recitations (akkhanam).

(6) Hand music (panisaram).

(7) The chanting of bards (vetals).

(8) Tam-tam playing (kumbhathunam).

(9) Fair scenes (sobhanagarkam).

(10) Acrobatic feats by Kandalas (Kandala-vamsa-dhopanam).

(11) Combats of elephants, horses, buffaloes, bulls, goats, rams, cocks and quails.

(12) Bouts at quarter staff, boxing, wrestling. (13-16) Sham-fights, roll-calls, manoeuvres, reviews.

They were addicted to games and recreations; that is to say,

(1) Games on boards with eight, or with ten rows of squares.

(2) The same games played by imagining such boards in the air.

(3) Keeping going over diagrams drawn on the ground so that one-steps only where one ought to go.

(4) Either removing the pieces or men from a help with one's nail, or putting them into a heap, in each case without shaking it. He who shakes the heap, loses.

(5) Throwing dice.

(6) Hitting a short stick with a long one.

(7) Dipping the hand with the fingers stretched out in lac, or red dye, or flour water, and striking the wet hand

on the ground or on a wall, calling out 'what shall it be?' and showing the form required—elephants, horses.

(8) Games with balls.

(9) Blowing through toy pipes made of leaves.

(10) Ploughing with toy ploughs.

(11) Turning summersaults.

(12) Playing with toy windmills made of palm leaves.

(13) Playing with toy measures made of palm leaves. (14, 15) Playing with toy carts or toy bows.

(16) Guessing at letters traced in the air, or on a playfellow's back.

(17) Guessing the playfellow's thoughts.

(18) Mimicry of deformities.

They were addicted to the use of high and large couches that is to say:

(1) Moveable settees, high, and six feet long (Asandi).

(2) Divans with animal figures carved on the supports (Pallanko).

(3) Goat's hair coverings with very long fleece (Gonako).

(4) Patchwork counterpanes of many colours (Kittaka).

(5) White blankets (Patika).

(6) Woollen coverlets embroidered with flowers (Patalika).

(7) Quilts stuffed with cotton wool (Tulika).

(8) Coverlets embroidered with figures of lions, tigers, & c., (Vikatika).

(9) Rugs with fur on both sides (Uddalom).

(10) Rugs with fur on one side (Ekantalomi).

(11) Coverlets embroidered with gems (Katthissam).

(12) Silk coverlets (Koseyyam).

(13) Carpets large enough for sixteen dancers (Kittakam). (14-16) Elephant, horse and chariot rugs.

(17) Rugs of antelope skins sewn together (Aginepaveni).

(18) Rugs of skins of the plantain antelope.

(19) Carpets with awnings above them (Sauttarakkhadam).

(20) Sofas with red pillows for the head and feet". The

> Brahmins were addicted to the use of means for adorning and beautifying themselves; that is to say : Rubbing in scented powders on one's body, shampooing it, and bathing it, patting the limbs with clubs after the manner of wrestlers, the use of mirrors, eye-ointments, garlands, rouge, cosmetics, bracelets, necklaces, walking-sticks, reed cases for drugs, rapiers, sunshades, embroidered slippers, turbans, diadems, whisks of the yak tail and long-fringed white robes. The Brahmins were addicted to such low conversation as these :

Tales of kings, of robbers, of ministers of state ; tales of war, of terrors, of battles ; talk about foods and drinks, clothes, beds, garlands, perfumes ; talks about relationships, equipages, villages, towns, cities and countries ; tales about women, and about heroes ; gossip at street corners, or places whence water is fetched ; ghost stories ; desultory talk ; speculations about the creation of the land or sea, or about existence and non-existence. The Brahmins were addicted to the use of wrangling phrases: such as:

"You don't understand this doctrine and discipline, I do." "How should you know about this doctrine and discipline?" "You have fallen into wrong views. It is I who am in the right." " I am speaking to the point, you are not." "You are putting last what ought to come first, and first what ought to come last."

"What you've ex-cogitated so long, that is all quite upset." " You are proved to be wrong." " Set to work to clear your views." " Disentangle yourself if you can."

The Brahmins were addicted to taking messages, going on errands, and acting as go-betweens; to wit, on kings, ministers of state, Kshatriyas, Brahmans, or young men, saying: 'Go there, come hither, take this with you, bring that from there.'

'The Brahmins were tricksters, drone out (of holy words for pray), diviners, and exorcists, ever hungering to add gain to gain.'

The Brahmins earned their living by wrong means of livelihood, by low arts, such as these:

(1) Palmistry—prophesying long life, prosperity, & c., (or the reverse from marks on a child's hands, feet, & c.)

(2) Divining by means of omens and signs.

(3) Auguries drawn from thunderbolts and other celestial portents.

(4) Prognostication by interpreting dreams.

(5) Fortune-telling from marks on the body.

(6) Auguries from the marks on cloth gnawed by mice.

(7) Sacrificing to Agni.

(8) Offering oblations from a spoon.

(9-13) Making offerings to gods of husks, of the red powder between the grain and the husk, of husked grain ready for boiling, or ghee and of oil.

(14) Sacrificing by spewing mustard seeds, & c., into the fire out of one's mouth.

(15) Drawing blood from one's right knee as a sacrifice to the gods.

(16) Looking at the knuckles, & c., and, after muttering a charm, divining whether a man is well born of luck or not.

(17) Determining whether the site for a proposed house or pleasance, is luck or not.

(18) Advising on customary law.

(19) Laying demons in a cemetery.

(20) Laying ghosts.

(21) Knowledge of the charms to be used when lodging in an earth house.

(22) Snake charming.

(23) The poison craft.

(24) The scorpion craft.

(25) The mouse craft.

(26) The bird craft.

(27) The crow craft.

(28) Foretelling the number of years that man has yet to live.

(29) Giving charms to ward off arrows.

(30) The animal wheel.

The Brahmins earned their living by wrong means of livelihood, by low arts, such as these:

Knowledge of the signs of good and bad qualities in the following things and of the marks in them denoting the health or luck of their owners : to wit, gems, staves, garments, swords, arrows, bows, other weapons, women, men, boys, girls, slaves, slave-girls, elephants, horses, buffaloes, bulls, oxen, goats, sheep, fowls, quails, iguanas, herrings, tortoises, and other animals.

The Brahmins, earned their living by wrong means of livelihood by low arts such as soothe saying, to the effect that,

The chiefs will march out.

The home chiefs will attack and the enemies retreat.

The enemies' chiefs will attack, and ours will retreat.

The home chiefs will gain the victory, and ours will suffer defeat.

The foreign chiefs will gain the victory on this side, and ours will suffer defeat.

Thus will there be victory on this side, defeat on that. The Brahmins, while living on food provided by the faithful, earn their living by wrong means of livelihood, by such low arts as fore-telling:

(1) There will be an eclipse of the Moon.

(2) There will be an eclipse of the Sun.

(3) There will be an eclipse of a star (Nakshatra).

(4) There will be aberration of the Sun or the Moon.

(5) The Sun or the Moon will return to its usual path.

(6) There will be aberrations of the stars.

(7) The stars will return to their usual course.

(8) There will be a jungle fire.

(9) There will be a fall of meteors.

(10) There will be an earthquake.

(11) The god will thunder.

(12-15) There will be rising and setting, clearness and dimness of the Sun or the Moon or the stars, or foretelling of each of these fifteen phenomena that they will betoken such and such a result."

The Brahmins earned their living by wrong means of the livelihood, by low arts, such as these:

- Foretelling an abundant rainfall.
- Foretelling a deficient rainfall.
- Foretelling a good harvest.
- Foretelling scarcity of food.
- Foretelling tranquillity.
- Foretelling disturbances.
- Foretelling a pestilence.
- Foretelling a healthy season.
- Counting on the fingers.
- Counting without using the fingers Summing up large totals.
- Composing ballads, poetising.
- Casuistry, sophistry.

The Brahmins, while living on food provided by the faithful, earn their living by wrong means of livelihood by low arts, such as:

(1) Arranging a lucky day for marriages in which the bride or bridegroom is brought home.

(2) Arranging a lucky day for marriages in which the bride or bridegroom is sent forth.

(3) Fixing a lucky time for the conclusion of treaties of peace (or using charms to procure harmony).

(4) Fixing a lucky time for the outbreak of hostilities (or using charms to make discord).

(5) Fixing a lucky time for the calling in of debts (or charms for success in throwing dice).

(6) Fixing a lucky time for the expenditure of money (or charms to bring ill luck to an opponent throwing dice).

(7) Using charms to make people lucky.

(8) Using charms to make people unlucky.

(9) Using charms to procure abortion.

(10) Incantations to keep a man's jaws fixed.

(11) Incantations to bring on dumbness.

(12) Incantations to make a man throw up his hands.

(13) Incantations to bring on deafness.

(14) Obtaining oracular answers by means of the magic mirror.

(15) Obtaining oracular answers through a girl possessed.

(16) Obtaining oracular answers from a god.

(17) The worship of the Sun.

(18) The worship of the Great One.

(19) Bringing forth flames from one's mouth.

(20) Invoking Siri, the goddess of Luck. The Brahmins earned their living by wrong means of livelihood, by low arts, such as these:

- (1) Vowing gifts to a god if a certain benefit be granted.
- (2) Paying such vows.
- (3) Repeating charms while lodging in an earth house.
- (4) Causing virility.
- (5) Making a man impotent.
- (6) Fixing on lucky sites for dwellings.
- (7) Consecrating sites.
- (8) Ceremonial rinsing of the mouth.
- (9) Ceremonial bathing.
- (10) Offering sacrifices.
- (11-14) Administering emetics and purgatives.
- (15) Purging people to relieve the head (that is by giving drugs to make people sneeze).
- (16) Oiling people's ears (either to make them grow or to heal sores on them).
- (17) Satisfying people's eyes (soothing them by dropping medicinal oils into them).
- (18) Administering drugs through the nose.
- (19) Applying collyrium to the eyes.
- (20) Giving medicinal ointment for the eyes.
- (21) Practising as an oculist.
- (22) Practising as a surgeon.

(23) Practising as a doctor for children.

(24) Administering roots and drugs.

(25) Administering medicines in rotation.

2

Reformers and Their Fate

This is a typed bound copy consisting of 87 pages. The Ambatta Sutta starts at page 69 of the manuscript and after page 70, pages are numbered from A to Z. The beginning of page 71 starts with Lohikka Sutta.—Editors.

1. Aryan Society. II. Buddha and Reform. III. I

It was Sir T. Madhava Raw who speaking of Hindu Society of his time said :

"The longer one lives, observes, and thinks, the more deeply does he feel that there is no community on the face of the earth which suffers less from political evils and more from self-inflicted or self-accepted or self-created, and therefore avoidable evils, than the Hindu Community."

This view expresses quite accurately and without exaggeration the necessity of social reform in Hindu Society.

The first Social Reformer and the greatest of them all is Gautama Buddha. Any history of Social Reform must begin with him and no history of Social Reform in India will be complete which omits to take account of his great achievements.

Siddhartha, surname Gautama, was born in the Sakya clan at Kapilvastu in Northern India, on the borders of Nepal in 563 B.C. Tradition says he was a prince. He received education fit for a prince, was married and had a son. Oppressed by the evils and misery then prevalent in the Aryan Society he renounced the world at the age of twenty-nine and left his home in search for truth and deliverance. He became a mendicant and studied with two distinguished teachers, but finding that their teachings did not satisfy him he left them and became an ascetic. He gave up that also as being futile. By hard thinking he got insight into things and as a result of this insight he formulated his own

Dhamma. This was at the age of thirty-five. The remainder of his eighty years he spent in spreading his Dhamma and founding and administering an order of monks. He died about the year 483 B.C. at Kusinara surrounded by his devoted followers.

To the carrying out of his mission, the Buddha devoted all his days after the achievement of enlightenment. His time was divided between feeding the lamp of his own spiritual life by solitary meditation—just as Jesus spent hours in lonely prayer—and active preaching to large audiences of his monks, instructing the more advanced in the subtle points of inner development, directing the affairs of the Order, rebuking breaches of discipline, confirming the faithful in their virtue, receiving deputation, carrying on discussions with learned opponents, comforting the sorrowful, visiting kings and peasants, Brahmins and outcasts, rich and poor. He was a friend of publicans and sinners, and many a public harlot, finding herself understood and pitied, gave up her evil ways to take refuge in the "Blessed One". Such a life demanded a variety of moral qualities and social gifts, and among others a combination of democratic sentiments with an aristocratic *Savoir Faire* which is seldom met with. In reading the dialogues one can never forget that Gotama had the birth and upbringing of an aristocrat. He converses not only with Brahmins and pundits but with princes and ministers and kings on easy and equal terms. He is a good diner-out, with a fund of anecdotes and apparently a real sense of humour, and is a welcome quest at every house. A distinguished Brahmin is pictured as describing him thus :

'The venerable Gotama is well born on both sides, of pure descent..... is handsome, pleasant to look upon, inspiring trust, gifted with great beauty of complexion, fair in colour, fine in presence, stately to behold, virtuous with the virtue of the Arhats, gifted with goodness and virtue and with a pleasant voice and polite address, with no passion of lust left in him nor any fickleness of mind. He bids all men welcome, is congenial, conciliatory, not supercillious, accessible to all, not backward in conversation. ' But what appealed most to the India of his time, and has appealed most to India through the ages, is expressed by the Brahmin in these words : "The monk Gotama has gone forth into the religious life, giving up the great clan of his relatives, giving up much money and gold, treasure both buried and above ground. Truly while he was still a young man, without a grey hair on his head, in the beauty of his early manhood he went forth from the household life into the homeless state."

"Such a life as his, demanded not only pleasant manners, sympathy and kindness, but firmness and courage. When the occasion required it, he could be calmly severe with those who worked evil for the Order. Physical pain, he bore not only with equanimity but with no diminution of his inner joy. Courage also was needed and was found ; as, for example, in the Buddha's calm attitude during Devadatta's various attempts to assassinate him, in facing threats of murder, and in the conversion of the famous bandit in the Kingdom of Kosala, whom all the countryside feared, and whom the Buddha visited, alone and unarmed, in his lair, changing him from a scourge of the kindorn to a peaceful member of the Order. Neither pain, danger, nor insults marred his spiritual peace. When he was reviled he reviled not again. Nor was he lacking in tender thoughtfulness for those who needed his comfort and support."

He was beloved of all. Repeatedly he is described or describes himself, as one born into the world for the good of the many, for the happiness of the many, for the advantage, the good, the happiness of gods and men, out of compassion for the world.

He left an indelible mark on the Aryan Society and although his name has gone out of India the impression of his teaching still remains.

His religion spread like wild fire. It soon became the religion of the whole of India. But it did not remain confined to India. It reached every corner of the then known world. All races accepted it. Even the Afghans were once Buddhists. It did not remain confined to Asia. There is evidence to show that Buddhism was the religion of Celtic Britain. What was the cause of this rapid spread of Buddhism? 0n this point what Prof. Hopkins has said is worth quoting. This is what he says:

"The cause, then, of the rapid spread of Buddhism at the beginning of its career lies only in the conditions of its teaching and the influential backing of its founder. It was the individual Buddha that captivated men ; it was the teaching that emanated from him that fired enthusiasm ; it was his position as an aristocrat that made him acceptable to the aristocracy, his magnetism that made him the idol of the people. From every page stands out the strong, attractive personality of this teacher and winner of hearts. No man ever lived so godless yet so godlike. Arrogating to himself no divinity, despairing of future bliss, but without fear as without hope, leader of thought but despising lovingly the folly of the world, exalted but adored, the universal brother, he wandered among men, simply, serenely, with gentle irony subduing them that opposed him, to congregation after congregation speaking with majestic sweetness, the master to each, the friend of all. His voice was singularly vibrant and eloquent; his very tones convinced the hearer, his looks inspired awe. From the tradition it appears that he must have been one of those whose personality alone suffices to make a man not only a leader but also a god to the hearts of his fellows. When such a one speaks he obtains hearers. It matters little what he says, for he influences the motions, and bends whoever listens to his will. But if added to this personality, if encompassing it. there be the feeling in the minds of others that what this man teaches is not only a variety, but the very hope of their salvation ; if for the first time they recognise in his words the truth that makes of slaves free men, of classes a brotherhood, then it is not difficult to see wherein lies the lightning like speed with which the electric current passes from heart to heart. Such a man was Buddha, such was the essential of his teaching: and such was the inevitable rapidity of Buddhistic expansion and the profound influence of the shock that was produced by the new faith upon the moral consciousness of Buddha's people."

To understand the great reform, which he brought about by his teaching, it is necessary to have some idea of the degraded condition of the Aryan civilisation at the time when Buddha started on the mission *of* his life.

The Aryan Community of his time was steeped in the worst kind of debauchery: social, religious and spiritual.

To mention only a few of the social evils, attention may be drawn to gambling. Gambling had become as widespread among the Aryans as drinking. Every king had a hall of gambling attached to his palace. Every king had an expert gambler in his employment as a companion to play with. King *Virat* had in his employment *Kank* as an expert gambler. Gambling was not merely a pastime with kings. They played with heavy stakes. They staked kingdoms, dependents, relatives, slaves, servants. King Nala staked everything in gambling with *Paskkar* and lost everything. The only thing he did not stake was himself and his wife Damayanti. Nala had to go and live in the forest as a beggar. There were kings who went beyond Nala. The Mahabharat tells how Dharma the eldest of the Pandavas gambled and staked everything, his brothers and also his and their wife Draupadi. Gambling was a matter of honour with the Aryans and any invitation to gamble was regraded as an injury to one's honour and dignity. Dharma gambled with such disastrous consequences although he was warned beforehand. His excuse was that he was invited to gamble and that as a man of honour he could not decline such an invitation.

This vice of gambling was not confined to kings. It had infected even the common folk. Rig-Veda contains lamentations of poor Aryan ruined by gambling. The habit of gambling had become so common in Kautilya's time that there were gambling houses licensed by the king from which the king derived considerable revenue.

Drinking was another evil which was rampant among the Aryans. Liquors were of two sorts *Soma* and *Sura*. *Soma* was a sacrificial wine. The drinking of the Soma was in the beginning permitted only to Brahmins, Kshatriyas and Vaishyas. Subsequently it was permitted only to Brahmins and Kshatriyas. The Vaishyas were excluded from it and the Shudras were never permitted to taste it. Its manufacture was a secret known only to the Brahmins. *Sura* was open to all and was drunk by all. The Brahmins also drank *Sura*. Shukracharya the priest to the *Asuras* drank so heavily that in his drunken state he gave the life-giving *Mantras*—known to him only and with which he used to revive the *Asuras* killed by the *Devas*— to *Katch* the son of *Brahaspati* who was the priest of the Devas. The Mahabharat mentions an occasion when both *Krishna* and *Arjuna* were dead drunk. That shows that the best among the Aryan Society were not only not free from the drink habit but that they drank heavily. The most shameful part of it was that even the Aryan women were addicted to drink. For instance *Sudeshna* the wife of king *Virat* tells her maid *Sairandhri* to go to *Kichaka's* palace and bring *Sura* as she was dying to have a drink. It is not to be supposed that only queens indulged in drinking. The habit of drinking was common among women of all classes and even Brahmin women were not free from it. That liquor and dancing was indulged in by the Aryan women is clear from the *Kausitaki Grihya Sutra* 1. 1 1-12, which says, "Four or eight women who are not widowed after having been regaled with wine and food are to dance for four times on the night previous to the wedding ceremony."

Turning to the Aryan Society it was marked by class war and class degradation. The Aryan Society recognised four classes, the Brahmins, Kshatriyas, Vaishyas and Shudras. These divisions were not merely horizontal divisions, all on a par with each other in the matter of social relationship. These divisions, had become vertical, one above the other. Being placed above or below there was both jealousy and rivalry among the four classes. This jealousy and rivalry had given rise even to enmity. This enmity was particularly noticeable between the two highest classes, namely, the Brahmins and the Kshatriyas and there was a regular class *war* between the two, so intense that it would delight the heart of any Marxian to read the descriptions thereof. Unfortunately there is no detailed history of this class war between the Brahmins and the Kshatriyas. Only a few instances have been recorded. Vena, Pururavas, Nahusha, Sudas, Sumukh and Nimi were some of the Kshatriya kings who came into the conflict with the Brahmins. The issues in these conflicts were different.

The issue between Vena and the Brahmins was whether a King could command and require the Brahmins to worship him and offer sacrifice to him instead of the Gods. The issue between Pururavas and the Brahmins was whether a Kshatriya King could confiscate the property of the Brahmin. The issue between Nahusha and the Brahmins was whether a Kshatriya king could order a Brahmin to do a servile job. The issue between Nimi and the Brahmins was whether the king was bound to employ only his family priest at the sacrificial ceremony. The issue between Sudas and the Brahmins was whether the king was bound to employ only a Brahmin as a priest.

This shows how big were the issues between the two classes. No wonder that the struggle between them was also the bitterest. The wars between them were not merely occasional riots. They were wars of extermination. It is stated that Parashuram a Brahmin fought against the Kshatriyas twenty-one times and killed every Kshatriya.

While the two classes were fighting among themselves for supremacy, they both combined to keep down the Vaishyas and the Shudras. The Vaishya was a milch cow. He lived only to pay taxes. The Shudra was a general beast *of* burden. These two classes existed for the sole purpose of making the life of the Brahmins and Kshatriyas glorious and happy. They had no right to live for themselves. They lived to make the life of their betters possible.

Below these two classes there were others. They were the Chandalas and Shwappakas. They were not untouchables but they were degraded. They were outside the pale of society and outside the pale of law. They had no rights and no opportunities. They were the rejects of the Aryan Society.

The sexual immorality *of* the Aryan Society must shock their present day descendants. The Aryans of pre-Buddhist days had no such rule of prohibited degrees, as we have today to govern their sexual or matrimonial relationship.

According to the Aryan Mythology, Brahma is the creator. Brahma had three sons and a daughter. His one son Daksha married his sister. The daughters born of this marriage between brother and sister were married some to Kashyapa the son of Marichi the son of Brahma and some to Dharma the third son of Brahma.

In the Rig-Veda there is an episode related of Yama and Yami brother and sister. According to this episode Yami the sister invites her brother Yama to cohabit with her and becomes angry when he refuses to do so.

A father could marry his daughter. *Vashishta* married his own daughter *Shatrupa* when she came of age. *Manu* married his daughter *Ila*. *Janhu* married his daughter *Janhavi*. *Surya* married his daughter *Usha*· There was polyandri not of the ordinary type. The polyandri prevalent among the Aryans was a polyandri when Kinsmen cohabited with one woman. *Dhahaprachetani* and his son *Soma* cohabited with *Marisha* the daughter of *Soma*·

Instances of grandfather marrying his grand-daughter are not wanting. Daksha gave his daughter in marriage to his father Brahma and from that marriage was born the famous Narada. Dauhitra gave his 27 daughters to his father Soma for cohabitation and procreation.

The Aryans did not mind cohabiting with women in the open and within sight of people. The Rishis used to perform certain religious rites which were called Vamdevya vrata. These rites used to be performed on the Yadnya Bhumi. If any woman came there and expressed a desire for sexual intercourse and asked the sage to satisfy her, the sage used to cohabit with her then and there in the open on the Yadnya Bhumi. Instances of this may be mentioned; the case of the sage Parashara who had sexual intercourse with Satyavati and also of Dirghatapa. That such a custom was common is shown by the existence of the word Ayoni. The word Ayoni is understood to mean of immaculate conception. That is not however the original meaning of the word. The original meaning of the word Yoni is house. Ayoni means conceived out of the house i.e. in the open. That there was nothing deemed to be wrong in this is clear from the fact that both Sita and Draupadi were Ayonija. That this was very common is clear from the fact that religious injunctions had to be issued against such a practice.

There was prevalent among the Aryans the practice of renting out their women to others for a time. As an illustration may be mentioned the story of Madhavi. The king Yayati gave his daughter Madhavi as an offering to his guru Galav. Galav rented out the girl Madhavi to three kings each a period. Thereafter he gave her in marriage to Vishwamitra. She remained with him until a son was born to her. Thereafter Galav took away the girl and gave her back to her father Yayati.

Besides the practice of letting out women to others temporarily at a rent, there was prevalent among the Aryans another practice namely, allowing procreation by the best amongst them. Raising a family was treated by them as though it was a breeding or stock raising. Among the Aryas there was a class of persons called *Devas* who were Aryans but of a superior status and prowess. The Aryans allowed their women to have sexual intercourse with any one of the class of Devas in the inerest of good breeding. This practice prevailed so extensively that the Devas came to regard prelibation in respect of the Aryan women as their prescriptive right. No Aryan woman could be married unless this right of prelibation had been redeemed and the woman released from the control of the Devas by offering what was technically called *Avadan*. The Laja Hoame which is performed in every Hindu marriage and the details of which are given in the Ashwalayan Grahya Sutra is a relic of this act of the redemption of the Aryan woman from the right of prelibation of the Devas. The *Avadan* in the Laja Hoame is nothing but the price for the extinguishment of the right of the Devas over the bride. The *Saptapadi* performed in all Hindu marriages and which is regarded as the most essential ceremony without which there is no lawful marriage has an integral connection with this right of prelibation of the Devas. Saptapadi means walking by the bridegroom seven steps with the bride. Why is this essential? The answer is that the Devas if they were dissatisfied with the compensation could claim the woman before the seventh step was taken. After the seventh step was taken, the right of the Devas was extinguished and the bridegroom could take away the bride and live as husband and wife without being obstructed or molested by the Devas.

There was no rule of chastity for maidens. A girl could have sexual intercourse with and also progeny from anybody without contracting marriage. This is evident from the root meaning of the word *Kanya* which means a girl. *Kanya* comes from the root *Kam* which means a girl free to offer herself to any man. That they did offer themselves to any man and had children without contracting regular marriage is illustrated by the case of *Kunti* and *Matsyagandha*. Kunti had children from different men before she was married to Pandu and Matsyagandha had sexual intercourse with the sage Parashara before she was married to *Shantanu* the father of Bhishma.

Bestiality was also prevalent among the Aryans. The story of the sage Dam having sexual intercourse with a female deer is well known. Another instance is that of Surya cohabiting with a mare. But the most hideous instance is that of the woman having sexual intercourse with the horse in the Ashvamedha Yadna.

The religion of the Aryan consisted of the *Yadna* or sacrifice. The sacrifice was a means to enter into the godhead of the gods, and even to control the gods. The traditional sacrifices were twenty-one in number divided into three classes of seven each. The first were sacrifices of butter, milk, corn, etc. The second class covered *Soma* sacrifices and third animal sacrifices. The sacrifice may be of short duration or long duration lasting for a year or more. The latter was called a *Sattra.* The argument in favour of the sacrifice is that eternal holiness is won by him that offers the sacrifice. Not only a man's self but also his Manes stood to benefit by means of sacrifice. He gives the Manes pleasure with his offering, but he also raises their estate, and sends them up to live in a higher world.

The sacrifice was by no means meant as an aid to the acquirement of heavenly bliss alone. Many of the great sacrifices were for the gaining of good things on earth. That one should sacrifice without the ulterior motive of gain is unknown. Brahmanic India knew no thank offering. Ordinarily the gain is represented as a compensating gift from the divinity, whom they sacrifice. The sacrifice began with the recitation : " He offers the sacrifice to the god with this text : 'Do thou give to me (and) I (will) give to thee ; do thou bestow on me (and) I (will) bestow on thee'. "

The ceremony of the sacrifice was awe-inspiring. Every word was pregnant with consequences and even the pronunciation of the word or accent was fateful. There are indications, however, that the priest themselves understood that, much in the ceremonial was pure hocus-pocus, and not of much importance as it was made out to be.

Every sacrifice meant fee to the priest. As to fee, the rules were precise and their propounds were unblushing. The priest performed the sacrifice for the fee alone, and it must consist of valuable garments, kine, horses or gold—when each was to be given was carefully stated. The priests had built up a great complex of forms, where at every turn fees were demanded. The whole expense, falling on one individual for whose benefit the sacrifice was performed, must have been enormous. How costly the whole thing became can be seen from the fact that in one place the fee for the sacrifice is mentioned as one thousand cows. For this greed, which went so far that he proclaimed that he who gives a thousand cows obtains all things of heaven. The priest had a good precedent to cite, for, the gods of heaven, in all tales told of them, ever demand a reward from each other when they help their neighbour gods. If the Gods seek rewards, the priest has a right to do the same.

The principal sacrifice was the animal sacrifice. It was both costly and barbaric. In the Aryan religion there are five sacrificial animals mentioned. In this list of sacrificial animals man came first. The sacrifice of a man was the costliest. The rules of sacrifice required that the individual to be slaughtered must be neither a. priest nor a slave. He must be a Kshatriya or Vaishya. According to the ordinary valuation of those times the cost of buying a man to be sacrificed was one thousand cows. Besides being costly and barbaric, it must have been revolting because the sacrificers had not only to kill the man but to eat him. Next to man came the horse. That also was a costly sacrifice because the horse was a rare and a necessary animal for the Aryans in their conquest of India. The Aryans could hardly afford such a potent instrument of military domination to be offered as sacrifice. The sacrifice must have been revolting in as much as one of the rituals in the horse-sacrifice was the copulation of the horse before it was slaughtered with the wife of the sacrificer.

The animals most commonly offered for sacrifice were of course the cattle which were used by the people for their agricultural purposes. They were mostly cows and bullocks.

The Yadnas were costly and they would have died out of sheer considerations of expense involved. But they did not. The reason is that the stoppage of Yadna involved the question of the loss of the Brahmin's fees. There could be no fees if the Yadna ceased to be performed and the Brahmin would starve. The Brahmin therefore found a substitute for the costly sacrificial animals. For a human sacrifice the Brahmin allowed as a substitute for a live man, a man of straw or metal or earth. But they did not altogether give up human sacrifice for fear that this Yadna might be stopped and they should lose their fees. When human sacrifice became rare, animal sacrifice came in as a substitute. Animal sacrifice was also a question of expense to the laity. Here again rather than allow the sacrifice to go out of vogue, the Brahmins came forward with smaller animals for cattle just as cattle had been allowed to take the place of the man and the horse. All this was for the purpose of maintaining the *Yadna* so that the Brahmin did not lose his fees which was his maintenance. So set were the Brahmins on the continuance of the Yadna that they were satisfied with merely rice as an offering.

It must not however be supposed that the institution of substitutes of the Yadnas of the Aryans had become less horrid. The introduction of substitutes did not work as a complete replacement of the more expensive and more ghastly sacrifice by the less expensive and the more innocent. All that it meant was that the offering may be according to the capacity of the sacrificer. If he was poor his offering may be rice. If he was well to do it might be a goat. If he was rich it might be a man, horse, cow or a bull. The effect of the subsitutes was that the Yadna was brought within the capacity of all so that the Brahmin reaped a larger harvest of feast on the total. It did not have the effect of stopping animal sacrifice. Indeed animals continued to be sacrificed by the thousands.

The Yadna often became a regular carnage of cattle at which the Brahmins did the work of butchers. One gets some idea of the extent of this carnage of innocent animals from references to the Yadnas which one comes across in Buddhist literature. In the Suttanipat a description is given of the Yadna that was arranged to be performed by Pasenadi, king of Kosala. It is stated that there were tied to the poles for slaughter at the Yadna five hundred oxen, five hundred bulls, five hundred cows, five hundred goats and five hundred lambs and that the servents of the king who were detailed to do the jobs according to the orders given to them by the officiating Brahmin priests were doing their duties with tears in their eyes.

The Yadna besides involving a terrible carnage was really a kind of carnival. Besides roast meet there was drink. The Brahmins had Soma as well as Sura. The others had Sura in abundance. Almost every Yadna was followed by gambling and what is most extraordinary is that, side by side there went on also sexual intercourse in the open. Yadna had become debauchery and there was no religion left in it. The Aryan religion was just a series of observances. Behind these observances there was no yearning for a good and a virtuous life. There was no hunger or thirst for rightousness. Their religion was without any spiritual content. The hymns of the Rig Veda furnish very good evidence of the absence of any spiritual basis for the Aryan religion. The hymns are prayers addressed by the Aryans to their gods. What do they ask for in these prayers? Do they ask to be kept away from temptation? Do they ask for deliverance from evil? Do they ask for forgiveness of sins? Most of the hymns are in praise of Indra.

They praise him for having brought destruction to the enemies of the Aryans. They praise him because he killed all the pregnant wives of Krishna, an Asura. They praise him because he destroyed hundreds of villages of the Asuras. They praise him because he killed lakhs of Dasyus. The Aryans pray to Indra to carry on greater destruction among the Anaryas in the hope that they may secure to themselves the food supplies of the Anaryas and the wealth of the Anaryas. Far from being spiritual and elevating, the hymns of the Rig-Veda are saturated with wicked thoughts and wicked purposes. The Aryan religion never concerned itself with what is called a righteous life.

Such was the state of the Aryan Society when Buddha was born. There are two pertinent questions regarding Buddha as a reformer who laboured to reform the Aryan Society. What were the chief planks in his reform? To what extent did he succeed in his reform movement? To take up the first question.

Buddha felt that for the inculcation of a good and a pure life, example was better than precept. The most important thing he did was to lead a good and a pure life so that it might serve as a model to all. How unblemished a life he led can be gathered from the *Brahma-Jala Sutta.* It is reproduced below because it not only gives an idea of the pure life that Buddha led but it also gives an idea of how impure a life the Brahmins, the best among the Aryans led.

Brahma Jala Sutta

1. Thus have I heard. The Blessed One was once going along the high road between Rajagaha and Nalanda with a

great company of the brethren with about five hundred brethren. And Suppiya the mendicant too was going along the high road between Rajagaha and Nalanda with his disciple the young Brahmadatta. Now just then Suppiya the mendicant was speaking in many ways in dispraise of the Buddha, in dispraise of the Doctrine, in dispraise of the Order. But young Brahmadatta, his pupil, gave utterance, in many ways, to praise of the Buddha, to praise of the Doctrine, to praise of the Order. Thus they two, teacher and pupil, holding opinions in direct contradiction of one to the other, were following, step by step, after the Blessed one and the company of the brethren.

2. Now the Blessed one put up at the royal rest house in the Ambalatthika pleasance to pass the night, and with him the company of the brethren. And so also did Suppiya the mendicant, and with him his young disciple Brahmadatta. And there, at the rest houses, these two carried on the same discussion as belore.

3. And in the early dawn a number of the brethren assembled as they rose up in the pavilion ; and this was the trend of the talk that sprang up among them as they were seated there. 'How wonderful a thing is it, brethren, and how strange that the Blessed One, he who knows and sees, the Arahat the Buddha Supreme, should so clearly have perceived how various are the inclination of men! For see how while Suppiya the mendicant speaks in many ways in dispraise of the Buddha, the Doctrine, and the Order, his own disciple, young Brahmadatta, speaks, in as many ways, in praise of them. So do these two, teacher and pupil, follow step by step after the Blessed One and the company of the brethren, giving utterance to views in direct contradiction of one to the other.

4. Now the Blessed One on realising what was the drift of their talk, went to the pavilion, and took his seat on the mat spread out for him. And when he had sat down he said : "What is the talk *on* which you are engaged sitting here and what is the subject of the conversation between you?" And they told him all. And he said:

5. Brethren, if outsiders should speak against me, or against the Doctrine, or against the Order, you should not on that account either bear malice, or suffer heart burning, or feel ill-

will. If you, on that account, should be angry and hurt, that would stand in the way of your own self-conquest. If, when others speak against us, you feel angry at that, and displeased, would you then be able to judge how far that speech of theirs is well said or ill? 'That would not he so, Sir.' 'But when outsiders speak in dispraise of me, or of the Doctrine, or of the Order, you should unravel what is false and point it out as wrong, saying, "For this *or* that reason this is not the fact, that is not so, such a thing is not found among us, is not in us."

6. But also, brethren, if outsiders should speak in praise of me, in praise of the Doctrine, in praise of the Order, you should not, on that account, be filled with pleasure *or* gladness, or be lifted up in heart. Were you to be so that also would stand in the way of your self-conquest. When outsiders speak in praise of me, or of the Doctrine, or of the Order, you should acknowledge what is right to be the fact saying: "For this or that reason this is the fact, that is so, such a thing is found among us, is in us."

7. It is in respect only of trifling things, of matters of little value, of mere morality, that an unconverted man, when praising the Tathagata, would speak. And what are such trifling, minor details of mere morality that he would praise? (4) (The Moralities. Part 1).

8. "Putting away the killings of living things, Gotama the recluse holds aloof from the destruction of life. He has laid the cudgel and the sword aside, and ashamed of roughness, and full of mercy, he dwells compassionate and kind to all creatures that have life. "It is thus that the unconverted man, when speaking in praise of the Tathagata, might speak.

Or he might say: "Putting, away the taking of what has not been given, Gotama the recluse lived aloof from grasping what is not his own. He takes only what is given, and expecting that gifts will come, he passes his life in honesty and purity of heart."

Or he might say: "Putting away in-chastity, Gotama the recluse is chaste. He holds himself aloof, far off, from the vulgar practice, from the sexual act."

9. Or he might say: "Putting away lying words, Gotama the recluse holds himself aloof from falsehood. He speaks truth

from the truth he never swerves ; faithful and trustworthy, he breaks not his word to the world".

Or he might say: "Putting away slander. Gotama the recluse holds himself aloof from calumny. What he hears here he repeats not elsewhere to raise a quarrel against the people here; what he hears elsewhere he repeats not here to raise a quarrel against the people there. Thus does he live as a binder together of those who are divided, an encourage of those who are friends, a peacemaker, a lover of peace, impassioned for peace, a speaker of words that make for peace."

Or he might say: "Putting away rudeness of speech, Gotama the recluse holds himself aloof from harsh language. Whatsoever word is blameless, pleasant to the ear, lovely, reaching to the heart, urbane, pleasing to the people, beloved of the people such are words he speaks."

Or he might say : "Putting away frivolous talk, Gotama the recluse holds himself aloof from vain conversation. In season he speaks, in accordance with the facts, words full of meaning, on religion, on the discipline of the Order. He speaks, and at the right time, words worthy to be laid up in one's heart, fitly illustrated, clearly divided, to the point."

10. Or he might say: "Gotama the recluse holds himself aloof from causing injury to seeds or plants.

He takes but one meal a day, not eating at night, refraining from food after hours (after midday).

He refrains from being a spectator at shows at fairs with nautch dances, singing, and music.

He abstains from wearing, adorning, or ornamenting himself with garlands, scents, and unguents.

He abstains from the use of the large and lofty beds.

He abstains from accepting silver or gold.

He abstains from accepting uncooked grain.

He abstains from accepting raw meat.

He abstains from accepting women or girls.

He abstains from accepting bondmen or bond-women.

He abstains from accepting sheep or goats.

He abstains from accepting fowls or swine.

He abstains from accepting elephants, cattle, horses and mare.

He abstains from accepting cultivated fields or waste.

He abstains from the acting as a go-between or messenger.

He abstains from buying and selling.

He abstains from cheating with scales or bronzes or measures.

He abstains from the crooked ways of bribery, cheating, and fraud.

He abstains from maiming, murder, putting in bonds, highway robbery, dacoity, and violence."

Such are the things, brethren, which an unconverted man, when speaking in praise of the Tathagata might say. '

Here ends the Kula Sila (the Short Paragraphs on Conduct).

II. Or he might say: "Whereas some recluses and Brahmans, while living on food provided by the faithful, continue addicted to the injury of seedlings and growing plants whether propagated from roots or cuttings or joints or buddings or seeds—Gotarna the recluse holds aloof from such injury to seedlings and growing plants. "

12. Or he might say: "Whereas some recluses and Brahmans, while living on food provided by the faithful, continue addicted to the use of the things stored up; stores, to wit, of foods, drinks, clothing, equipages, bedding, perfumes, and curry-stuffs—Gotama the recluse holds aloof from such use of things stored up."

13. Or he might say: "Whereas some recluses and Brahmans, while living on food provided by the faithful, continue addicted to visiting shows ; that is to say,

(1) Nautch dances (nakkarn),

(2) Singings of songs (gitam)

(3) Instrumental music (vaditam)

(4) Shows at fairs (pekham)

(5) Ballads recitations (akkhanam)

(6) Hand music (paniseram)

(7) The chanting of bards (vetala)

(8) Tam-tam playing (kumbhathunam) (9) Fair scences (sobhanagarkarn)

(10) Acrobatic feats by Kandalas (Kandala-vamsa-dhopanam)

(11) Combats of elephants, horses, buffaloes, bulls, goats, rams.

Cocks and quails.

(12) Bouts at quarterstaff, boxing, wrestling.

(13)-(16) Sham-fights, roll-calls, manoeuvres, reviews. Gotama the recluse holds aloof from visiting such shows." 14. Or he might say: "Whereas some recluses and Brahmans, while living on food provided by the faithful, continue addicted to games and recreations, that is to say.

(1) Games on hoards with eight, or with ten rows of squares.

(2) The same games played by imagining such boards in the air.

(3) Keeping going over diagrams drawn on the ground so that one-steps only where one ought to go.

(4) Either removing the pieces or men from a heap with *one's* nail or putting them into a heap in each case without shaking it. He, who shakes the heap, loses.

(5) Throwing dice.

(6) Hitting a short stick with a long one.

(7) Dipping the hand with the fingers stretched out in lac or red dye, or flour water, and striking the wet hand on the ground or on a wall calling out 'What shall it be?' and showing the form requires—elephants, horses etc.,

(8) Games with balls.

(9) Blowing through toy pipes made of leaves.

(10) Ploughing with toy ploughs.

(11) Turning summersaults.

(12) Playing with toy windmills made of palm leaves.

(13) Playing with toy measures made of palm leaves.

(14, 15) Playing with toy carts or toy bows.

(16) Guessing at letters traced in the air, or on a playfellow's back.

(17) Guessing the playfellow's thoughts.

(I8) Mimicry of deformities. Gotama the recluse holds aloof from such games and recreations."

15. Or he might say: "Whereas some recluses and Brahmans, while living on food provided by the faithful, continue addicted to the use of high and large couches: that is to say,

(1) Moveable settees, high, and six feet long (Asandi).

(2) Divans with animal figures carved on the supports (Pallanko).

(3) Goats' hair coverings with very long fleece (Ganako).

(4) Patchwork counterpanes of many colour (Kittaka).

(5) White blankets (Patika).

(6) Woollen coverlets embroidered with flowers (Patalika).

(7) Quilts stuffed with cottonwood (Tulika).

(8) Coverlets embroidered with figures of lions, tigers, &c., (Vikatika).

(9) Rugs with fur on both sides (Uddalomi).

(10) Rugs with fur on one side (Ekantalomi).

(11) Coverlets embroidered with gems (Katthissam).

(12) Silk coverlets (Koseyyam).

(13) Carpets large enough for sixteen dancers (Kuttakam).

(14-16) Elephant, horse, and chariot rugs.

(17) Rugs of antelope skins sewn together (Aginapaveni).

(18) Rugs of skins of the plantain antelope.

(19) Carpets with awnings above them (Sauttarakkhadam).

(20) Sofas with red pillows for the head and feet."

16. Or he might say: "Whereas some recluses and Brahmans, while living on food provided by the faithful, continue addicted to the use of means for adorning and beautifying themselves: that is to say:

Rubbing in scented powders on one's body, shampooing it, and bathing it patting the limbs with clubs after the manner of wrestlers. The use of mirrors, eye-ointments, garlands, rouge, cosmetics, bracelets, necklaces, walking sticks, reed cases for drugs, rapiers, sunshades, embroidered slippers, turbans, diadems, whisks of the yak's tail, and long-fringed white robes. Gotama the recluse holds aloof from such means of adorning and beautifying the person."

17. Or he might say: "Whereas some recluses and Brahmans while living on food provided by the faithful, continue addicted to such low conversation as these:

Tales of kings, of robbers, of ministers of state, tales of war, of terrors, of battles; talk about foods and drinks, clothes, beds, garlands, perfumes, talks about relationships, equipages, villages, towns, cities, and countries. Tales about women, and about heroes; gossip at street corners, or places whence water is fetched: ghost stories; desultory talk; speculations about the creation of the land or sea, or about existence and non-existence.

Gotama the recluse holds aloof from such low conversation."

18. Or he might say: "Whereas some recluses and Brahmans, while living on food provided by the faithful, continue addicted to the use of wrangling phrases: such as:

"You don't understand this doctrine and discipline, I do."

"How should you know about this doctrine and discipline?"

"You have fallen into wrong views. It is I who am in the right."

"I am speaking to the point, you are not."

"You are putting last what ought to come first, and first what ought to come last."

"What you've excoriated so long, that's all quite upset."

"Your challenge has been taken up."

"You are proved to be wrong." "Set to work to clear your views."

"Disentangle yourself if you can."

Gotama the recluse holds aloof from such wrangling phrases."

19. Or he might say, "Whereas some recluses and Brahmans, while living on food provided by the faithful, continue addicted to taking messages, going on errands, and acting as go-betweens; to wit, on kings, ministers of state, Kshatriyas, Brahmans, or young men, saying. Go there, come-hither, take this with you, bring that from thence.'

Gotama the recluse abstains from such servile duties." 20. Or he might say: "Whereas some recluses and Brahmans, while living on food provided by the faithful, are tricksters, droners out (of holy words for pay), diviners, and exorcists, ever hungering to add gain to gain.

Gotam the recluse holds aloof from such deception and patter." Here ends the Majjhima Sila (the Longer Paragraphs on Conduct).

21. Or he might say: "Whereas some recluses and Brahmans, while living on food provided by the faithful, earn their living by wrong means of livelihood, by low arts, such as these:

(1) Palmistry—prophesying long life, prosperity, &c., (or the reverse), from marks on a child's hands, feet, &c.

(2) Divining by means of omens and signs.

(3) Auguries had drawn from thunderbolts and other celestial portents.

(4) Prognostication by interpreting dreams.

(5) Fortune telling from marks on the body.

(6) Auguries from the marks on cloth gnawed by mice.

(7) Sacrificing to Agni.

(8) Offering oblations from a spoon. (9-13) Making offerings to gods of husks, of the red powder between the grain and the husk, of husked grain ready for boiling, of ghee and of oil.

(14) Sacrificing by spewing mustard seeds, &c., into the fire out of one's mouth.

(15) Drawing blood from one's right knee as a sacrifice to the gods.

(16) Looking at the knuckles, &c., and, after muttering a charm, divining whether a man is well born of luck or not.

(17) Determining whether the site, for a proposed house or pleasance, is lucky or not.

(18) Advising on customary law.

(19) Laying demons in a cemetery.

(20) Laying ghosts.

(21) Knowledge of the charms to be used when lodging in an earth house.

(22) Snake charming.

(23) The poison craft.

(24) The scorpion craft.

(25) The mouse craft.

(26) The bird craft.

(27) The crow craft.

(28) Foretelling the number of years that a man has yet to live.

(29) Giving charms to ward off arrows.

(30) The animal wheel.

Gotama the recluse holds aloof from such low arts."

22. Or he might say: "Whereas some recluses and Brahmans while living on food provided by the faithful, earn their living by wrong means of livelihood, by low arts, such as these:

Knowledge of the signs of good and bad qualities in the following things, and of the marks in them denoting the health or luck of their owners to wit, gems, staves, garments, swords, arrows, bows, other weapons, women, men, boys, girls, slaves, slave-girls, elephants, horses, buffaloes, bulls, oxen, goats, sheep, fowls, quails, iguanas, herrings, tortoises, and other animals.

Gotama the recluse holds aloof from such low arts."

23. Or he might say: "Whereas some recluses and Brahmans, while living on food provided by the faithful, earn their living by wrong means of livelihood by low arts, such as sooth saying to the effect that:

The chiefs will march out.

The home chiefs will attack, and the enemies retreat.

The enemies' chiefs will attack, and ours will retreat.

The home chiefs will gain the victory, and ours will suffer defeat.

The foreign chiefs will gain the victory on this side, and ours will suffer defeat.

Thus will there be victory on this side, defeat on that.

Gotama the recluse holds aloof from such low arts."

24. Or he might say: "Whereas some recluses and Brahmans,

while living on food provided by the faithful, earn their living by wrong means of livelihood, by such low arts as foretelling:

(1) There will be an eclipse of the Moon.

(2) There will be an eclipse of the Sun.

(3) There will be an eclipse of a Star (Nakshatra).

(4) There will be aberration or the Sun or the Moon.

(5) The Sun or the Moon will return to its usual path.

(6) There will be aberrations of the Stars.

(7) The Stars will return to their usual course.

(8) There will be a fall of meteors.

(9) There will be a jungle fire.

(10) There will be an earthquake.

(11) The God will thunder.

(12-15) There will be rising and setting, clearness and dimness of the Sun or the Moon or the stars, or foretelling of each of these fifteen phenomena that they will betoken such and such a result."

Gotama the recluse holds aloof from such low arts.

25. Or he might say: "Whereas some recluses and Brahmans, while living on food provided by the faithful, earn their living by wrong means of the livelihood, by low arts, such as these:

- Foretelling an abundant rainfall.
- Foretelling a deficient rainfall.
- Foretelling agood harvest.
- Foretelling scarcity of food.
- Foretelling tranquility.
- Foretelling disturbances.
- Foretelling a pestilence.
- Foretelling a healthy season.
- Counting on the fingers.
- Counting without using the fingers.
- Summing up large totals.
- Composing ballads, poetising, Casuistry, sophistry.

Gotama the recluse holds aloof from such low arts." 26. Or he might say: "Whereas some recluses and Brahmans, while living on food provided by the faithful, earn their living by wrong means of livelihood, by low arts, such as:

(1) Arranging a lucky day for marriages in which the bride or bridegroom is brought home.

(2) Arranging a lucky day for marriages in which the bride or bridegroom is sent forth.

(3) Fixing a lucky time for the conclusion of treaties of peace (or using charms to procure harmony)

(4) Fixing a lucky time for the outbreak of hostilities (or using charms to make discord).

(5) Fixing a lucky time for the calling in of debts (or charms for success in throwing dice).

(6) Fixing a lucky time for the expenditure of money (or charms to bring ill luck to an opponent throwing dice).

(7) Using charms to make people lucky.

(8) Using charms to make people unlucky.

(9) Using charms to procure abortion.

(10) Incantations to keep a man's jaws fixed.

(11) Incantations to bring on dumbness.

(12) Incantations to make a man throw up his hands.

(13) Incantations to bring on deafness.

(14) Obtaining oracular answers by means of the magic mirror.

(15) Obtaining oracular answers through a girl possessed.

(16) Obtaining oracular answers from a god.

(17) The worship of the Sun.

(18) The worship of the Great One.

(19) Bringing forth flames from one's mouth.

(20) Invoking Siri, the goddess of Luck.

Gotama the recluse holds aloof from such low arts."

27. Or he might say: "Whereas some recluses and Brahmans, while living on food provided by the faithful, earn their living by wrong means of livelihood, by low arts, such as these:

(1) Vowing gifts to a god if a certain benefit be granted,

(2) Praying such vows.

(3) Repeating charms while lodging in an earth house.

(4) Causing virility.

(5) Making a man impotent.

(6) Fixing on lucky sites for dwellings.

(7) Consecrating sites.

(8) Ceremonial rinsing of the mouth.

(9) Ceremonial bathing.

(10) Offering sacrifices.

(11-14) Administering emetics and purgatives.

(15) Purging people to relieve the head (that is by giving drugs to make people sneeze).

(16) Oiling people's ears (either to make them grow or to heal sores on them).

(17) Satisfying people's eyes (soothing them by dropping medicinal oils into them).

(I8) Administering drugs through the nose.

(19) Applying collyrium to the eyes.

(20) Giving medical ointment for the eyes.

(21) Practising as an oculist.

(22) Practising as a surgeon.

(23) Practising as a doctor for children.

(24) Administering roots and drugs.

(25) Administering medicines in rotation.

Gotama the recluse holds aloof from such low arts.

"These brethren are the trifling matters, the minor details of morality, of which the unconverted man, when praising the Tathagata, might speak.'

Here end the Long Paragraphs on Conduct.

This was indeed the highest standard for a moral life for an individual to follow. So high a standard of moral life was quite unknown to the Aryan Society of his day.

He did not stop merely with setting an example by leading a life of purity. He also wanted to mould the character of the ordinary men and women in society. For their guidance he devised a form of baptism which was quite unknown to the

Aryan Society. The baptism consisted in the convert to Buddhism undertaking to observe certain moral precepts laid down by Buddha. These precepts are known as Panch Sila or the five precepts. They are; (1) Not to kill, (2) Not to steal, (3) Not to lie, (4) Not to be unchaste and (5) Not to drink intoxicants.

These five precepts were of the laity.

For the Monks there were five additional precepts:

(6) Not to eat at forbidden times,

(7) Not to dance, sing, or attend theatrical or other spectacles,

(8) To abstain from the use of garlands, scents, and ornaments,

(9) To abstain from the use of high or broad beds, and

(10) Never to receive money.

These *Silas* or precepts formed the moral code which it was intended should regulate the thoughts and actions of men and women.

Of these the most important one was the precept not to kill. Buddha took care to make it clear that the precept did not merely mean abstention from taking life. He insisted that the precept must be understood to mean positive sympathy, good will, and love for every thing that breathes.

He gave the same positives and extended content to other precepts. One of the Buddha's lay followers once reported to him the teaching of a non-Buddhist ascetic, to the effect that the highest ideal consisted in the absence of evil deeds, evil words, evil thoughts, and evil life. The Buddha's comment upon this is significant. "If, said he, "this were true, then every suckling child would have attained the ideal of life. Life is knowledge of good and evil; and after that the exchange of evil deeds, words, thoughts, and life, for good ones. This is to be brought about only by a long and determined effort of the will".

Buddha's teachings were not merely negative. They are positive and constructive. Buddha was not satisfied with a man following his precepts. He insisted upon encouraging others to follow them. For example in the *Auguttara Nikaya* the Buddha is quoted as distinguishing between a good man and a very good man by saying that one who abstains from killing, stealing, in-chastity, lying and drunkenness may be called good ; but only he deserves to be called very good who abstains from these evil things himself and also instigates others to do the like..........

As has been well said the two cardinal virtues of Buddhism are love and wisdom.

How deeply he inculcated the practice of love as a virtue is clear from his own words. "As a mother at the risk of her life watches over her own child, her only child, so also let every one cultivate: a boundless loving mind towards all beings. And let him cultivate good will towards, the entire world, a boundless (loving) mind above and below and across, unobstructed, without hatred, without enmity. This way of living is the best in the world." So taught Buddha.

"Universal pity, sympathy for all suffering beings, good will to every form of sentient life, these things characterised the Tathagath (Buddha) as they have few others of the sons of men ; and he succeeded in a most surprising degree in handing on his point of view to his followers.

Buddha held to the doctrine of wisdom as firmly as he did to the doctrine of love. He held that moral life began with knowledge and ended with wisdom. he "came to save the world, and his method for the accomplishment of this end was the destruction of ignorance and the dissemination of knowledge as to the true values of life and the wise way to live. "Buddha did not arrogate to himself the power to save people. People had to do that for themselves. And the way to save lay through knowledge. So much insistence did he place upon knowledge that he did not think that morality without knowledge was virtue.

There are three things against which Buddha carried on a great campaign.

He repudiated the authority of the Vedas.......... Secondly he denounced the *Yudna* as a form of religion. The attitude of Buddha towards Yadna is well stated in the Jatakamala in the form of a story. The story runs thus :

The Story of the Sacrifice

Those hearts are pure do not act up to the enticement of the wicked. Knowing this, pure-heartiness is to be striven after. This will be taught by the following:

Long ago the Bodhisattva it is said, was a king who had obtained his kingdom in the order of hereditary succession. He had reached this state as the effect of his merit, and ruled his realm in peace, not disturbed by any rival, his sovereignty being universally acknowledged. His country was free from any kind of annoyance, vexation or disaster, both his home relations and those with foreign countries being quite in every respect; and all his vessels obeyed his commands.

1. This monarch having subdued the passions, his enemies, felt no inclination for such profits as are to be blamed when enjoyed, but was with his whole heart intent on promoting the happiness of his subjects. Holding virtuous practice (dharma) the only purpose of his actions, he behaved like a Muni.

2. For he knew the nature of mankind, that people set a high value on imitating the behaviour of the highest. For this reason, being desirous of bringing about salvation for his subjects, he was particularly attached to the due performance of his religious duties. 3. He practised almsgiving kept strictly the precepts of moral conduct (sila), cultivated forbearance, strove for the benefit of the creatures. His mild countenance being in accordance with his thoughts devoted to the happiness of his subjects, he appeared like the embodied Dharma.

Now it once happened that though protected by his arm, his realm, both in consequence of the faulty actions of its inhabitants and inadvertence on the part of the angels charged with the care of rain, was afflicted in several districts by drought and the troublesome effects of such a disaster. Upon this the king, fully convinced that his plague had been brought about by the violation of righteousness by himself or his subjects, and taking much to heart the distress of his people, whose welfare was the constant object of his thoughts and cares, took the advice of men of acknowledged competence, who were reputed for their knowledge in matters of religion. So keeping counsel with the elders among the Brahmans, headed by his family priest (purohita) and his ministers, he asked them for some means of putting an end to that calamity. Now they believing a solemn sacrifice as is enjoined by the Veda to be a cause of abundant rain, explained to him that he must perform such a sacrifice of a frightful character, inasmuch as it requires the massacre of many hundreds of living beings. But after being informed of everything concerning such a slaughter as is prescribed for the sacrifice, his innate compassion forbade him to approve of their advice in his heart; yet out of civility, unwilling to offend them by harsh words of refusal, he slipped over this point, turning the conversation upon other topics. They, on the other hand, no sooner caught the opportunity of conversing with the king on matters of religion, than they once more admonished him to accomplish the sacrifice, for they did not understand his deeply hidden mind.

4. "You constantly take care not to neglect the proper time of performing your different royal duties, established for the sake of obtaining the possession of land and ruling it. The due order of these actions of yours is in agreement with the precepts of Righteousness (dharma).

5. "How then is this that you who (in all other respects) are so clever in the observance of the triad (of dharma, artha, and kama), bearing your bow to defend the good of your people, are so careless and almost sluggish as to that bridge to the world of the Devas, the name of which is 'sacrifice'?

6. " Like servants, the kings (your vassel) revere your commands, thinking them to be the surest gage of success. Now the time is come, 0 destroyer of your foes, to gather by means of sacrifice superior blessings, which are to procure for you a shining glory.

7. 'Certainly, that holiness which is the requisite for a dikshita is already yours, by reason of your habitual practice of charity and your strictness in observing the restraint (of good conduct). Nevertheless, it would be fit for you to discharge your debt to the Devas by such sacrifices as are the subject matter of the Veda. The deities being satisfied by duly and faultlessly performed sacrifice, honour the creatures in return by (sending) rain. Thus considering, take to mind the welfare of your subjects and your own, and consent to the performance of a regular sacrifice which will enhance your glory.'

8. Thereupon he entered upon this thought: ' Very badly guarded is my poor person indeed, being given in trust to such leaders. While faithfully believing and loving the law, I should uproot my virtue of tender heartiness by reliance upon the words of others. For, truly.'

9. Those who are reputed among men to be the best refuge are the very persons who intend to do harm, borrowing their arguments from the Law. Alas! Such a man, who follows the wrong path shown by them, will soon find himself driven to straits, for he will be surrounded by evils.

10. What connections may there be, forsooth, between righteousness and injuring animals? How my residence in the world of the Devas or propitiation of the deities have anything to do with the murder of victims?

II. The animal slaughtered according to the rites with the prescribed prayers, as if those sacred formulas were so many darts to wound it, goes to heaven, they say, and with this object it is killed. In this way that action is interpreted to be done according to the Law. Yet it is a lie.

12.For how is it possible that in the next world one should reap the fruits of what has been done by others? And by what reason will the sacrificial animal mount to heaven, though he has not abstained from wicked actions, though he has not devoted himself to the practice of good ones, simply because he has been killed in sacrifice, and not on the ground of his own actions?

13. And should the victim killed in sacrifice really go to heaven, should we not expect the Brahmans to offer themselves to be immolated in sacrifice? A similar practice, however, is nowhere seen among them. Who, then, may take to heart the advice proffered by these counsellors?

14. As to the Celestials, should we believe that they who are wont to enjoy the fair ambrosia of incomparable scent, flavour, magnificence, and effective power, served to them by the beautiful Apsaras, would abandon it to delight in the slaughter of a pitiable victim, that they might feast on the omentum and such other parts of his body as are offered to them in sacrifice?

Therefore, it is the proper time to act so and so.' Having thus made up his mind, the king feigned to be eager to undertake the sacrifice; and in approval of their words he spoke to them in this manner; 'Verily, well protected am I, well gratified, having such counsellors as Your Lordships are, thus bent on securing my happiness! Therefore I will have a human sacrifice (purushamedha) of a thousand victims performed. Let my officials, each in his sphere of business, be ordered to bring together the requisites necessary for that purpose. Let also an inquiry be made of the most fitting ground whereon to raise the tents and other buildings for the sattra. Further, the proper time for the sacrifice must be fixed (by the astrologers) examining the auspicious lunar days, karanas, muhurtas, and constellations.'

The purohita answered; `In order to succeed in your enterprise, Your Majesty ought to take the Avabhritha (final bath) at the end of one sacrifice; after which you may successively undertake the others. For if the thousand human victims were to be seized at once, your subjects, to be sure, would blame you and be stirred up to great agitation on their account.' These words of the purohita having been approved by the (other) Brahmans, the king replied: ' Do not apprehend the wrath of the people, Reverands. I shall take such measures as to prevent any agitation among my subjects.'

15. After this the king convoked an assembly of the townsmen and the lands men, and said: 'I intend to perform a human sacrifice of a thousand victims. But nobody behaving honestly is fit to be designated for immolation on my part. With this in mind, I give you this advice. Whomsoever of you I shall henceforward perceive transgressing the boundaries of moral conduct, despising my royal will him I order to be caught to be a victim at my sacrifice, thinking such a one the stain of his family and a danger to my country. With the object of carrying this resolution into effect, I shall cause you to be observed by faultless and sharp-sighted emissaries, who have shaken off sleepy carelessness and will report to me concerning your conduct. '

16. Then the foremost of the assembly, folding their hands and bringing them to their foreheads, spoke:

'Your Majesty, all your actions tend to the happiness of your subjects, what reason can there be to despise you on that account? Even (God) Brahma cannot but sanction your behaviour. Your Majesty, who is the authority of the virtuous, be our highest authority. For this reason anything which pleases Your Majesty must please us too. Indeed, you are pleased with nothing else but our enjoyment and our good.'

After then, notables both of the town and the country had accepted his command in this manner; the king dispersed about his towns and all over his country, officers notified as such by their outward appearance to the people with the charge of laying hold of the evil doers, and everywhere he ordered proclamations to be made by beat of drum day after day, of this kind.

17. The King, a granter of security as he is, warrants safety to every one who constantly cultivates honesty and good conduct, in short, to the virtuous, yet, intending to perform a human sacrifice for the benefit of his subjects, he wants human victims by thousands to be taken out of those who delight in misconduct.

18. 'Therefore, whosoever henceforward, licentiously indulging in misbehaviour, shall disregard the command of our monarch, which is even observed by the kings, his vassals, shall be brought to the state as a sacrificial victim by the very force of his own actions, and people shall witness his miserable suffering, when he shall pine with pain, his body being fastened to the sacrificial post.'

When the inhabitants of that realms became aware of their king's careful search after evil-doers with the aim of destining them to be victims at his sacrifice-for they heard the most frightful royal proclamation day after day and saw the king's servants, who were appointed to look out for wicked people and to seize them. Appearing every now and then everywhere they abandoned their attachment to bad conduct, and grew intend on strictly observing the moral precepts and self-control. They avoided every occasion of hatred and enmity and settling their quarrels and differences, cherished mutual love and mutual esteem. Obedience to the words of parents and teachers, a general spirit of liberality and sharing with others, hospitality, good manners, modesty, prevailed among them. In short, they lived as it was in the Krita Yuga.

19. The fear of death had awakened in them thoughts of the next world; the risk of tarnishing the honour of their families had stirred their care of guarding their reputation; the great purity of their hearts had strengthened their sense of shame. These factors being at work, people were soon distinguished by their spotless behaviour.

20. Even though every one became more than ever intends on keeping a righteous conduct, still the king's servants did not diminish their watchfulness in the pursuit of the evildoers. This also contributed to prevent people from falling short of righteousness.

21. The king learning from his emissaries this state of things in his realm, felt extremely rejoiced. He bestowed rich presents on those messengers as a reward for the good news they told him, and enjoined his ministers, speaking something like this :

22. The protection of my subjects is my highest desire, you know. Now they have become worthy to be recipients of sacrificial gifts, and it is for the purpose of my sacrifice that I have provided this wealth. Well, I intend to accomplish my sacrifice in the manner, which I have considered to be the proper once. Let every one who wishes for money, that it may be fuel for his happiness, come and accept it from my hand to his heart's content. In this way the distress and poverty, which is vexing our country, may be soon driven out. Indeed, whenever I consider my own strong determination to protect my subjects and the great assistance I derive from you, my excellent companions in that task, it often seems to me as though those sufferings of my people, by exciting my anger, were burning in my mind like a blazing fire.'

24. The ministers accepted the royal command and anon went to execute it. They ordered alms-halls to be established in all villages, towns, and markets, likewise at all stations on the roads. This being done, they caused all who begged in order to satisfy their wants, to be provided day after day with a gift of those objects, just as had been ordered by the king.

25. So poverty disappeared, and the people, having received wealth from the part of the king, dressed and adorned with manifold and fine garments and ornaments, exhibited the splendour of festival days.

26. The glory of the king, magnified by the eulogies of the rejoiced recipients of his gifts, spread about in all directions in the same way, as the flower dust of the lotuses carried forth by the small waves of a lake, extends itself over a larger and larger surface.

27. And after the whole people, in consequence of the wise measures taken by their ruler, had become intent on virtuous behaviour, the plagues and calamities, overpowered by the growth of all such qualities as conduce to prosperity, faded away, having lost their hold.

28. The seasons succeeded each other in due course, rejoicing everybody by their regularity, and like kings newly established, complying with the lawful order of things. Consequently the earth produced the various kinds of corn in abundance, and there was fullness of pure and blue water and lotuses in all water basins.

29. No epidemics afflicted mankind; the medicinal herbs possessed their efficacious virtues more than ever; monsoons blew in due time and regularly; the planets moved along in auspicious paths.

30. Nowhere there existed any danger to be feared, either from abroad, or from within, or such as might be caused by dangerous derangement of the elements. Continuing in righteousness and self-control, cultivating good behaviour and modesty, the people of that country enjoyed as it were the prerogatives of the Krita Yuga. By the power, then, of the king performing his sacrifice in this manner in accordance with (the precepts of) the Law, the sufferings of the indigent were put to an end together with the plagues and calamities, and the country abounded in a prosperous and thriving population offering the pleasing aspect of felicity. Accordingly people never wearied of repeating benedictions on their king and extending his renown in all directions.

One day, one of the highest royal officials, whose heart had been inclined to the (True) Belief, spoke thus to the king: "This is a true saying, in truth.

31. "Monarchs, because they always deal with all kinds of business, the highest, the lowest, and the intermediate, by far surpass in their wisdom any wise men.

"For, Your Majesty, you have obtained the happiness of your subjects both in this world and in the next, as the effect of your sacrifice being performed in righteousness, free from the blameable sin of animal-slaughter. The hard times are all over and the sufferings of poverty have ceased, since men have been established in the precepts of good conduct. Why use many words? Your subjects are happy.

32. "The black antelope's skin which covers your limbs has the resemblance of the spot on the bright Moon's surface, nor can the natural loveliness of your demeanour be hindered by the restraint imposed on you by your being a dikshita. Your head, adorned with such hair-dress as is in compliance with the rites of the diksha, possesses no less lustre than when it was embellished with the splendour of the royal umbrella. And, last not least, by your largesse's you have surpassed the renown and abated the pride of the famous performer of a hundred sacrifices.

33. "As a rule, Oh, you wise ruler, the sacrifice of those who long for the attainment of some good, is a vile act, accompanied as it is by injury done to living beings. Your sacrifice, on the contrary, this monument of your glory, is in complete accordance with your lovely behaviour and your aversion to vices.

34. "Oh! Happy are the subjects who have their protector in you! It is certain that no father could be a better guardian to his children." Another said:

35." If the wealthy practise charity, they are commonly impelled to do so by the hopes they put in the cultivation of that virtue; good conduct too, may be accounted for by the wish to obtain high regard among men or the desire of reaching heaven after death. But such a practice of both, as is seen in your skill in securing the benefit of others, cannot be found but in those who are accomplished both in learning and in virtuous exertions. "In such a way, then, those whose hearts are pure do not act up to the enticement of the wicked. Knowing this, pure-heartiness is to be striven after." (In the spiritual lessons for princes, also this is to be said: ' Who to his subjects wishing good, himself exerts, Thus brings about salvation, glory, happiness. No other should be of a king the businesses.

And it may be added as follows: '(The prince) who strives after material prosperity, ought to act in accordance with the precepts of religion, thinking, a religious conduct of his subjects to be the source of prosperity.'

Further this is here to be said: 'Injuring animals never tends to bliss, but charity, self-restraint, continence and the like have this power; for this reason he who longs for bliss must devote himself to these virtues. 'And also when discoursing on the Tathagata : 'In this manner the Lord showed his inclination to care for the interests of the world, when he was still in his previous existences.')

Another powerful attack against Yadna is contained in his discourses known as Kutadanta Sutta. It is as follows :

The Wrong Sacrifice and the Right

1. Thus have I heard. The Blessed One once, when going on a tour through Magadha, with a great multitude of the brethren, with about five hundred brethren, came to a Brahman village in Magadha called Khanumata. And there at Khanumata he lodged in the Ambalatthika pleasance.

Now at that time the Brahman Kutadanta was dwelling at Khanumata, a place teeming with life, with much grassland and woodland and water and corn, on a royal domain presented him by Seniya Bimbisara the king of Magadha, as a royal gift, with power over it as if he were the king.

And just then a great sacrifice was being got ready on behalf of Kutadanta the Brahman. And a hundred bulls, and a hundred steers, and a hundred heifers, and a hundred goats, and a hundred rams had been brought to the post for the sacrifice.

2. Now the Brahmans and householders of Khanumata heard the news of the arrival of the Samana Gotama. And they began to leave Khanumata in companies and in bonds to go to the Ambalatthika pleasance.

3. And just then Kutandanta the Brahman had gone apart to the upper terrace of his house for his siesta; and seeing the people thus to go by, he asked his door-keeper the reason. And the doorkeeper told him.

4. Then Kutandanta thought: 'I have heard that the Samana Gotarna understands about the successful performance of a sacrifice with its threefold method and its sixteen accessory instruments. Now I don't know all this, and yet I want to carry out a sacrifice. It would be well for me to go to the Samana Gotama, and ask him about it. '

So he sent his doorkeeper to the Brahmans and householders of Khanumata, to ask them to wait till he could go with them to call upon the Blessed One.

5. But there were at that time a number of Brahmans staying at Khanumata to take part in the great sacrifice. And when they heard this they went to Kutadanta, and persuaded him on the same grounds as the Brahmans had laid before Sonadanda, not to go. But he answered them in the same terms as Sonadanda had used to those Brahmans. Then they were satisfied, and went with him to call upon the Blessed One.

9. And when he was seated there Kutadanta the Brahman told the Blessed One what he had heard, and requested him to tell him about success in performing a sacrifice in its three modes and with its accessory articles of furniture of sixteen kinds.

'Well then, O Brahman, give ear and listen attentively and I will speak.'

'Very well, Sir, `said Kutadanta in reply; and the Blessed One spoke as follows:

10. 'Long ago, O Brahman, there was a king by name Wide-realm (Maha Vigita), mighty, with great wealth and large property; with stores of silver and gold, of aids to enjoyment, of goods and corn; with his treasure-houses and his garners full. Now when King Wide-realm was once sitting alone in meditation, he became anxious at the thought: "I have in abundance all the good things a mortal can enjoy. The whole wide circle of the earth is mine by conquest to possess. 'Twere well if I were to offer a great sacrifice that should ensure me weal and welfare for many days. "

And he had the Brahman, his chaplain, called; and telling him all that he had thought, he said: "Be I would faun, O Brahman, offer a great sacrifice-let the venerable one instruct me how-for my weal and my welfare for many days."

11. Thereupon the Brahman who was chaplain said to the king: "The king's country, Sirs, is harassed and harried. There are decoits abroad who pillages the villages and townships, and who makes the roads unsafe. Were the king, so long as that is so, to levy a fresh tax, verily his majesty would be acting wrongly. But perchance his majesty might think. 'I'll soon put

a stop to these scoundrels' game by degradation and banishment, and fines and bonds and death! ' But their license cannot be satisfactorily put a stop to. The remnant left unpunished would still go on harassing the realm. Now there is one method to adopt to put a thorough end to this disorder. Whosoever there be in the king's realm who devote themselves to keeping cattle and the farm, to them let his majesty the king give food and seed-corn. Whosoever there be in the king's realm who devote themselves to trade, to them let his majesty the king give capital. Whosoever there be in the king's realm who devote themselves to government service, to them let his majesty the king give wages and food. Then those men following each his own business, will no longer harass the realm; the king's revenue will go up ; the country will be quiet and at peace ; and the populace, pleased one with another and happy; dancing their children in their arms, will dwell with open doors."

'Then King Wide-realm, O Brahman, accepted the word of his chaplain, and did as he had said. And those men, following each his business, harassed the realm no more. And the King's revenue went up. And the country became quiet and at peace. And the populace pleased one with another and happy, dancing their children in their arms, dwelt with open doors.'

12. 'So King Wide-realm had his chaplain called, and said: "The disorder is at an end. The country is at peace. I want to offer that great sacrifice—let the venerable one instruct me how—for my weal and my welfare for many days."

' Then let his majesty the king send invitations to whomsoever there may be in his realm who are Kshatriyas, vassals of his, either in the country or the towns ; or who are ministers and officials of his, either in the country or the towns ; or who are Brahmans of position, either in the country or the towns ; or who are householders of substance, either in the country or the towns, saying : "I intend to offer a great sacrifice. Let the venerable ones give their sanction to what will be to me for weal and welfare for many days."

'Then King Wide-realm, O Brahman, accepted the word of his chaplain, and did as he had said. And they each—Kshatriyas and ministers and Brahmans and householders—made alike reply: "Let his majesty the king celebrate the sacrifice. The time is suitable O King! " ' Thus did these four, as colleagues by consent, become wherewithal to furnish forth that sacrifice,

13. 'King Wide-realm was gifted in the following eight ways:

'He was well born on both sides, on the mother's side and on the father's, of pure descent back through seven generations, and no slur was cast upon him, and no reproach, in respect of birth.'

'He was handsome, pleasant in appearance, inspiring trust, gifted with great beauty of complexion, fair in colour, fine in presence, stately to behold.'

' He was mighty, with great wealth, and large property, with stores of silver and gold, of aids to enjoyment, of goods and corn, with his treasure-houses and his garners full.'

' He was powerful, in command of an army, loyal and disciplined in four divisions (of elephants, cavalry, chariots, and bow men), burning up, methinks, his enemies by his very glory.'

' He was a believer, and generous, a noble giver, keeping open house, a well in spring whence Samanas and Brahmans, the poor and the wayfarers, beggars, and petitioners might draw, a doer of good deeds. '

'He was learned in all kinds of knowledge.' ' He knew the meaning of what had been said, and could explain, " This saying has such and such a meaning, and that such and such ".

' He was intelligent, expert and wise and able to think out things present or past or future.

' And these eight gifts of his, too, became where withal to furnish forth that sacrifice.'

14. 'The Brahman, his chaplain was gifted in the following four ways :

' He was well born on both sides, on the mother's and on the father's, of pure descent back through seven generations, with no slur cast upon him, and no reproach in respect of birth.

' He was a student repeater who knew the mystic verses by heart, master of the three Vedas, with the indices, the ritual, the phonology, and the exegesis (as a fourth), and the legends as a fifth, learned in the idioms and the grammar, versed in Lokayata (Mature-lore) and in the thirty marks on the body of a great man.

' He was virtuous, established in virtue, gifted with virtue that had grown great.

' He was intelligent, expert, and wise; foremost, or at most the second, among those who hold out the ladle. ' ' Thus these four gifts of his, too became wherewithal to furnish forth that sacrifice.'

15. 'And further, O Brahman, the chaplain, before the sacrifice had begun, explained to King Wide-realm the three modes:

Should his majesty the King, before starting on the great sacrifice, feel any such regret as : "Great, alas, will be the portion of my wealth used up herein, "let not the king harbour such regret. Should his majesty the King, whilst he is offering the great sacrifice, feel any such regret as : "Great, alas, will be the portion of my wealth used up herein "let not the king harbour such regret. Should his majesty the King, when the great sacrifice has been offered, feel any such regret as "Great, alas, will be the portion of my wealth used up herein, "let not the king harbour such regret.'

'Thus did the chaplain, O Brahman, before the sacrifice, had begun, explained to King Wide-realm the three modes.'

16. 'And further, 0 Brahman, the chaplain, before the sacrifice had begun, in order to prevent any compunction that might afterwards in ten ways, arise as regards those who had taken part therein, said : "Now there will come to your sacrifice, Sire, men who destroy the life of living things, and men who refrain there from, men who take what has not been given, and men who refrain there from, men who speak lies, and men who do not—men who slander and men who do not—men who speak rudely and men who do not—men who chatter vain things and men who refrain there from—men who covet and men who covet not—men who harbour illwill and men who harbour it not—men whose views are wrong and men whose views are right. Of each of these let them, who do evil, alone with their evil. For them who do well let your majesty offer,

for them, Sire, arrange the rites, for them let the king gratify, in them shall our heart within find peace."

17. 'And further, O Brahman, the chaplain, whilst the king was carrying out the sacrifice, instructed and aroused and incited and gladdened his heart in sixteen ways : "Should there be people who should say of the king, as he is offering the sacrifice : 'King Wide-realm is celebrating sacrifice without having invited the four classes of his subjects, without himself having the eight personal gifts, without the assistance of a Brahman who has the four personal gifts.' Then would they speak not acording to the fact. For the consent of the four classes has been obtained, the king had the eight, and his Brahman has the four, personal gifts. With regard to each and every one of these sixteen conditions the king may rest assured that it has been fulfilled. He can sacrifice, and be glad, and possess his heart in peace."

18. 'And further, O Brahman, at that sacrifice neither were any oxen slain, neither goats, nor fowls, nor fatted pigs, nor were any kinds of living creatures put to death. No trees were cut down to be used as posts, no Dabha grasses mown to strew around the sacrificial spot. And the slaves and messengers and workmen there employed were driven neither by rods nor fear, nor carried on their work weeping with tears upon their faces. Who so chose to help, he worked ; who so chose not to help, worked not. What each chose to do he did; what they chose not to do, that was left undone, With ghee and oil, and butter and milk, and honey and sugar only was that sacrifice accomplished.

19. 'And further, O Brahman, the Kshatriya vassels, and the ministers and officials, and the Brahmans of position, and the householders of substance, whether of the country or of the towns, went to King, Wide-realm, taking with them much wealth, and said, "This abundant wealth, Sire, have we brought hither for the king's use. Let his majesty accept it at our hands!"

"Sufficient wealth have I, my friends, laid up, the produce of taxation that is just. Do you keep yours, and take away more with you! "

When they had thus been refused by the king, they went aside, and considered thus one with the other: "It would not be seem us now, were we to take this wealth away again to our own homes. King Wide-realm is offering a great sacrifice. Let us too make an after-sacrifice!"

20. ' So the Kshatriyas established a continual largesse to the east of the king's sacrificial pit, and the officials to the south thereof, and the Brahmans to the west thereof, and the householders to the north thereof. And the things given, and the manner of their gift, was in all respects like unto the great sacrifice of King Wide-realm himself.'

'Thus, O Brahman, there was a fourfold co-operation, and King Wide-realm was gifted with eight personal gifts, and his officiating Brahman with four. And there were three modes of the giving of that sacrifice. This, 0 Brahman, is what is called the due celebration of a sacrifice in its threefold mode and with its furniture of sixteen kinds.

21. 'And when he had thus spoken, those Brahmans lifted up their voices in tumult, and said: "How glorious the sacrifice, how pure its accomplishment! "But Kutadanta the Brahman sat there in silence.

Then those Brahmans said to Kutadanta : ' Why do you not approve the good words of the Samana Gotarna as well-said?'

' I do not fail to approve ; for he who approves not as well-said that which has been well spoken by the Samana Gotama, verily his head would split in twain. But I was considering that the Samana Gotama does not say : "Thus have I heard," nor "Thus behoves it to be," but says only, " Thus it was then, " or "It was like that then". So I thought ; "For a certainty the Samana Gotama himself must at that time have been King Wide-realm, or the Brahman who officiated for him at that sacrifice. Does the Venerable Gotama admit that he who celebrates such a sacrifice, or causes it to be celebrated, is reborn at the dissolution of the body, after death, into some state of happiness in heaven ? "

'Yes, O Brahman, that I admit. And at that time I was the Brahman who, as chaplain, had that sacrifice performed.'

22. 'Is there, O Gotama, any other sacrifice less difficult and less troublesome, with more fruit and more advantage still

than this? ' ' Yes, 0 Brahman, there is.' 'And what, 0 Gotama, may that be?'

'The perpetual gifts kept up in a family where they are given specifically to virtuous recluses.'

23. 'But what is the reason, O Gotama, and what the cause, why such perpetual giving specifically to virtuous recluses, and kept up in a family, are less difficult and troublesome of greater fruit and greater advantage than that other sacrifice with its three modes and its accessories of sixteen kinds ? '

' To the latter sort of sacrifice, 0 Brahman, neither will the Arhata go, nor such as have entered on the Arhat way. And why not? Because in it beating with sticks takes place, and seizing by the throat. But they will go to the former, where such things are not. And therefore are such perpetual gifts above the other sort of sacrifice.'

24. ' And is there, O Gotama, any other sacrifice less difficult, and less troublesome, of greater fruit and of greater advantage than either of these.' ' Yes, 0 Brahman, there is.' ' And what, 0 Gotama, may that be ? '

'The putting up of a dwelling place (Vihara) on behalf of the Order in all the four directions.'

25. And is there, O Gotama, any other sacrifice less difficult and less troublesome, of greater fruit and of greater advantage than each and all of these three?' 'Yes, 0 Brahman, there is.' ' And what, 0 Gotama, may that be ? '

' He who with trusting heart takes a Buddha as his guide, and the Truth, and the Order—that is a sacrifice better than open largeses, better than perpetual alms, better than the gift of a dwelling place.'

26. 'And is there, O Gotama, any other sacrifice less difficult and less troublesome, of greater fruit and of greater advantage than all these four?'

'When a man with trusting heart takes upon himself the precepts-abstinence from destroying life; abstinence from taking what has not been given ; abstinence from evil conduct in respect of lusts ; abstinence from lying words; abstinence from strong, intoxicating, maddening drinks, the root of carelessness, that is a sacrifice better than open largesses, better than perpetual alms, better than the gift of dwelling places, better than accepting guidance.'

27. 'And is there, O Gotama, any other sacrifice less difficult and less troublesome, of greater fruit and of greater advantage than all these five?' 'Yes, O Brahman, there is.' 'And what, 0 Gotama, may that be?'

(The answer is the long passage from the Samana-phale Sutta 40, p. 62 (of the text,) down to 75 (p. 74) on the First Ghana, as follows :

1. The Introductory paragraphs on the appearance of a Buddha, his preaching, the conversion of ahearer, and his renunciation of the world.

2. The Silas (minor morality).

3. The paragraph on Confidence.

4. The paragraph on 'Guarded is the door of his senses.'

5. The paragraph on ' Mindful and self possessed.'

6. The paragraph on Content.

7. The paragraph on Solitude.

8. The paragraph on the Five Hindrances.

9. The description of the First Ghana.) 'This, 0 Brahman, is a sacrifice less difficult and less troublesome, of greater fruit and greater advantage than the previous sacrifices,

(The same is then said the Second, Third, and Fourth Ghanas, in succession (as in the Samannao-phalo Sutas 77-82) and of the Insight arising from knowledge *(ibid* 83, 84), and further (omitting direct mention either way of 85-96 inclusive) of the knowledge of the destruction of the Asavas the deadly intoxications or floods *(ibid.* 97-98).

' And there is no sacrifice man can celebrate, 0 Brahman, higher and sweeter than this.'

28. And when he had thus spoken, Kutadanta the Brahman said to the Blessed One :

' Most excellent, 0 Gotama, are the words of thy mouth, most excellent ! Just as if a man were to set up what has been thrown down, or were to reveal that which has been hidden away, or were to point out the right road to him who has gone astray, or were to bring a light into the darkness so that those who had eyes could see external forms—just even so has the truth been made known to me in many a figure by the Venerable Gotama. I, even I, betake myself to the Venerable Gotama as my guide, to the Doctrine and the Order. May the Venerable One accept me as a disciple, as one who, from this day forth, as long as life endures has taken him as his guide. And I myself, O Gotama, will have the seven hundred bulls, and the seven hundred steers, and the seven hundred heifers, and the seven hundred goats, and the seven hundred rams set free. To them I grant their life. Let them eat green grass and drink fresh water, and may cool breezes waft around them.'

29. Then the Blessed One discoursed to Kutadanta the Brahman in due order; that is to say, he spoke to him of generosity, of right conduct, of heaven, of the danger, the vanity, and the defilement of lusts, of the advantages of renunciation. And when the Blessed One became aware that Kutadanta the Brahman had become prepared, softened, unprejudiced, upraised, and believing in heart then did he proclaim the doctrine the Buddhas alone have won; that is to say, the doctrine of sorrow, of its origin, of its cessation and of the Path. And just as a clean cloth, with all stains in it washed away, will readily take the dye, just even so did Kutadanta the Brahman, even while seated there, obtain the pure and spotless Eye for the Truth. And he knew whatsoever has a beginning, in that is inherent also the necessity of dissolution.

30. And then the Brahman Kutadanta, as one who had seen the Truth, had mastered it, understood it, dived deep down into it. Who had passed beyond doubt, and put away perplexity and gained full confidence, who had become dependent on no other for his knowledge of the teaching of the Master, addressed the Blessed One and said :

' May the venerable Gotama grant me the favour of taking his tomorrow meal with me and also the members of the Order with him. '

And the Blessed One signified, by silence, his consent. Then the Brahman Kutadanta, seeing that the Blessed One had accepted, rose from his seat, and keeping his right towards him as he passed, he departed thence. And at daybreak he had sweet food, both hard and soft, made ready at the pit prepared for his sacrifice and had the time announced to the Blessed One: 'It is time, 0 Gotama and the meal is ready. ' And the Blessed One, who had dressed early in the morning, put on his outer robe, and taking his bowl with him, went with the brethren to Kutadanta's sacrificial pit, and sat down there on the seat prepared for him. And Kutadanta the Brahman satisfied the brethren with the Buddha at their head, with his own hand, with sweet food, both hard and soft, till they refused any more. And when the Blessed One had finished his meal, and cleansed the bowl and his hands, Kutadanta the Brahman took a low seat and seated himself beside him. And when he was thus seated, the Blessed One instructed and aroused and incited and gladdened Kutadanta the Brahman with religious discourse ; and then arose from his seat and departed thence.

Thirdly Buddha denounced the caste system. The Caste System in its present form was not then existing. The bar against inter-dining and inter-marriage had not then become operative. Things were flexible and not rigid as they are now. But the principle of inequality which is the basis of the caste system had become well established and it was against this principle that Buddha carried on a determined and a bitter fight. How strongly was he opposed to the pretensions of the Brahmins for superiority over the other classes and how convincing were the grounds of his opposition are to be found in many of his dialogues. The most important one of these is known as the Ambattha Sutta.

3

The Decline and Fall of Buddhism

Dr. B. R. Ambedkar had written "The Decline and Fall of Buddhism", as a part of the treatise, `Revolution and Counter-Revolution '. We have found only 5 pages in our papers which were not even corrected. Copy of this essay has been received from Shri S. S. Rege, which shows some corrections in Dr. Ambedkar's handwriting. This essay is of 18 typed pages which is included here.—' Editors.

The disappearance of Buddhism from India has been a matter of great surprize to everybody who cares to think about the subject and is also a matter of regret. But it lives in China, Japan, Burma, Siam, Annam, Indo-China, Ceylon and parts of Malaya-Archipalego. In India alone, it has ceased to exist. Not only it has ceased to live in India but even the name of Buddha has gone out of memory of most Hindus. How could such a thing have happened ?

This is an important question for which there has been no satisfactory answer. Not only there is no satisfactory answer, nobody has made an attempt to arrive at a satisfactory answer. In dealing with this subject people fail to make a very important distinction. It is a distinction between the fall of Buddhism and the decline of Buddhism. It is necessary to make this distinction because the fall of Buddhism is one, the reasons for which are very different from those which brought about its downfall. For the fall is due to quite obvious causes while the reasons for its decline are not quite so obvious.

There can be no doubt that the fall of Buddhism in India was due to the invasions of the Musalmans. Islam came out as the enemy of the *'But'*. The word *'But'* as everybody knows is an Arabic word and means an idol. Not many people however know what the derivation of the word *'But' is 'But'* is the Arabic corruption of Buddha. Thus the origin of the word indicates that in the Moslem mind idol worship had come to be identified with the Religion of the Buddha. To the Muslims, they were one and the same thing. The mission to break the idols thus became the mission to destroy Buddhism. Islam destroyed Buddhism not only in India but wherever it went.

Before Islam came into being Buddhism was the religion of Bactria, Parthia, Afghanistan, Gandhar and Chinese Turkestan, as it was of the whole of Asia. In all these countries Islam destroyed Buddhism. As Vicent Smith points out :

"The furious massacre perpetrated in many places by Musalman invaders were more efficacious than Orthodox Hindu persecutions, and had a great deal to do with the disapperance of Buddhism in several provinces (of India),"

Not all will be satisfied with this explanation. It does seem inadequate. Islam attacked both, Bramhanism and Buddhism. It will be asked why should one survive and the other perish. The argument is plausible but not destructive of the validity of the thesis. To admit that Bramhanism survived, it does not mean that the fall of Buddhism was not due to the sword of Islam. All that it means is that, there were circumstances which made it possible for Bramhanism and impossible for Buddhism to survive the onslaught of Islam. Fortunately for Bramhanism and unfortunately for Buddhism that was the fact.

Those who will pursue the matter will find that there were three special circumstances which made it possible for Bramhanism and impossible for Buddhism to survive the calamity of Muslim invasions. In the first place Bramhanism at the time of the Muslim invasions had the support of the State. Buddhism had no such support. What is however more important is the fact that this State support to Bramhanism lasted till Islam had become a quiet religion and the flames of its original fury as a mission against idolatory had died out.

Secondly the Buddhist priesthood perished by the sword of Islam and could not be resusciated. On the other hand it was not possible for Islam to annihilate the Bramhanic priesthood. In the third place the Buddhist laity was persecuted by the Bramhanic rulers of India and to escape this tyranny the mass of the Buddhist population of India embraced Islam and renounced Buddhism. Of these circumstances there is not one which is not supported by history.

Among the Provinces of India which came under Muslim domination, Sind was the first. It was ruled by a Shudra king. But the throne was usurped by a Bramhin who established his own dynasty which naturally supported the Bramhanic religion at the time of the invasion of Sind by Ibne Kassim in 712 A.D. The ruler of Sind was Dahir. This Dahir belonged to the dynasty of Brahmin rulers.

Heuen Tsang had noticed that the Punjab was in his time ruled by a Kshatriya Buddhist dynasty. This dynasty ruled Punjab till about 880 A.D. In that year the throne was usurped by a Brahmin army commander by name Lalliya who founded the Brahmin Shahi dynasty. This dynasty ruled the Punjab from 880 A.D. to 1021 A.D. It will thus be seen that at the time when the invasions of the Punjab were commenced by Sabuktagin and Mohammad, the native rulers belonged to the Bramhanic religion and Jayapala (960-980 A.D.) Anandpal (980-1000 A.D.) and Trilochanpal (1000-21 A.D.) of whose struggles with Sabuktagin and Mahammad we read so much were rulers belonging to the Bramhanic faith.

Central India began to be infested by Muslim invasions which commenced from the time of Mohammad and continued under the leadership of Shahabuddin Ghori. At that time Central India consisted of different kingdoms. Mewad (now known as Udepur) ruled by the Gulohits, Sambhar (now divided into Bundi, Kota and Sirohi) ruled by the Chauhans, Kanauj ruled by the Pratihars, Dhar ruled by the Parmars, Bundelkhand ruled by Chandellas, Anhilwad ruled by the Chavdas, Chedi ruled by the Kalachuris. Now the rulers of all these kingdoms were Rajputs and the Rajputs for reasons which are mysterious and which I will discuss later on had become the staunchest supporters of the Bramhanic religion.

About the time of these invasions Bengal had fallen into two kingdoms, Eastern and Western. West Bengal was ruled by the Kings of the Pal dynasty and East Bengal was ruled by the Kings of the Sena dynasty.

The Palas were Kshatriyas. They were Buddhist but as Mr. Vadiya says "probably only in the beginning or in name". As to the Sena kings there is a difference of opinion. Dr. Bhandarkar says they were Brahmins who had taken to the military profession of the Kshatriyas. Mr. Vaidya insists that the Sena Kings were Aryan Kshatriyas or Rajputs belonging to the Lunar race. In any case there is no doubt that the Senas like the Rajputs were supporters of the orthodox faith.

"South of the river Nerbudda, then existed about the time of the Muslim invasions four kingdoms (1) The Deccan Kingdom of Western Chalukyas, (2) The Southern Kingdom of the Cholas (3) The Silahara Kingdom in Konkan on the West Coast and (4) The Ganga Kingdom of Trikalinga on the East Coast. These Kingdoms flourished during 1000-1200 A.D. which is the period of the Muslim invasions. There were under them, certain feudatory Kingdons which rose to power in the 12th Century A.D. and which became independent and powerful in the 13 the Century. They are (1) Devagiri ruled by the Yadavas, (2) Warangal ruled by Kakatiyas (3) Halebid ruled by Hoyasalas (4) Madura ruled by the Pandyas and (5) Travancore ruled by the Cheras. All these ruling dynasties were followers of orthodox Brahmanism. The Muslim invasions of India commenced in the year 1001 A.D.

The last wave of these invasions reached Southern India in 1296 A.D. when Allauddin Khilji subjugated the Kingdom of Devagiri. The Muslim conquest of India was really not completed by 1296. The wars of subjugation went on between the Muslim conquerors and the local rulers who though defeated were not reduced. But the point which requires to bear in mind is that during this period of 300 years of Muslim Wars of conquests, India was governed all over by princes who professed the orthodox faith of Bramhanism. Bramhanism beaten and battered by the Muslim Invaders could look to the rulers for support and sustenance and did get it. Buddhism beaten and battered by the Muslim invaders had no such hope. It was an uneared for orphan and it withered in the cold blast of the native rulers and was consumed in the fire lit up by the conquerors.

The Musalman invaders sacked the Buddhist Universities of Nalanda, Vikramasila, Jagaddala, Odantapuri to name only a few. They raised to the ground Buddhist monasteries with which the country was studded. The Monks fled away in thousands to Napal, Tibet and other places outside India. A very large number were killed outright by the Muslim commanders. How the Buddhist priesthood perished by the sword of the Muslim invaders has been recorded by the Muslim historians themselves. Summarizing the evidence relating to the slaughter of the Budhist Monks perpetrated by the Musalman General in the course of his invasion of Bihar in 1197 A.D. Mr. Vincent Smith says:

"The Musalman General, who *had* already made his name a terror by repeated plundering expeditions in Bihar, seized the capital by a daring stroke. The almost contemporary historian met one of the survivors of the attacking party in A.D. 1243, and learned from him that the Fort of Bihar was seized by a party of only two hundred horsemen, who boldly rushed the postern gate and gained possession of the place. Great quantities of plunder were obtained, and the slaughter of the 'shaven headed Brahmans', that is to say the Buddhist monks, was so thoroughly completed, that when the victor sought for some one capable of explaining the contents of the books in the libraries of the monasteries, not a living man could be found who was able to read them. 'It was discovered', we are told, 'that the whole of that fortress and city was a college, and in the Hindi tongue they call a college Bihar."

Such was the slaughter of the Buddhist priesthood perpetrated by the Islamic invaders. The axe was struck at the very root. For by killing the Buddhist priesthood Islam killed Buddhism. This was the greatest disaster that befell the religion of Buddha in India. Religion like any other ideololgy can be attained only by propaganda. If propoganda fails, religion must disappear. The priestly class, however detestable it may be, is necessary to the sustenance of religion. For it is by its propoganda that religion is kept up. Without the priestly class religion must disappear. The sword of Islam fell heavily upon the priestly class. It perished or it fled outside India. Nobody remained to keep the flame of Buddhism burning. It may be said that the same thing must have happened to the Brahmanic priesthood. It is possible, though not to the same extent. But there is this difference between the constitution of the two religions and the difference is so great that it contains the whole reason why Brahmanism survived the attack of Islam and why Buddhism did not. This difference relates to the constitution of the clergy.

The Bramhanic priesthood has a most elaborate organization. A clear and succinct account of it has been given by the late Sir Ramkrishna Bhandarkar in the pages of the Indian Antiquary.

'Every Brahmanic family, ' he writes, ' is devoted to the study of a particular Veda, and a particular Sakha (recension) of a Veda ; and the domestic rites of the family are performed according to the ritual described in the Sutra connected with that Veda. The study consists in getting by heart the books forming the particular Veda. In Northern India, where the predominant Veda is the White Yagush and the Sakha that of the Madhyandinas, this study has almost died out, except at Banaras, where Brahmanic families from all parts of India are settled. It prevails to some extent in Gujarat, but to a much greater extent in the Maratha country; and in Tailangana there is a large number of Brahmans who still devote their life to this study. Numbers of these go about to all parts of the country in search of dakshina (fee, alms), and all well-to-do natives patronize them according to their means, by getting them to repeat portions of their Veda, which is mostly the Black Yagush, with Apastamba for their Sutra. Hardly a week passes here in Bombay in which no Tailangana Brahman comes to me to ask for dakshina. On each occasion I get the men to repeat what they have learned, and compare it with the printed texts in my possession.

'With reference to their occupation, Brahmans of each Veda are generally divided into two classes, Grihasthas and Bhikshukas. The former devote themselves to a worldly avocation, while the latter spend their time in the study of their sacred books and the practice of their religious rites.

'Both these classes have to repeat daily the Sandhya-vandana or twilight-prayers, the forms of which are somewhat different for the different Vedas. But the repetition of the Gayatri-mantra 'Tat Savitur Vareynam' etc., five, then twenty eight, or a hundred and eight times, which forms the principal portion of the ceremony, is common to all.

'Besides this, a great many perform daily what is called Brahmayagna, which on certain occasions is incumbent on all. This for the Rig-Veda consists of the first hymn of the first mandal, and the opening sentences of the Aitareya Brahmana, the five parts of the Aitereya Aranyaka, the Yagus-samhita, the Sama-samhita, the Atharva-samhita, Asvalayana Kalpa Sutra, Nirukta, Khandas, Nighantu, Jyotisha, Siksha, Panini, Yagnavalkya Smriti, Mahabharata, and the Sutras of Kanada, Jaimini, and Badarayan.' The point to be remembered is that in the matter of officiation there is no distinction between a Bhikshuka and a Grahastha. In Brahmanism both are priest and the Grahastha is no less entitled to officiate as a priest than a Bhikshu is. If a Grahastha does not choose to officiate as a priest, it is because he has not mastered the mantras and the ceremonies or because he follows some more lucrative vocation. Under Brahmanic dispensation every Brahmin who is not an outcast has the capacity to be a priest. The Bhikshuka is an actual priest, a Grahastha is a potential priest. All Brahmins can be recruited to form the army of Bramhanic priesthood. Further no particular training or initiation ceremony is necessary for a Brahmin to act as a priest. His will to officiate is enough to make him function as a priest. In Brahmanism the priesthood can never become extinct. Every Brahmin is a potential priest of Brahmanism and be drafted in service when the need be. There is nothing to stop the rake's life and progress. This is not possible in Buddhism. A person must be ordained in accordance with established rites by priests already ordained, before he can act as a priest. After the massacre of the Buddhist priests, ordination became impossible so that the priesthood almost ceased to exist. Some attempt was made to fill the depleted ranks of the Buddhist priests. New recruits for the priesthood had to be drawn from all available sources. They certainly were not the best. According to Haraprasad Shastri,

"The paucity of Bhiksus brought about a great change in the composition of the Buddhist priesthood. It was the married clergy with families, who were called Aryas, that took the place of the Bhiksus proper, and began to cater to the religious needs of the Buddhists generally. They commenced attaining the normal status of Bhiksus through the performance of some sacraments. (lntro.pp.l9.7, quoting Tatakara Guptas' Adikarmaracana : 149, pp. 1207-1208). They officiated at the religious ceremonies but at the same time, in addition to their profession of priesthood, earned their livelihood through such avocations as those of a mason, painter, sculptor, goldsmith, and carpenter.

These artisan priests who were in later times larger in numbers than the Bhiksus proper became the religious guides of the people. Their avocations left them little time and desire for the acquisition of learning, for deep thinking, or for devotion to Dhyana and other spiritual exercises. They could not be expected to raise the declining Buddhism to a higher position through their endeavours nor could they check its course towards its ruin through the introduction of salutary reforms." It is obvious that this new Buddhist priesthood had neither dignity nor learning and were a poor match for the rival, the Brahmins whose cunning was not unequal to their learning.

The reason why Brahmanism rose from the ashes and Buddhism did not, is to be accounted for, not by any inherent superiority of Brahmanism over Buddhism. It is to be found in the peculiar character of their priesthood. Buddhism died because its army of priests died and it was not possible to create. Though beaten it was never completely broken. Every Brahmin alive became priest and took the place of every Brahmin priest who died.

As to the conversion to the faith of Islam by the Buddhist population as a cause of the fall of Buddhism, there can hardly be much doubt.

In his Presidential address to the early Medieval and Rajput section of the Indian History Congress held at Allahabad in 1938, Prof. Surendra Nath Sen very rightly observed that there were two problems relating to the Medieval History of India for which no satisfactory answers were forthcoming as yet. He mentiond two : one connected with the origin of the Rajputs and the other to the distribution of the Muslim population in India. Referring to the second, he said :

"But I may be permitted to deal with one question that is not wholly of antiquarian interest today. The distribution of Muslim population in India demands some explanation. It is commonly believed that Islam followed the route of conquest and the subjugated people were forced to accept the faith of their rulers. The predominance of the Muslims in the Frontier Province and the Punjab lends some colour to this contention. But this theory cannot explain an overwhelming Muslim majority in Eastern Bengal. It is quite likely that the North-Western Frontier Province was peopled by Turkish folks during the Kushan days, and their easy conversion to Islam may be explained by racial affinity with the new conquerors; but the Muslims of Eastern Bengal are certainly not racially akin to the Turks and the Afghans, and the conversion of the Hindus of that region must have been due to other reasons." What are these other reasons ? Prof. Sen then proceeds to lay bare these reasons which are found in Muslim Chronicles. He takes the case of Sind for which there is direct testimony and says:

"According to the Chachnama, the Buddhists of Sind suffered all sorts of indignities and humiliations under their Brahman rulers, and when the Arabs invaded their country, the Buddhists lent their whole hearted suport to them. Later on, when Dahir was slain and a Muslim Government was firmly established in his country, the Buddhists found to their dismay that, so far as their rights and privileges were concerned, the Arabs were prapared to restore status quo ante bellum and even under the new order the Hindus received a preferential treatment. The only way out of this difficulty was to accept Islam because the converts were entitled to all the privileges reserved for the ruling classes. So the Buddhists of Sind joined the Muslim fold in large numbers." Prof. Sen then adds this significant passage:

"It cannot be an accident that the Punjab, Kashmir, the district around Behar Sharif, North-East Bengal where Muslims now predominate, were all strong Buddhist Centres in the pre-Muslim days. It will not be fair to suggest that the Buddhists succumbed more easily to political temptations than the Hindus and the change of religion was due to the prospects of the improvement of their political status."

Unfortunately the causes that have forced the Buddhist population of India to abandon Buddhism in favour of Islam have not been investigated and it is therefore impossible to say how far the persecution of the Brahmanic Kings was responsible for the result. But there are not wanting indications which suggest that this was the principal cause. We have positive evidence of two Kings engaged in the campaign of persecuting the Buddhist population.

The first to be mentioned is Mihirkula. He belonged to the Huns who invaded India about 455 A.D. and established their kingdom in Northern India with Sakala, the modern Sialkot in the Punjab as the capital. Mihirkula ruled about 528 A.D. As Vincent Smith says: "All Indian traditions agree in representing Mihirkula as a blood thirsty tyrant. `The Attila of India', stained to a more than ordinary degree with 'implicable cruelty' noted by historians as characteristic of the Hun temperament."

Mihirkula, to use the language of Smith, :-"exhibited ferocious hostility against the peaceful Buddhist cult, and remorselessly overthrew the *stupas* and monasteries, which he plundered of their treasures".

The other is Sasanka, the King of Eastern India. He ruled about the first decade of the seventh century and was defeated in a conflict with Harsha. In the words of Vincent Smith.

"Sansanka, who has been mentioned as the treacherous murderer of Harsha's brother, and probably was a scion of the Gupta dynasty, was a worshipper of Shiva, hating Buddhism, which he did his best to extirpate. He dug up and burnt the holy Bodhi tree at Buddha Gaya, on which, according to legend, Asoka had lavished inordinate devotion; broke the stone marked with the footprints of Buddha at Pataliputra; destroyed the convents, scattered the monks, carrying his persecutions to the foot of the Nepalese hills ". The seventh century seems to be a century of religious persecution in India. As Smith points out:

"A terrible persecution of the cognate religion Jainism occurred in Southern India in the seventh century".

Coming nearer to the time of the Muslim invasions, we have the instance of Sindh where presecution was undoutedly the cause. That these persecutions continued upto the time of the Muslim invasions may be presumed by the fact that in Northern India the Kings were either Brahmins or Rajputs both of whom were anti Buddhists. That the Jains were persecuted even in the 12th century is amply supported by history. Smith refers to Ajayadeva, a Saiva King of Gujarat who came to the throne in A.D. 1174-6 and began his reign by a merciless persecution of the Jains, torturing their leader to death. Smith adds, "Several other well-established instances of severe persecution might be cited."

There is therefore nothing to vitiate the conclusion that the fall of Buddhism was due to the Buddhist becoming coverts to Islam as a way of escaping the tyranny of Brahmanism. The evidence, if it does not support the conclusion, at least makes it probable. If it has been a disaster, it is a disaster for which Brahmanism must thank itself.

Literature of Brahminism

We have come across scattered pages of this essay, numbering from 6 to 14 and 17 to 39. These pages seem to be a continuation of the subject dealt with under the title 'The Decline and Fall of Buddhism'. Some of the pages are the first copies while the rest are the carbon copies. There are 14 more pages dealing with the Vedanta Sutras and Bhagvat Gita. The size and quality of the paper on which 3 chapters i.e. (1) The Decline and Fall of Buddhism, (2) The Literature of Brahminism and (3) Vedanta Sutras and Bhagvat Gita are typed, appear to be similar but distinct from the size and quality of other Chapters in this part.—Editors.

The facts which supply the reasons must be gleaned from the literature of Brahmanism which grew up after its political trimuph under Pushyamitra.

The literature falls under six categories (1) Manu Smriti (2) Gita. (3) Shankaracharya's Vedant (4) Mahabharat (5) Ramayana and (6) the Puranas. In analysing this literature, I propose to bring out only such facts as are capable of being suggested by inference, the reason or reasons for the decline of Buddhism.

There is nothing unusual or unfair in this. For literature is the mirror in which the life of a people can be said to be reflected. There is one point which I feel I must clear up. It relates to the period when this literature came into existence.

Not all will agree that the literature referred to came into being after the revolution of Pushyamitra. On the contrary most Hindus, whether orthodox or not, learned or not, have an inerradicable belief that their sacred literature is a very old one in point of time. Indeed it seems to be an article of faith with every Hindu which necessitates a belief in a very high antiquity of their sacred literature

As to the age of Manu I have given references to show that Manu Smriti was written by Sumati Bharagava after 185 B.C. i.e. after the Revolution of Pushyamitra. I need say nothing more on the subject.

The date of the Bhagavat Gita is a subject about which there has been a difference of opinion.

Mr. Telang was of opinion that the Geeta must be older than the third century B.C. though he was not able to say how much. Mr. Tilak. ....

In the opinion of Prof. Garbe, the Geeta as we have it, is different from what it originally was. He agrees that the conviction that the Bhagwat Geeta has not reached us in its original form but has undergone essential transformations, is now, however, shared by many Indologists outside India. According to Prof. Garbe, one hundred and forty-six verses in the Bhagwat Geeta are new and do not belong to the original Geeta. As to the date of its composition Prof. Garbe says that it "cannot possibly be placed before the second Century A.D."

Prof. Kausambi insists that the Geeta was composed in the reign of King Baladitya. Baladitya belonged to the Gupta Dynasty which supplanted the Andhra Dynasty in the year. .... Baladitya came to the throne in the year 467 A.D. His reasons for so late a date are two. Before Shankaracharya—who was born in 788 A.D. and who died in 820 A.D.—wrote his commentary on the Bhagwat Geeta, it was an unknown composition. It was certainly not mentioned in the *Tatvasangraha* by Shantarakshit who wrote his treatise only 50 years before the advent of Shankaracharya. His second reason is this. Vasubandhu was the originator of a school of thought known as '*Vijnyan Vad*'. The *Bramha- Sutra- Bhashya* contains a criticism of the Vijnyan Vad of Vasubandu. The Geeta contains a reference to the Bramha-Sutra-Bhashya. The

Geeta must therefore be after Vasubandu and after the Bramha-Sutra-Bhashya. Vasubandhu was the preceptor of the Gupta King Baladitya. That being so, the Geeta must have been composed during or after the reign of Baladitya.

Nothing more need be said about the date of Shankaracharya. The age in which he lived and wrote is now generally accepted. Something about his life needs to be said. But I will reserve that for another place.

The question of determining the date of the composition of the Mahabharata is next to impossible. Only an attempt to fix the period of its composition can be made. The Mahabharat has undergone three editions and with each editor the title and subject matter has changed. In its original form it was known as *'Jaya'*, Triumph.

This original name occurs even in the third edition both in the beginning as well *as* in the end. The original edition of the book known as *'Jaya'* was composed by one Vyas. In its second edition it was known as Bharat. The Editor of this second edition was one Vaishampayana. Vaishampayan's edition was not the only second edition of the Bharata. Vyas had many pupils besides Vaishampayana ; Sumantu, Jaimini, Paila and Shuka were his other four pupils. They all had learned at the feet of Vyas. Each one of them produced his own. Thus there were four other editions of Bharata. Vaishampayana recast the whole and brought out his own version. The third editor is Sauti. He recast Vaishampayana's version of Bharata. Sauti's version ultimately came to have the name of *Mahabharata*. The book has grown both in size and in the subject matter aswell. The *'Jaya'* of Vyas was amall work having not more than 8800 Shlokas. In the hands of Vaishampayana it grew into 24000 verses. Sauti expanded it to contain 96836 Shlokas. As to subject matter the original as composed by Vyas was only a story of the war between the Kauravas and the Pandavas. In the hands of Vaishyampayana the subject became two-fold. To the original story there was added the sermon. From a purely historical work, it became a diadactic work aiming to teach a right code of social, moral and religious duties. Sauti the last Editor made it an all-embracing repository of legendary lore. All the smaller floating legends and historical stories which existed independently of the Bharata were brought together by Sauti so that they might not be lost or that they may be found togeher. Sauti had another ambition, that was to make the Bharata a storehouse of learning and knowledge. This is the reason why he added sections on all branches of knowledge, such as politics, geography, archary etc. Taking into account Sauti's habit of repetition, it is no wonder that the Bharata in his hand became Mahabharata.

Now as to the date of its composition. There is no doubt that the war between the Kauravas and the Pandavas is a very ancient event. But that does not mean that the composition of Vyas is as old as the event or contemporaneous with the event. It is difficult to assign specific dates to the different editions. Taking it as a whole Prof. Hopkins says :

"The time of the whole Mahabharata generally speaking may then be from 200-400 A.D. This, however, takes into account neither subsequent additions, such as we know to have been made in later times, nor the various recasting in verbal form, which may safely be assumed to have occurred at the hands of successive copyists."

But there are other circumstances which definitely point to a later date.

The Mahabharat contains a reference to the Huns. It was Skandagupta who fought the Huns and defeated them in or about the year 455 A.D.. Notwithstanding this the invasions of the Huns continued till 528 A.D. It is obvious that the Mahabharat was being written about his time or therefter.

There are other indications which suggest a much later date. The Mahabharat refers to the Mlenchhas or the Muslims. In the 190th Adhyaya of the Vana Parva of the Mahabharat there is a verse 29 wherein the author says that "the whole world will be Islamic. All Yadnas, rites and ceremonies and religious celebrations will cease". This is a direct reference to the Muslims and although the verse speaks of what is to happen in the future, the Mahabharat being a Purana must as in the case of the Purana be taken to speak of the event that has happened. This verse so interpreted show that the Mahabharat was being written after the date of the Muslim invasions of India. There are other references which point to the same conclusion. In the same Adhyaya verse 59, it is said that "Oppressed by the Vrashalas, the Brahmins struck with fear and finding no one to protect them, will roam all over the world groaning and crying in agony".

The Vrashalas referred to in this verse cannot be the Buddhists. There is no particle of evidence that the Brahmins were ever oppressed. On the contrary the evidence is that the Brahmins, during the Buddhists regime, were treated with the same liberality as the Buddhist Bhikshus. The reference to the Vrashalas means the uncultured must be to the Islamic invaders.

There occur other verses in the same Adhyaya of the Vanaparva. They are 65, 66 and 67. In these verses it is said that, "Society will become disarranged. People will worship *Yedukas.* They will boycott Gods. The Shudras will not serve the twice-born. The whole world will be covered with Yedukas. The Yug will come to an end."

What is the meaning of the term *'Yedukas'?* By some it has been taken to mean a Buddhist *Chaitya.* But according to Mr. Kausambi this is wrong. Nowhere either in the Buddhist literature or in the Vedic literature is the word Yeduka used in the sense of `Chaitya'. On the contrary according to the Amarkosh as commented upon by Maheshwar Bhatt the word Yeduka means a wall which contains a wooden structure to give it strength. So understood Kausambi contends that the word Yeduka must mean `Idgaha' of the Musalmans before which they say their prayers. If this is a correct interpretation then it is obvious that parts of the Mahabharata were written after the invasion of Mohammad Ghori. The first Muslim invasion took place in 712 A.D. under lbne Kassim. He captured some of the towns in Northern India but did not cause much destruction. He was followed by Mohammad of Gazni. He caused great destruction of Temples and Viharas and massacred priests of both religions. But he did not engage himself in building Mosques or Idgahas. That was done by Mohammad Ghori. From this it can be said that the writing of the Mahabharata was not complete till 1200 A.D.

It seems that like the Mahabharata, the Ramayana has also gone through three editions. There are two sort of references to the Ramayana in the Mahabharata. In one case the reference is to 'Ramayana' without any mention of the author. In other the reference is to the Ramayana of Valmilki. But the present

Ramayana is not the Ramayana of Valmiki. In the opinion of Mr. C. V. Vaidya :

"That the present Ramayana, even as it is approved and adopted by the searching and all-respected commentator Kataka, is not the Ramayana originally written by Valmiki, not even the most orthodox thinker will be disposed to doubt. Whoever even cursorily reads the poem cannot but be struck with the inconsistencies, the severances of connections, juxta-positions of new and old ideas which abound so greatly in the present Ramayana, whether we take the Bengal or the Bombay text of it. And one cannot but come to the conclusion that the Ramayana of Valmiki was substantially reconstructed at some subsequent date."

As in the case of the Mahabharata there has been an accretion to the subject matter of the Ramayana. Originally it was just a story of the war between Rama and Ravana over the abduction of Rama's wife Sita by Ravana. In the second edition it became a story with a sermon. From a purely historical work it also became a didactic work aiming to teach a right code of Social, Moral and religious duties. When it assumed the form of a third edition it was, again, like the Mahabharat, made a repository of legends, knowledge, learning, philosophy and other arts and sciences.

With regard to the date of the composition of the Ramayana one proposition is well established namely that the episode of Rama is older than the episode of the Pandus. But that the composition of the Ramayana has gone on paripassu along with the composition of the Mahabharata. Portions of Ramayana may be earlier than the Mahabharata. But there can be no doubt that a great part of the Ramayana was composed after a great part of the Mahabharata had already been composed.

The literature from which I propose to draw upon consists of (1) The Bhagwat Geeta (2) The Vedant Sutras (3) The Mahabharat (4) The Ramayana and (5) The Puranas. In analysing this literature I propose to bring out only such facts as are capable of being suggested by inference a reason or reasons for the decline of Buddhism.

Before proceeding to examine the subject matter of this lirerature I must deal with the question of the period when this literature came into existence. Not all will agree that the literature referred to came into being after the revolution of Pushyamitra. On the contrary most Hindus whether orthodox or not, learned or not, have an in-eradicable belief that their sacred literature is a very old one in point of time. Indeed it seems to be an article of faith with every Hindu which necessitates a belief in a very high antiquity of their sacred literature.

Bhagwat Gita

Beginning with the Bhagwat Gita, the date of its composition has been a matter of controversy. Mr. Telang was of opinion that we should "take the second century B.C. as a terminous before which the Gita must have been composed". The late Mr. Tilak was convinced that the date of the present Gita must be taken as not later than 500 years before the Saka era" which means that the present Gita was composed somewhere about. . . .. According to Prof. Garbe the date of the composition of the Bhagwat Gita must be placed somewhere between 200 and 400 A.D. There is another view propounded by Mr. Kausambi and is based on quite indisputable data.

Prof. Kausambi insists that the Gita was composed in the reign of Gupta King Baladitya. Baladitya belonged to the Gupta dynasty which supplanted the Andhra Dynasty in the year..... Baladitya came to the throne in the year 467 A.D. His reasons for so late a date for the composition of the Gita are two. Before Sankaracharya—who was

born in 788 A.D. and who died in 820 A.D.—wrote his commentary on the Bhagwat Gita, it was an unknown composition. It was certainly not mentioned in the *Tatvasangraha* by Shantarakshit who wrote his treatise only 50 years before the advent of Sankaracharya. His second reason is this. Vasubandhu was the originator of a school of thought known as '*Vijnan Vad*". The Brahma-Sutra-Bhashya contains a criticism of the Vijnan Vad of Vasubandhu. The Gita contains a reference to the Brahma-Sutra-Bhashya. The Gita must therefore be after Vasubandhu and after the Brahma-Sutra-Bhashya. Vasubandhu was the preceptor of the Gupta King Baladitya. That being so the Bhagwat Gita must have been composed or at any rate portions of Gita must have been added to the original edition during or after the reign of Baladitya i.e. about 467 A.D.

While there is a difference of opinion regarding the date of the composition of the Bhagwat Gita, there is no difference of opinion that the Bhagwat Gita has gone through many editions. All share the conviction that the Bhagwat Gita has not reached us in its original form but has undergone essential transformations at the hands of different editors who have added to it from time to time. It is equally clear that the editors through whose hands it has gone were not of equal calibre. As Prof. Garbe points out.

"The Gita is certainly `no artistic work which the all comprehending vision of a genious has created.' The play of inspiration is indeed often times perceptible; not seldom, however, there are merely high-sounding, empty words with which an idea that has been already quite often explained, is repeated: and occasionally the literary expression is exceedingly faulty. Verses are bodily taken over from the Upanishad literature, and this is certainly what a poet filled with inspiration would never have done. The workings of Sattva, Rajas and Tamas are systematized with a truly Indian pedantry, and much indeed besides this could be brought forward to prove that the Gita is not the product of a genuinely poetic creative impulse..."

Hopkins speaks of the Bhagwat Gita as characteristic in its sublimity as in its puerilities, in its logic as in its want of it. . . .Despite its occasional power and mystic exaltation, the Divine Song in its present state as a poetical production is unsatisfactory. The same thing is said over and over again, and the contradictions in phraseology and meaning are as numnerous as the repetitions, so that one is not surprised to find it described as "the wonderful song, which causes the hair to stand on end".

This is not to be rejected as the view of foreigners. It is fully supported by Prof. Rajwade who goes to show that some of those who had a hand in the composition of the Bhagwat Gita were ignorant of the rules of grammar.

While all are agreed that there have been different editions of the Gita under different editors, they are not agreed as to what parts of the Gita are original and what parts of the Gita are additions subsequently made. In the opinion of the late Rajaram Shastri Bhagwat the original Gita consisted only of 60 Shlokas. Humboldt was inclined to the view that originally the Gita consisted of only the first eleven Adhyayas (chapters) and that 12 to 18 Adhyayas were subsequent additions made to the original. Hopkins" view is that the first fourteen Adhyayas constitute the heart of the poem. Prof. Rajwade thinks that Adhyayas 10 and II are spurious. Prof. Garbe says that 146 verses in the Bhagwat Gita are new and do not belong to the original Gita which means that more than one-fifth of the Gita is new.

Regarding the author of the Gita there is none mentioned. The Gita is a conversation between Arjuna and Krishna which took place on the battle field, in which Krishna propounds his philosophy to Arjuna. The conversation is reported by Sanjaya to Dhritarashtra, the father of the Kauravas. The Gita should have been a part of the Mahabharata, for, the incident which formed the occasion for it, is natural to it, but it does not find a place there. It is a seperate indepenent work. Yet there is no author to whom it is attributed. All that we know, is that Vyas asks Sanjaya to report to Dhritarashtra the conversation that took place between Arjuna and Krishna. One may therefore say that Vyas is the author of the Gita.

Vedant Sutras

As has already been said, the Vedic lirerature consists of the Vedas, the Brahmanas, the Aranyakas, and the Upanishadas. From the point of their subject matter, this literature falls into two classes (1) literature which deals with religious observances and rites and ceremonies technically called Karma Kanda and (2) literature which deals with the knowledge about God to use the Vedic equivalent; the Bramhanas, technically called 'Gnanakanda'. The Vedas and the Bramhanas fall under the first category of literature, while the Aranyakas and the Upanishadas fall under the second.

This Vedic literature had grown to enormous proportions and what is important is that, it had grown in a wild manner. Some system, some coordination was necessary to bring order out of this chaos. As a result of the necessity for this coordination, there grew up a branch of inquiry called "Mimansa" i.e. an inquiry into the connected meaning of sacred texts i.e. the Vedic literature. Those who thought it necessary to undertake such a task of systematization and coordination divided themselves into two schools, those who systematized the '*Karmakand*" portion and these who systematized the "*Gnanakand*' portion of the Vedic literature. The result was that there grew up two branches of the Mimansa Shastra, one called *Purva Mimansa* and the other *Ultara Mimansa.* As the names suggest, the Purva Mimansa deals with the early portion of the Vedic literature namely the *Vedas* and the *Bramhanas.* That is why it is called Purva (early) Mimansa. The Uttara Mimansa deals with the later portions of the Vedic literature namely the Aranyakas and Upanishads. That is why it is called Uttara (later) Mimansa.

The literature connected with the two branches of the Mimansa Shastra is immense. Of this, two collections of Sutras stand out as the principal and leading works in this field of Mimansa. The authorship of one is attributed to Jaimini and that of the other is ascribed to Badarayana. Jaimini's Sutras deal with 'Karmakanda" and Badarayan's deal with 'Gnanakand'.There is no doubt that there were prior to Jaimini and Badarayana, other authors who had written treatises on these subjects. Nonetheless the sutras of Jaimini and Badarayana are taken as the standard works on the two Branches of the Mimansa Shastra.

Although the Sutras of both relate to that branch of inquiry called Mimansa, Jaimini's sutras are called *Mimansa Sutras* while those of Badarayana are called *Vedanta Sutras.* The term 'Vedanta' is taken to mean "the end of the Veda", or the doctrines set forth in the closing chapter of the Vedas which comprise the Upanishads and as the Upanishads constitute "the final aim of the Vedas." The Sutras of Badarayana which go to systematize and coordinate them have come to be called *Vedanta Sutras,* or the doctrines set forth in the closing chapter of the Vedas which asked Sanjaya to report to. This is the origin of the Vedanta Sutras.

Who is this Badarayana? Why did he compose these Sutras, and when did he compose them? Beyond the name nothing is known about Badarayana. It is not even certain that it is the real name of the author. There is a considerable uncertainty regarding the authorship of these Sutras even among his chief commentators.

Some say that the author is Badarayana. Others say that the author of the Sutra is Vyas. The rest say that Badarayana and Vyas are one and the same person. Such is the bewildering conflict of opinion regarding the author of the Sutras.

Why did he compose these Sutras? That the Brahmins should undertake to systematize the Karmakand portion of the Vedic literature one can quite understand. The Bramhins were deeply concerned with the Karmakand. Their very existence, their livelihood depended upon the systematization of the Karmakand portion of the Vedic literature.

The Brahmins on the other hand had no interest in the 'Gnankand' portion of the Vedic literature. Why should they have made an attempt to systematize it ? The question has not even been raised. But it is an important question and the answer to that must also be very important. Why the question is important and what the answer is I shall discuss later on.

There are two other questions with regard to the Vedanta Sutras. First is this. Is this work theological in character or is it purely philosophical in its nature? Or is it an attempt to tie down pure philosophy to the apron strings of established theology and thereby to make it innocuous and harmless. The other question relates to the commentaries on the Vedanta Sutras.

There have been altogether five commentaries on the Vedanta Sutras by five eminent men all of whom are called Acharyas (doctors of learning) by reason of their intellectual eminence.

They are (1) Shankaracharya (788 A.D. to 820 A.D.), (2) Ramanujacharya (1017 A.D. to 1137 A.D.), (3) Nimbarkacharya (died about 1162 A.D.), (4) Madhavacharya (1197-1276 A.D.) and (5) Vallabhacharya (born 1417 A.D.).

The commentaries of these Acharyas on the Vedanta Sutras have become far more important than the Vedanta Sutras.

The point of some significance is that on the text of one and the same collection of the Vedanta Sutras, an attempt has been made by those five Acharyas to found five different systems of thought.

According to Shankara, the Vedanta Sutras teach absolute monism. According to Ramanuja, qualified monism. According to Nirnbarka, monodualism. According to Madhava, dualism and according to Vallabha, pure monism. I will not discuss here what these terms mean. All I want to say is why should five different schools should have arisen as a result of five different interpretation of the same collection of Sutras. Is it a mere matter of grammar ? Or is there any other purpose behind these several interpretations.

There is also another question which arises out of the plurality of commentaries. While there are five different commentaries each propounding five different ways of looking at God and the individual soul really speaking there are only two, the view taken by Shankaracharya and the view taken by the other four. For though the four differ among themselves, they are all united in their opposition to Shankaracharya on two points (1) The complete oneness between God and individual soul and (2) the world is an illusion. Here comes the third question. Why did Shankaracharya propound so unique a view of the Vedanta Sutras of Badarayana? Is it the result of a critical study of the Sutras? Or is it a wishful interpretation designed to support a preconceived purpose?

I am only raising this question. I don't propose to deal with them here. Here I am concerned with the age of this literature, is it Pre-Buddhist or Post-Buddhist.

As to the date of the composition of the Vedanta Sutras the initial difficulty is that like the Bhagwat Gita it has also gone through several recensions. According to some there have been three recensions of the Vedanta Sutras. That being so nothing definite can be said regarding the date of its composition. The views expressed are only approximations. There can be no doubt that the Vedanta Sutras are composed after the rise of Buddhism for the Sutras do allude to Buddhism. They must not be after Manu for Manu refers to them in his Smriti. Prof. Keith holds that they must have been written about 200 A.D. and Prof. Jacobi believes that the Sutras must have been composed between 200 A.D. and 450 A.D.

Mahabharata

The question of determining the date of the composition of the Mahabharata is next to impossible. Only an attempt to fix the period of its composition can be made. The Mahabharata has undergone three editions and with each editor the title and subject matter has changed. In its original form it was known as '*Jaya*' Triumph. This original name occurs even in the third edition, both in the beginning as well as in the end. The original edition of the book known as '*Jaya*' was composed by one Vyas. In its second edition it was known as Bharat. The editor of this second edition was one Vaishampayana. Vaishampayana's Edition was not the only second edition of the Bharata. Vyas had many pupils besides Vaishampayana; Sumantu, Jaimini, Paila and Shuka were his other four pupils. They all had learned at the feet of Vyas. Each one of them produced his own edition. Thus there were four other editions of Bharata. Vaishampayana recast the whole and brought out his own version. The third Editor is Sauti. He recast Vaishampayana's version of Bharata. Sauti's version ultimately came to have the name of *Mahabharata*.

The book has grown both in size and in the subject matter as well. The 'Jaya' of Vyas was a small work having not more than 8,800 Shlokas. In the hands of Vaishampayana it grew into 24,000 verses. Sauti expanded it to contain 96,836 Shlokas. As to subject matter, the original as composed by Vyas was only a story of the war between the Kauravas and the Pandavas. In the hands of Vaishampayana the subject became two-fold. To the original story there was added the sermon. From a purely historical work it became a diadactic work aiming to teach a right code of social, moral and religious duties. Sauti the last Editor made it an all embracing repository of legendary lore. All the smaller floating legends and historical stories which existed independently of the Bharata were brought together by Sauti so that they might not be lost or that they may be found together. Sauti had another ambition, that was to make the Bharata a storehouse of learning and knowledge. This is the reason why he added sections on all branches of knowledge, such as politics, geography, archary etc. Taking into account Sauti's habit of repetition it is no wonder that the Bharata in his hand became Mahabharata.

Now as to the date of its composition. There is no doubt that the war between the Kauravas and the Pandavas is a very ancient event. But that does not mean that the composition of Vyas is as old as the event or contempraneous with the event. It is difficult to assign specific dates tu the different editions. Taking it as a whole Prof. Hopkins says :

"The time of the whole Mahabharata generally speaking may then be from 200-400 A.D. This, however, takes into account neither subsequent additions, such as we know, to have been made in later times, nor the various recasting in verbal form, which may safely be assumed to have occurred at the hands of successive copyists."

But there are other circumstances which definitely point to a later date.

The Mahabharata contains a reference to the Huns. It was Skandagupta who fought the Huns and defeated them in or about the year 455. Notwithstanding this, the invasions of the Huns continued till 528 A.D. It is obvious that the Mahabharata was being written about this time or thereafter.

There are other indications pointed out by Mr. Kausarnbi which suggest a much later date. The Mahabharata refers to the Mlenchhas or the Muslims. In the 190th Adhyaya of the Vana Parva of the Mahabharata, there is a verse 29 wherein the author says that "the whole world will be Islamic. All Aryan rites and ceremonies and religious celebrations will cease". This is a direct reference to the Muslims and although the verse speaks of what is to happen in the future, the Mahabharata being a Purana must as in the case of the Purana be taken to speak of the event has happened. This verse so interpreted show that the Mahabharata was being written after the date of the Muslim invasions of India. There are other references which point to the same conclusion. In the same Adhyaya verse 59 it is said that "Oppressed by the Vrashalas, the Brahmins struck with fear, and finding no one to protect them will roam all over the world groaning and crying in agony ".

The Vrashalas referred to in this verse cannot be the Buddhists. There is no particle of evidence that the Brahmins were ever oppressed. On the contrary the evidence is that the Brahmins during the Buddhist regimes were treated with the same liberality as the Buddhist Bhikshus. The reference to the Vrashalas which means the uncultured must be to the Islamic invaders. If that is so, then part of the Mahabharata was certainly composed after the Muslim invasions of India began.

There occur other verses in the same Adhyaya of the Vanaparva which points to the same conclusion. They are 65, 66 and 67. In these verses it is said that "Society will become disarranged. People will worship *Yedukas.* They will boycott Gods. The Shudras will not serve the twice born. The whole world will be covered with Yedukas. The Yug will come to an end".

Great significance attaches to the term *'Yedukas'.* By some it has been taken to mean a Buddhist *Chaitya,* on the ground that *Yeduka* means bone and particularly the bones of Buddha and subsequently Chaitya because a Chaitya contains the bones of the Buddha. But according to Mr. Kausambi this is wrong. Nowhere either in the Buddhist lirerature or in the Vedic literature is the word Yeduka used in the sense of 'Chaitya'. On the contrary, according to Amarkosh as commented upon by Maheshwar Bhatt, the word Yeduka means a wall which contains a wooden structure to give it strength. So understood Kausambi contends that the word Yeduka must mean 'Idgaha' of the Musalmans before which they say their prayers. If this is a correct interpretation then it is obvious that part of the Mahabharata was written after the Muslim invasions, particularly after those of Mahamad Ghori. The first Muslim invasion took place in 721 A.D. under Ibne Kassim. He captured some of the towns in Northern India but did not cause much destruction of Temples and Viharas and massacred priests of both the religions. But he did not engage himself in building Mosques or Idgahas. That was done by Mahamad Ghori. So that, it can well be said, that the writing of the Mahabharata was going on till 1200 A.D.

Ramayana

It is a fact that like Mahabharata, the Ramayana has also gone through three editions. There are two sorts of references to the Ramayana in the Mahabharata. In one case the reference is to Ramayana without any mention of the author. The other reference is to the Ramayana of Valmiki. But the present

Ramayana is not the Ramayana of Valmiki. In the opinion of Mr. C. V. Vaidya:

" That the present Ramayana, even as it is approved and adopted by the searching and all-respected commentator Kataka, is not the Ramayana originally written by Valmiki, not even the most orthodox thinker will be disposed to doubt. Whoever even cursorily reads the poem, cannot but be struck with the inconsistencies, the severances of connections, juxtapositions of new and old ideas which abound so greatly in the present Ramayana, whether we take the Bengal or the Bombay text of it. And one cannot but come to the conclusion that the Ramayana of Valmiki was substantially reconstructed at some subsequent date."

As in the case of the Mahabharata, there has been an accretion to the subject matter of the Ramayana. Originally it was just a story of the war between Rama and Ravana over the abduction of Rama's wife Sita by Ravana. In the second edition it became a story with a sermon. From a purely historical work, it also became a didactic work aiming to teach a right code of Social, Moral and religious duties. When it assumed the form of a third edition, it was again, like the Mahabharata, made a repository of legends, knowledge, learning, philosophy and other arts and sciences.

With regard to the date of the composition of the Ramayana, one proposition is well established namely that the episode of Rama is older than the episode of the Pandus. But that the composition of the Ramayana has gone on peripassu along with the composition of the Mahabharata. Portions of Ramayana may be earlier than the Mahabharata. But there can be no doubt that a great part of the Ramayana was composed after a great part of the Mahabharata had already been composed.

PURANAS

The Puranas today number 18. This is however not the original number. According to traditions, there is no reason to doubt, there was only one Purana to start with. Tradition alleges that this Purana was older than the Vedas. The Atharva Veda refers to this *Purana* and the Bramhanda Puran says that it is more ancient than the Vedas. It was a lore which the King was expected to know for the Satapada. Brarnhana says the Adhvaryu was required to recite the Purana to the King on the 10th day of the Yajna.

The origin of the 18 Puranas is attributed to Vyas who it is said recast the original single Purana and by additions and substractions made 18 out of one. The making of the 18 Puranas is thus the second stage in the evolution of the Puranas. The edition of each of these 18 Puranas as published or uttered by Vyas is called the Adi Purana i.e. the original edition as brought out by Vyas. After Vyas composed these 18 Puranas, he taught them to his disciple Romaharsana. Romaharsana prepared his own edition of the Puranas and taught it to his six disciples. Romaharsana's edition of the Puranas thus became the third edition of the Puranas. Of the six disciples of Romaharsana, three: Kasyapa, Savarni and Vaisampayana, made three separate editions which may be called the fourth edition of the Puranas which we call by their names. According to the Bhavishya Purana, the Puranas came to be revised sometime during the reign of King Vikramaditya.

As to the subject matter of the Puranas. The *Purana* from the oldest time is a recognised department of knowledge. For instance it was distinguished from Itihas or history. By Itihas what was understood was past occurances connected with a ruling king. By *Akhyana* was meant the recital of an event the occurance of which one had witnessed. By *Upakhyana* was meant the recital of something one has heard. *Gat has* meant songs about dead ancestors and about nature and universe.

Kalpashudi are ancient ways of acting regarding Shraddha and Kalpa. The Purana was distinguished from all these branches of knowledge. The Purana was concerned with five subjects. (1) Sarga (2) Prati Sarga (3) Vamsha (4) Manvantar and (5) Vamshacharitra. Sarga means creation of the universe, Pratisarga means the dissolution of the Universe. Vamsha means Geneology, Manvantar means the Ages of the different Manus, particularly the fourteen successive Manus who were the progenitors or sovereigns of the Earth. Vamshacharitra means the account of royal dynasties.

There has been a considerable addition made in the scope and subject matter of the Puranas. For the Puranas which we have are no longer confined to these subjects. In addition to these subjects they contain other subjects which fall entirely outside their prescribed scope. Indeed there has been such a change in the fundamental notion regarding the scope of the Puranas so that some of them do not contain any treatment of the regular subjects but deal wholly with the new or extra subjects. The extra subjects include the following main topics:

(I) Smriti Dharma which include discussion of:

(1) Varnashrama-dharma,

(2) Achara,

(3) Ahnika,

(4) Bhashyabhasya,

(5) Vivaha,

(6) Asaucha,

(7) Shradha

(8) Dravya-Suddhi

(9) Pataka,

(10) Prayaschitta,

(11) Naraka,

(12) Karma Vipaka and

(13) Yuga Dharma.

(II) Vrata Dharma—Observance of holy vows and holy days

(III) Kshetra Dharma—Pilgrimages to holy places and

(IV) Dana Dharma—Gifts to holy persons. In addition to this, there are two other topics the new subject matter with which one finds the Puranas to be deeply concerned.

The first of these two topics relates to sectarian worship. The Puranas are votaries of a particular deity and advocate the cause of a particular deity and the sect devoted to his worship. Five Puranas advocate worship of Vishnu, Eight worship of Shiva, One worship of Brahma, *One* worship of Surya, Two worship of Devi and One worship of Genesh.

The second topic which the Puranas have made a part of their subject matter is the history of the Avatars of the God. The Puranas make a distinction between identification of two Gods and the incarnation of a God. In the case of identification, the theory is that the God is one although he has two names. In the case of an incarnation, God becomes another being of the man or brute and does something miraculous. In reading this history of incarnations the fruitful source is Vishnu. For it is only Vishnu who has taken Avatars from time to time and done miraculous deeds and we find in the Puranas this new topic discussed in all its elaborate details.

It is no wonder if by the addition of these new subjects, the Puranas have been transformed out of recognition.

There is one other matter regarding the authorship of the Puranas which is noteworthy. It relates to the change in the authorship of the Puranas. Among the ancient Hindus, there were two separate sections among the literary class. One section consisted of the *Brahmins* and another section called *Sutas* who were non-Bramhins. Each was in charge of a separate department of literature. The Sutas had the monopoly of the Puranas. The Brahmins had nothing to do with the composition or the reciting of the Puranas. It was exclusively reserved for the Sutas and the Brahmins had nothing to do with it. Though the Sutas had specialized themselves in the making and the reciting of the Puranas, although they had acquired a hereditary and a prescriptive right to compose and recite the Puranas, there came a time when the Sutas were ousted from this profession by Brahmins who took it into their own hands and made a monopoly of it in their own favour. Thus there was a change in the authorship of the Puranas. Instead of the Sutas, it is the Brahmins who became their authors·

It is probably when the Puranas fell into the hands of the Brahmins that the Puranas have been finally edited and recast to make room for the new subjects. The editing and recasting has been of a very daring character. For in doing so they have added fresh chapters, substituted new chapters for old chapters and written new chapters with old names. So that by this process some Puranas retained their earlier materials, some lost their early materials, some gained new materials and some became totally new works.

The determination of the date of the composition of the Puranas is a problem which has hardly been tackled. All history written by the Brahmins is history without dates and the Puranas are no exception. The date of the Puranas has to be determined by circumstantial evidence co-related with events the dates of which are well settled. The dates of the composition of the different Puranas have not been examined as closely as those of the other parts of the Brahminic literature. Indeed scholars have paid no attention to the Puranas at all certainly nothing like what they have done in the matter of the Vedic literature. Mr. Hazara's is the only work I know of in which an attempt is made in the matter of determining the date of the composition of the Puranas. I give below the dates of the Puranas as found by him.

Puranas	Date of Composition
1. Markendeya	Between 200 and 600 A. D.
2. Vayu	Between 200 and 500 A. D.
3. Bramhanda	Between 200 and 500 A. D.
4. Vishnu	Between 100 and 350 A. D.
5. Matsya	Part about 325 A. D. Part about 1100 A. D.
6. Bhagwat	Between 500 and 600 A. D
7. Kurma	Between 550 and 1000 A. D.
8. Vamana	Between 700 and 1000 A. D.
9. Linga	Between 600 and 1000 A. D.
10. Varaha	Between 800 and 1500 A. D.
11. Padma	Between 600 and 950 A. D.
12. Brahanaradiya	Between 875 and 1000 A. D.
13. Agni	Between 800 and 900 A. D.
14. Garuda	Between 850 and 1000 A. D.
15. Bramha	Between 900 and 1000 A. D.
16. Skanda	After 700 A. D.
17. Bramha Vaivrata	After 700 A. D.
18. Bhavishya	After 500 A. D.

No more. precise date can be fixed for the Puranas at any rate for the present. New research in the field may narrow the higher and lower limits of their composition. The difference will only be a difference of degree. It will not be one of subversion of Eras.

This short survey is enough to remove any doubt as to the age of this literature that it is post-Buddhistic. The survey establishes one more point of great significance. This literature arose during the period subsequent to the triumph of Brahmins under the leadership of Pushyamitra. The survey brings out one other point. Vyas writes Mahabharata. Vyas tells Bhagwat

Gita, and Vyas also writes the Puranas. Mahabharata contains 18 Parvas, the Gita has 18 Adhyayas and the Puranas number 18. Is all this an Accident? Or is it the result of a design planned and worked out in concert ? We must wait and see.

The Vedanta Sutras

The vedanta Sutras of Badarayana as has been pointed out already constitute a department of study on the same line as the Karma Sutras of Jaimini. It is natural to ask how the founders of these two schools of thought comfort themselves towards each other. When one begins to inquire into the matter one comes across facts which are revealing. In the first place as Prof. Belvalkar points out, 'the Vedanta Sutras are very closely modelled upon the Karma Sutras' In the matter of methodology and terminology, Badarayana almost slavishly follows Jaimini. He accepts Jaimini rules of interpreting the text of the Shruti. He uses Jaimini's technical terms in the sense in which they have been used by Jaimini. He uses the very illustrations which are employed by Jaimini.

This is a matter for small wonder. But what is not a matter for small wonder is the attitude of the two schools towards each other in the matter of doctrine. Let me give an illustration.

Badarayana gives the following Sutras as illustrative of the position of Jaimini towards the Vedanta.

Because (the Self) is supplementary (to sacrificial acts), (the fruits of the knowledge of the Self) are mere praise of the agent, even as in other cases; thus says Jaimini.

"According to Jaimini the Vedas merely prescribe acts to attain certain purposes including Liberation, and nothing more. He argues that the knowledge of the Self does not yield any independent results, as Vedanta holds, but is connected with the acts through the agent. No one undertakes a sacrificial act unless he is conscious of the fact that he is different from the body and that after death he will go to heaven, where he will enjoy the results of his sacrifices. The Text dealing with Self-knowledge serve merely to enlighten the agent and so are subordinate to sacrificial acts. The fruits, however, which the Vedanta texts declare with regard to Self-knowledge, are merely praise, even as texts declare such results by way of praise, with respect to other matters. In short, Jaimini holds that by the knowledge that his Self will outlive the body, the agent becomes qualified for sacrificial actions, even as other things become fit in sacrifices through purificatory ceremonies. 3. Because we find (from the scriptures such) conduct (of men of realization).

"Janaka, emperor of Videha performed a sacrifice in which gifts were freely distributed" (Brih. 3.1.1.); "I am going to perform a sacrifice, Sirs" (Chh. 5.11.5.). Now both Janaka and Asvapati were knowers of the Self. If by this knowledge of the Self they had attained Liberation, there was no need for them to perform sacrifices. But the two texts quoted show that they did perform sacrifices. This proves that it is through sacrificial acts alone that one attains Liberation, and not through the knowledge of the Self, as the Vedantians hold. 4. That (viz, that knowledge of the Self stands in a subordinate relation to sacrificial acts) the scriptures directly declare, "That alone which is performed with knowledge, faith and meditation becomes more powerful" (Chh. 1.1.10); This text clearly shows that knowledge is a part of the sacrificial act. 5. Because the two (knowledge and work) go together (with the departing soul to produce the results).

"It is followed by knowledge, work, and past experience "(Brih. 4.4.2.). This text shows that knowledge and work go together with the soul and produce the effect which it is destined to enjoy. Knowledge independently is not able to produce any such effect." 6. Because (the scriptures) enjoin (work) for such (as know the purport of the Vedas).

"The scriptures enjoin work only for those who have a knowledge of the Vedas, which includes the knowledge of the Self. Hence knowledge does not independently produce any result." 7. And on account of prescribed rules.

"Performing works here let a man wish to live a hundred years" (Is. 2.); "Agnihotra is a sacrifice lasting up to old age and death:, for through old age one is freed from it or through death" (Sat. Br. 12.4.1.1.). From such prescribed rules also we find that Knowledge stands in a subordinate relation ro work.

What is the position of Badarayana towards Jaimini and Karma Kanda Shastras?

This is best illustrated by the reply which Badarayana gives to the attack by Jaimini on Vedanta as formulated by

Badarayana in the Sutras quoted above. The reply is contained in the following Sutras:

But because (the scriptures) teach (the Supreme Self to be) other (than the agent), Badarayana's (view is) correct; for that is seen (from the scriptures).

"Sutras 2-7 give the view of the Mimamsakas, which is refuted by Sutras 8-17.

The Vedanta texts do not teach the limited self, which is the agent, but the Supreme Self, which is different from the agent. Thus the knowledge of the Self which the Vedanta texts declare is different from that knowledge of the self which an agent possesses. The knowledge of such a Self, which is free from all limiting adjuncts, not only does not help, but puts an end to all actions. That the Vedanta texts teach the Supreme Self is clear from such texts as the following; "He who perceives all and knows all" (Mu. 1.1.9.); "Under the mighty rule of this immutable, O Gargi" etc. (Brih. 3.8.9.).

But the declarations of the Shruti equally support both views.

"This Sutra refutes the view expressed in Sutra 3. There it was shown that Janaka and others even after attaining Knowledge were engaged in work. This Sutra says the scriptural authority equally supports the view that for one who attained Knowledge there is no work. "Knowing this very Self the Brahmanas renounce the desire for sons, for wealth, and for the worlds, and lead a mendicant life" (Brih. 3.5.1.). "We also see from the scriptures that knowers of the Self like Yajnavalkya gave up work." 'This much indeed is (the means of) immortality, my dear'. Saying this Yajnavlkya left home" (Brih. 4.5.15). The work of Janaka and others was characterized by non-attachment, and as such it was practically no work; so the Mimarnsa argument is weak.

(The declaration of the scripture referred to in Sutra 4) is not universally true.

The declaration of the Shruti that knowledge enhances the fruit of the sacrifice does not refer to all knowledge, as it is connected only with the Udgitha, which is the topic of the section. (There is) division of knowledge and work, as in the case of a hundred (divided between two persons).

"This Sutra refutes Sutra 5. "It is followed by knowledge, work, and past experiences" (Brih. 4.4.2.). Here we have to take knowledge and work in a distributive sense, meaning that knowledge follows one and work another. Just as when we say a hundred be given to these two persons, we divide it into two halves and give each man fifty. There is no combination of the two. Even without this explanation Sutra 5 can be refuted. For the text quoted refers only to knowledge and work, which concern the transmigrating soul, and not an emancipated soul. For the passage, "Thus does the man who desires (transmigrate)" (Brih. 4.4.6.) shows that the previous text refers to the transmigrating self. And of the emancipated soul Shruti says, "But the man who never desires (never transmigrates)" etc. (Brih. 4.4.6.).

(The scriptures enjoin work) only on those who have read the Vedas.

"This Sutra refutes Sutra 6. Those who have read the Vedas and known about the sacrifices are entitled to perform work. No work is prescribed for those who have knowledge of the Self from the Upanishads. Such a knowledge is incompatible with work. 13. Because there is no special mention (of the Jaimini it does not (apply to him).

"This Sutra refutes Sutra 7. The text quoted there from the Isa Upanishad is a general statement, and there is no special mention in it that it is applicable to a Jnani also. In the absence of such a specification it is not binding on him.

Or rather the permission (to do work) is for praising (Knowledge).

"The injunction to do work for the knowers of the Self is for the glorification of this Knowledge. The praise involved in it is this : A knower of the Self may work all his life, but on account of this Knowledge he will not be bound by its effects. 15. And some according to their choice (have refrained from all work).

"In Sutra 3 it was said that Janaka and others were engaged in work even after Knowledge. This Sutra says that some have of their own accord given up all work. The point is that after Knowledge some may choose to work to set an example to others, while others may give up all work. There is no binding on the knowers of the Self as regards work. And (the scriptures say that the) destruction (of all qualifications for work results from Knowledge).

Knowledge destroys all ignorance and its products like agent, act, and result. "But when to the knower of Brahman everything has become the Self, then what should one see and through what" etc., (Brih. 4.5.15). The knowledge of the Self is antagonistic to all work and so cannot possibly be subsidiary to work. 17. And (Knowledge belongs) to those who observe continence (i.e. to Sannyasis); because (this fourth Ashrarna is mentioned) in the scriptures.

"The scriptures declare that Knowledge is gained in that stage of life in which continence is prescribed, i.e. the fourth stage or Sannyasa Asrama. To a Sannayasin there is no work prescribed except discrimination. So how can Knowledge be subservient to work? That there is a stage of life called Sannyasa we find from the scripütures themselves in texts like : "There are three branches of duty; sacrifice, study and charity are the first;. . . . All these attain to the worlds of the virtuous; but only one who is firmly established in Brahman attains immortality" (Chh. 2.33.1-2); "Desiring this world (the Self) alone monks renounce their homes" (Brih. 4..4.22). See also Mu. 1.2.11 and Chh. 5.10.1. Everyone can take to this life without being a householder etc. which shows the independence of Knowledge".

Many such Sutras can be found in Badarayana indicating the attitude of the two schools of thought towards each other. But one is enough as it is so very typical. If one stops to consider the matter the position becomes absolutely clear. Jaimini denounces Vedanta as a false Shastra a snare and a delusion, something superficial, unnecessary and insubstantial. What does Badarayana do in the face of this attack? He defends his own Vedanta Shastra. What one would expect from Badrayana is denunciation of the Karmakanda of Jaimini as a false religion. Badarayana shows no such courage. On the contrary he is very apologetic. He concedes that Jaimini's Karmakanda is based on the Scriptures and cannot be repudiated. All that he insists is that his Vedanta doctrine is also true because it has also the support of the Scriptures. Some explanation is necessary for this attitude of Badarayana.

Bhagwat Gita

The Bhagwat Gita forms part of the Bhishmaparvan of the great epic known as the Mahabharat. The epic is mainly concerned with the struggle for sovereignty between cousins, the Kauravas the sons of Dhritarashtra and the Pandavas the sons of Pandu. Pandu was the younger brother of Dhritarashtra. But as Dhritarashtra was blind the throne went to Pandu. After Pandu's death there arises a dispute between his sons and the sons of Dhritarashtra regarding the right of succession. The struggle for sovereignty culminated in the battle of Kurukshetra (near modern Panipat). In this battle Krishna sides with the Pandavas and acts as their guide, friend and philohopher,—nay acts as the charioteer of Arjuna, one of the Pandava brothers and who plays the part of the chief warrior in the battle on the side of the Pandavas.

The two armies of the Kauravas and the Pandavas were arrayed for battle on the field. Arjuna in his chariot with Krishna as a driver comes and takes his place in front of the Pandava army. Strong and valiant he gazes at the opposing army of the Kauravas and is struck by the horror of the dreadful fratricidal war in which he will have to kill his cousins and slay those whom he himself revers and to whom he is greatly attached and indebted, He becomes dejected, lays down his weapons and refuses to fight. Krishna begins to argue with him and provoke him to fight. This argument takes the form of a question and answer of a conversation between Arjuna and Krishna at the end of which Arjuna agrees to fight.

At the opening of the Bhagwat Gita we find old Dhritarashtra questioning Sanjaya about the battle. This is because Dhritarashtra the father of the Kauravas who though alive at the time when the battle was fought was a blind man and could not see and know things for himself. For the knowledge of the happenings he had to depend upon the reports of others. Anticipating the difficulty of getting someone to tell Dhritarashtra the authentic story, Vyas the author of the Mahabharata, it is said, bestowed on Sanjaya, the charioteer of Dhritrashtra, the power of knowing all that takes place on the battlefield— even the thoughts in men's minds- that he may make a faithful report to Dhritarashtra. That is why we find the episode of Bhagwat Gita related as a reply by Sanjaya to questions by Dhritarashtra. But the Gita is really a conversation between Arjuna and Krishna and is rightly called *Krishana Arjuna Samvad.*

In this Krishna-Arjuna-Samvad—which is the real name of the Bhagwat Gita— the main question over which there was disagreement was to fight or not to fight. There was no other question. This was the one and the only question which was the subject matter of discussion and argument between the two. Starting from this point of view it is obvious that the Gita could never have been intended by Krishna to be the occasion for moral instruction for the general public or the doctrinal exposition of any religious system or the catechism attached to any creed. Yet this is just what the Gita has come to be. Although the occasion was to decide to fight or not to fight, the Gita is said to contain what his religious doctrine Krishna is said to have preached to Arjuna.

The first question that crops up is who is this Krishna. To this one gets quite surprizingly a variety of answers from the Gita itself. At the start Krishna appears as a mere man with a completely human personality. He is a warrior by profession. He is a great warrior though he had chosen the humble duty of driving the chariot of Arjuna. From man he grows into superman directing and controlling the war and its frotunes. From superman he grows into a demigod and dictator. When all his arguments fail to move Arjuna to fight, he simply orders him to fight and the frightened Arjuna gets up and does his biddings. From demigod he rises to the position of God and is spoken of as Ishwara.

This shows the growth of the personality of Krishna. But what is important is that in the very same Gita, Krishna stands out as a representative of other forms of God. Four such representative characters in which Krishna appears are clear to any one who happens to read the Gita even casually.

Krishna is Vasudeo : *Bhagwat Gita :*

Ch.X.37. Of the Vrishnis I am Vasudeva; of the Pandavas, Dhananjaya; and also for the Munis, I am Vyasa; of the sages, Ushanas the sage. Krishna as Bhagwan :

Ch.X.12. The Supreme Brahman, the Supreme Abode, the Supreme Purifier, art Thou. Krishna is an Avtar of Vishnu :

Ch.X.21. Of the Adityas, I am Vishnu; of luminaries, the radiant Sun; of the winds, I am Marichi; of the asterisms, the Moon.

Ch.X1.24. On seeing Thee touching the sky, shining in many a colour, with mouths wide open, with large fiery eyes, I am terrified at heart, and find no courage nor peace, 0 Vishnu.

XI.30. Swallowing all the worlds on every side with Thy flaming mouths, Thou art licking Thy lips. Thy fierce rays, filling the whole world with radiance, are burning, 0 Vishnu. Krishna is also an Avtar of Shankara :

X.23. And of the Rudras I am Shankara; of the Yakshas and Rakshasas the Lord of wealth (Kuvera); of the Vasus I am Pavaka; and of mountains, Meru am 1.

Krishna is Bramhan :—

XV. 15. I am centred in the hearts of all; memory and perception as well as their loss come from Me. I am verily that which has to be known by all the Vedas, I indeed am the Author of the Vedanta, and the Knower of the Veda am 1.

XV. 16. There are two Purushas in the world,—The Perishable and the Imperishable. All beings are the Perishable, and the Kutastha is called Imperishable.

XV. 17. But (there is) another, the Supreme Purusha, called the Highest Self, the immutable Lord, who pervading the three worlds, sustains them.

XV. 18. As I transcend the Perishable and am above even the Imperishable, therefore am I in the world and in the Veda celebrated as the Purushottama, (the Highest Purusha).

XV. 19. He who free from delusion thus knows Me, the Highest Spirit, he knowing all, worships Me with all his heart, 0 descendant of Bharata.

Ask the next question, What is the doctrine that Krishna preaches to Arjuna? The doctrine preached by Krishna to Arjuna is said to be the doctrine of salvation for the human soul. While the question dealt with by Krishna is one relating to Salvation, Krishna teaches three different doctrines of Salvation.

Salvation is possible by *Dnyanmarg* as propounded by Samkhya Yog.

11.39. The wisdom of Self-realisation has been declared unto thee. Hearken thou now to the wisdom of Yoga, endued with which, 0 son of Pritha, thou shalt break through the bonds of Karma. Thus is the concluding verse of the discourse on Samkhya Yoga discussed in Chapter II, verses 11-16 and 18-30.

(2) Salvation is possible by *Karma* marg,

V.2. Both renunciation and performance of action lead to freedom : of these performance of action is superior to the renunciation of action.

(3) Salvation is possible by *Bhakti* Marg.

IX. 13. But the great souled ones, 0 son of Pritha, possessed of the Divine Prakriti, knowing Me to be the origin of beings, and immutable, worship Me with a single mind.

IX. 14. Glorifying Me always and striving with firm resolve, bowing down to Me in devotion, always steadfast, they worship Me. IX. 15. Others, too, sacrificing by the Yajna of knowledge (i.e. seeing the Self in all), worship Me the All Formed, as one, as distnct, as manifold.

IX. 17. I am the Father of this world, the Mother, the Sustainer, the Grandfather; the Purifier, the (one) thing to be known, (the syllable) 0m, and also the Rik Saman and Yajus.

IX.22. Persons who, meditating on Me as non-separate, worship Me in all beings, to them thus ever jealously engaged, I carry what they lack and preserve what they already have. There are two other features of the Bhagwat Gita which arrests one's attention.

(i) There is a sentiment of depreciation of the Vedas and Vedic rituals and sacrifices.

11.42-44. 0 Partha, no set determination is formed in the minds of those that are deeply attached to pleasure and power, and whose disctimination is stolen away by the flowery words of the unwise, who are full of desires and look upon heaven as their highest goal and who, taking pleasure in the panegyric words of the Vedas, declare that there is nothing else. Their (flowery) words are exuberant with various specific rites as the means to pleasure and power and are the causes of (new) births as the result of their works (performed with desire).

11.45 The Vedas deal with the three Gunas, Be thou free, 0 Arjun, from the triad of the Gunas, free from the apirs of opposites, ever balanced, free from (the thought of) getting and keeping, and established in the Self.

11.46. To the Brahmana who has known the Self, all the Vedas are of so much use, as a reservoir is, when there is a flood everywhere.

IX.21. Having enjoyed the vast Swarga-world, they enter the mortal world, on the exhaustion of their merit; Thus, abiding by the injunctions of the three (Vedas), desiring desires, they (constantly) come and go.

4

The Triumph of Brahmanism: Regicide or the Birth of Counter-Revolution

We have found only 3 typed pages under this title. Fortunately, a copy of the essay has been spared by Shri S. S. Rege for being included in this hook. While examining the pages we have noticed that the copy given by Mr. Rege also lacks page nos 3 to 7 and 9 to 17. The total typed pages of this essay have been numbered 92 inclusive of the missing pages. The title on the copy of Mr. Rege is the 'Triumph of Brahmanism'; whereas the first page of the script in our papers is also entitled as ' Regicide or the Birth of Counter-Revolution '. The classification of the subject into IX Chapters is noted in our copy whereas it is missing from the copy of Mr. Rege. Both the titles and the classification are recorded in the handwriting of Dr. Ambedkar. Hence, they are retained in this print. Incidentaly, the page nos 91017 were found fagged in other file. All those papers have now been introduced at proper place. Thus except page Nos. 4 to 7, the script is complete.—Editors.

I The Brahmanic Revolt against Buddhism. II Manu the apostle of Brahmanism. Ill Brahmanism and the Brahmin's Right to rule and regicide. IV Brahmanism and the privileges of Brahmins. V Brahmanism and the Creation of Caste. VI Brahmanism and the degradation of the Non-Brahmins. VII Brahmnism and the Suppression of the Shudra. VIII Brahmanism and the Subjection of Women. IX Brahmanism and the legalization of the social system.

Speaking about India, Prof. Bloomfield opens his lectures on the Religion of the Veda by reminding his audience that "India is the land of religions in more than one sense. It has produced out of its own resources, a number of distinctive systems and sects....

In another sense India is a land of religions. Nowhere else is the texture of life so much impregnated with religious convictions and practices... "

These observations contain profound truth. He would have given utterance to truth far more profound and arresting if he had said that India is a land of warring religions. For indeed there is no country in which Religion has played so great a part in its history as it has in the history of India. The history of India is nothing but a history of a mortal conflict between—Buddhism and Brahmanism. So neglected is this truth that no one will be found to give it his ready acceptance. Indeed there may not be wanting persons who would repudiate any such suggestion.

Let me therefore briefly recount the salient facts of Indian history. For it is important that everyone who was able to understand the history of India must know that it is nothing but the history of the struggle for supremacy between Brahmanism and Buddhism.

The history of India is said to begin with the Aryans who invaded India, made it their home and established their culture. Whatever may be the virtues of the Aryans, their culture, their religion and their social system, we know very little about their political history. Indeed notwithstanding the superiority that is claimed for the Aryans as against the Non-Aryans, the Aryans have left very little their political achievements for history to speak of.

The political history of India begins with the rise of a non-Aryan people called Nagas, who were a powerful people, whom the Aryans were unable to conquer, with whom the Aryans had to make peace, and whom the Aryans were compelled to recognize as their equals. Whatever fame and glory India achieved in ancient times in the political field, the credit for it goes entirely to the Non-Aryan Nagas. It is they who made India great and glorious in the annals of the world.

The first land mark in India's political history is the emergence of the Kingdom of Magadha in Bihar in the year 642 B.C. The founder of this kingdom of Magadha is known by the name of Sisunag and belonged to the non-Aryan race of Nagas.

From the small beginning made by Sisunag, this Kingdom of Magadha grew in its extent under the capable rulers of this Sisunag dynasty. Under Bimbisara the fifth ruler of this dynasty the kingdom grew into an Empire and came to be known as the Empire of Magadha. The Sisunag dynasty continued to rule the kingdom till 413 B.C. In that year the reigning Emperor of the Sisunag Dyansty Mahananda was killed by an adventurer called Nanda. Nanda usurped the throne of Magadha and founded the Nanda Dynasty.

This Nanda Dynasty ruled over the Empire of Magadha upto 322 B.C. The last Nanda king was deposed by Chandragupta who founded the Maurya Dynasty. Chandragupta was related to the family of the last ruling emperor of the Sisunag Dynasty so that it may be said that the revolution effected by Chandragupta was really a restoration of the Naga Empire of Magadha.

The Mauryas by their conquests enormously extended the boundaries of this Empire of Magadha which they inherited. So vast became the growth of this Empire under Ashoka, the Empire began to be known by another name. It was called the Maurya Empire or the Empire of Ashoka. *(From here onwards page Nos. 4 to 7 of the MS are missing.)*

It did not remain as one of the many diverse religions then in vogue. Ashoka made it the religion of the state. This of course was the greatest blow to Brahmanism. The Brahmins lost all state partonage and were neglected to a secondary and subsidiary position in the Empire of Ashoka.

Indeed it may be said to have been suppressed for the simple reason that Ashoka prohibited all animal sacrifices which constituted the very essence of Brahmanic Religion.

The Brahmins had not only lost state partonage but they lost their occupation which mainly consisted in performing sacrifices for a fee which often times was very substantial and which constituted their chief source of living. The Brahmins therefore lived as the suppressed and Depressed Classes for nearly 140 years during which the Maurya Empire lasted.

A rebellion against the Buddhist state was the only way of eseape left to the suffering Brahmins and there is special reason why Pushyamitra should raise the banner of revolt against the rule of the Mauryas. Pushyamitra was a Sung by Gotra.

The Sungas were Samvedi Brahmins, who believed in animal sacrifices and soma sacrifices. The Sungas were therefore quite naturally smarting under the prohibition on animal sacrifices throughout the Maurya Empire proclaimed in the very Rock Edict by Ashoka.

No wonder if Pushyamitra who as a Samvedi Brahmin was the first to conceive the passion to end the degradation of the Brahmin by destroying the Buddhist state which was the cause of it and to free them to practise their Brahmanic religion.

That the object of the Regicide by Pushyamitra was to destroy Buddhism as a state religion and to make the Brahmins the sovereign rulers of India so that with the political power of the state behind it Brahmanism may triumph over Buddhism is borne out by two other circumstances.

The first circumstance relates to the conduct of Pushyamitra himself. There is evidence that Pushyamitra after he ascended the throne performed the Ashvamedha Yajna or the horse sacrifice, the vedic rite which could only be performed by a paramount sovereign. As Vincent Smith observes :

"The exaggerated regard for the sanctity of animal life, which was one of the most cherished features of Buddhism, and the motive of Ashoka's most characterisitic legislation, had necessarily involved the prohibition of bloody sacrifices, which are essential to certain forms of Brahmanical worship, and were believed by the orthodox to possess the highest saving efficacy. The memorable horse sacrifices of Pushyamitra marked an early stage in the Brahmanical reaction, which was fully developed five centuries later in the time of Samudragupta and his successors."

Then there is evidence that Pushyamitra after his accession launched a violent and virulent campaign of persecution against Buddhists and Buddhism.

How pitiless was the persecution of Buddhism by Pushyamitra can be gauged from the Proclamation which he issued against the Buddhist monks. By this proclamation Pushyamitra set a price of 100 gold pieces on the head of every Buddhist monk.

Dr. Haraprasad Shastri speaking about the persecution of Buddhists under Pushyamitra says:

"The condition of the Buddhists under the imperial sway of the Sungas, orthodox and bigotted, can be more easily imagined than described. From Chinese authorities it is known that many Buddhists still do not pronounce the name of Pushyamitra without a curse."

If the Revolution of Pushyamitra was a purely political revolution there was no need for him to have launched a compaign of persecution against Buddhism which was not very different to the compaign of persecution launched by the Mahamad of Gazni against Hinduism. This is one piece of circumatantial evidence which proves that the aim of Pushyamitra was to overthrow Buddhism and establish Brahmanism in its place.

Another piece of evidence which shows that the origin and purpose of the revolution by Pushyamitra against the Mauryas was to destroy Buddhism and establish Brahmanism is evidenced by the promulgation of Manu Smriti as a code of laws.

The Manu Smriti is said to be divine in its origin. It is said to be revealed to man by Manu to whom it was revealed by the Swayambhu (i.e. the Creator). This claim, as will be seen from the reference already made to it, is set out in the Code itself. It is surprizing that nobody has cared to examine the grounds of such a claim.

The result is that there is a complete failure to realise the significance, place and position of the Manu Smriti in the history of India. This is true even of the historians of India although the Manu Smriti is a record of the greatest social revolution that Hindu society has undergone. There can however be no doubt that the claim made in the Manu Smriti regarding its authorship is an utter fraud and the beliefs arising out of this false claim are quite untenable.

The name Manu had a great prestige in the ancient history of India and it is with the object to invest the code with this ancient prestige that its authorship was attributed to Manu. That this was a fraud to deceive people is beyond question. The code itself is signed in the family name of Bhrigu as was the ancient custom. "The Text Composed by Bhrigu (entitled) "The Dharma Code of Manu" is the real title of the work. The name Bhrigu is subscribed to the end of every chapter of the Code itself. We have therefore the family name of the author of the Code. His personal name is not disclosed in the Book. All the same it was known to many. The Author of Narada Smriti writing in about the 4th Century A.D. knew the name of the author of the Manu Smriti and gives out the secret. According to Narada it was one Sumati Bhargava who composed the Code of Manu. Sumati Bhargava is not a legendary name, and must have been historical person for even Medhatithe the great commentator on the Code of Manu held the view that this Manu was 'a certain individual'. Manu therefore is the assumed name of Sumati Bhargava who is the real author of Manu Smriti.

When did this Sumati Bhargava compose this Code? It is not possible to give any precise date for its composition. But quite a precise period during which it was composed can be given. According to scholars whose authority cannot be questioned Sumati Bhargava must have composed the Code which he deliberately called Munu Smriti between 170 B.C. and 150 B.C. Now if one bears in mind the fact that the Brahmanic Revolution by Pushyamitra took place in 185 B.C. there remains no doubt that the code known as Manu Smriti was promulgated by Pushyamitra as embodying the principles of Brahmanic Revolution against the Buddhist state of the Mauryas. That the Manu Smriti forms the Institutes of Brahmanism and are a proof that Pushyamitra Revolution was not a purely personal adventure will be clear to any one who cares to note the following peculiarities relating to the Manu Smriti.

First thing to be noted is that the Manu Smriti is a new Code of law promulgated for the first time during the reign of Pushyamitra. There was a view once prevalent that there existed a code known as the Manava-Dharma-Sutra and that what is known as Manu Smriti is an adaptation of the old Manava Dharma Sutra. This view has been abandoned as there has been no trace of any such work. Two other works existed prior to the present Manu Smriti. One was known as Manava Artha Sastra, or Manava-Raja-Sastra or Manava-Raja-Dharma-Sastra. The other work was known as Manava-Grihya-Sutra. Scholars have compared the Manu Smriti. On important points the provisions of one are not only dissimilar but are in every way contrary to the provisions contained in the other. This is enough to show that Manu Smriti contains the new law of the new regime.

That the new regime of Pushyamitra was anti-Buddhist is betrayed by the open provisions enacted in the Manu Smriti against the Buddhists and Buddhism. Note the following provisions in Manu Smriti :—

IX. 225. ". . .. Men who abide in heresy . . . the king should banish from his realm."

IX. 226. "These robbers in disguise, living in the king's realm constantly injure the worthy subject by the performance of their misdeeds."

V. 89. "Libations of water shall not be offered to (the souls of) those who (neglect the prescribed rites and may be said to) have been born in vain, to those born in consequence of an illegal mixture of the castes, to those who are ascetics (of heretical sects) and to those who have committed suicide."

V.90. (Libations of water shall not be offered to the souls of) women who have joined a heretical sect.....

IV. 30. Let him (the householder) not honour, even by a greeting heretics.... logicians, (arguing against the Veda).

XII. 95. "All those traditions and all those despicable systems of Philosophy, which are not based on the Veda produce no reward after death, for they are declared to be founded on Darkness.

XII. 96. "All those (doctrines), differing from the (Veda), which spring up and (soon) perish, are worthless and false, because of modern date."

Who are the heretics to whom Manu refers and whom he wants the new king to banish from his realm and the

Householder not to honour in life as well as after death? What is this worthless philosophy of modern date, differing from the Vedas, based on darkness and bound to perish? There can be no doubt that the heretic of Manu is the Buddhist and the worthless philosophy of modern date differing from the Vedas is Buddhism. Kalluck Bhutt another commentator on Manu Smriti expressly states that the references to heretics in these Shlokas in Manu are to the Buddhists and Buddhism.

The third circumstance is the position assigned to the Brahmins in the Manu Smriti. Note the following provisions in Manu :—

I. 93. As the Brahmana sprang from (Bramha's) mouth, as he was the first born,and as he possesses the Veda, he is by right the lord of this whole creation.

I. 96. Of created beings the most excellent are said to be those which are animated; of the animated, those which subsist by intelligence; of the intelligent, mankind; and of men, the Brahmans.

I. 100. Whatever exists in the world is the property of the Bramhans ; on account of the excellence of his origin the Brahmana is, indeed, entitled to it all.

I. 101. The Brahmana eats but his own food, wears but his own apparel, bestows but his own in alms; other mortals subsist through the benevolence of the Brahmana.

X. 3. On account of his pre-eminance, on account of the superiority of his origin, on account of his observance of (particular) restrictive rules, and on account of his particular sanctification, the Brahmana is the lord of (all) castes.

XI. 35. The Bramhana is declared to be the creator of the world, the punisher, the teacher, and hence a benefactor of all created beings; to him let no man say anything unpropitious, nor use any harsh words.

Manu warns the King against displeasing the Bramhans in the following terms:—

IX. 313. Let him (the King) not, though fallen unto the deepest distress, provoke Bramhans to anger; for they, when angered, could instantly destroy him together with his army and his vehicles. Manu further proclaims,

XI. 31. A Bramhana who knows the law need not bring any (offence) to the notice of the king; by his own power alone he can punish those men who injure him.

XI. 32. His own power is greater than the power of the king; The Bramhana, therefore, may punish his foes by his own power alone.

This deification of the Brahmins, placing them even above the King would have been impossible unless the King himself was a Brahmin and in sympathy with the view expressed by Manu. Pushyamitra and his successors could not have tolerated these exaggerated claims of the Brahmins unless they themselves were Brahmins interested in the establishment of Bramhanism. Indeed it is quite possible that the Manu Smriti was composed at the command of Pushyamitra himself and forms the book of the philosophy of Bramhanism.

Taking all these facts into considerations there can remain no doubt; the one and only object of Pushyamitra's revolution was to destroy Buddhism and re-establish Bramhanism.

The foregoing summary of the political history of India would have been quite unnecessary for the immediate purpose of this chapter if I was satisfied with the way in which the history of India is written. But frankly I am not satisfied. For too much emphasis is laid on the Muslim conquest of India. Reels and reels have been written to show how wave after wave of Muslim invasions came down like avalanche and enveloped the people and overthrew their rulers. The whole history of India is made to appear as though the only important thing in it is a catalogue of Muslim invasions. But even from this narrow point of view it is clear that the Muslim invasions are not the only invasions worth study. There have been other invasions equally if not of greater importance. If Hindu India was invaded by the Muslim invaders so was Buddhist India invaded by Bramhanic invaders.

The Muslim invasions of Hindu India and the Bramhanic invasions of Buddhist India have many similarities. The Musalman invaders of Hindu India fought among themselves for their dynastic ambitions. The Arabs, Turks, Mongols and Afghans fought for supremacy among themselves. But they had one thing in common—namely the mission to destroy idolatory. Similarly the Bramhanic invadars of Buddhist India fought among themselves for their dynastic ambitions. The Sungas, Kanvas and the Andhras fought for supremacy among themselves.

But they, like the Muslim invaders of Hindu India, had one object in common that was to destroy Buddhism and the Buddhist Empire of the Mauryas. Surely if Muslim invasions of Hindu India are worthy of study at the hands of the historians, the invasions of Buddhist India by Bramhanic invaders are equally deserving of study. The ways and methods employed by the Bramhanic invaders of Buddhist India to suppress Buddhism were not less violent and less virulent than the ways and means adopted by Muslim invaders to suppress Hinduism. From the point of view of the permanent effect on the socia.l and spiritual life of the people, the Bramhanic invasions of Buddhist India have been so profound in their effect that compared to them, the effect of Muslim invasions on Hindu India have been really superficial and ephemeral. The Muslim invaders destroyed only the outward symbols of Hindu religion such as temples and Maths etc.

They did not extirpate Hinduism nor did they cause any subversion of the principles or doctrines which governed the spiritual life of the people. The effects of the Bramhanic invasions were a thorough-going change in the principles which Buddhism had preached for a century as true and eternal principles of spiritual life and which had been accepted and followed by the masses as the way of life. To alter the metaphor the Muslim invaders only stirred the waters in the bath and that too only for a while. Thereafter they got tired of stirring and left the waters with the sediments to settle. They never threw the baby—if one can speak of the principles of Hinduism as a baby—out of the bath.

Bramhanism in its conflict with Buddhism made a clean sweep. It emptied the bath with the Buddhist Baby in it and filled the bath with its own waters and placed in it its own baby. Bramhanism did not care to stop how filthy and dirty was its water as compared with the clean and fragrant water which flowed from the noble source of Buddhism. Bramhanism did not care to stop how hideous and ugly was its own baby as compared with the Buddhist baby. Bramhanism acquired by its invasions political power to annihilate Buddhism and it did annihilate.

Buddhism. Islam did not supplant Hinduism. Islam never made a thorough job of its mission. Bramhanism did. It drove out Buddhism as a religion and occupied its place.

These facts show that Brahmanic invasions of Buddhist India have a far greater significance to the Historian of India than the Muslim invasions of Hindu India can be said to have produced. Yet very little space is devoted by historians to the vissicitudes which befell Buddhist India built up by the Mauryas and even where that is done they have not cared to deal in a pointed manner with questions that quite naturally arise : questions such as, who were the Sungas, Kanavas and Andhras ; why did they destroy the Buddhist India which was built up by the Mauryas, nor has any attempt been made to study the changes that Brahmanism after its triumph over Buddhism brought about in the political and social structure.

Failure to appreciate this aspect of India's history is due to the prevalence of some very wrong notions. It has been commonly supposed that the culture of India has been one and the same all throughout history; that Brahmanism, Buddhism, Jainism are simply different phases and that there has never been any fundamental antagonism between them. Secondly it has been assumed that whatever conflicts have taken place in Indian politics were purely political and dynastic and that they had no social and spiritual significance. It is because of these wrong notions that Indian history has become a purely mechanical thing, a record of one dynasty succeeding another and one ruler succeeding another ruler. A corrective to such an attitude and to such a method of writing history lies in recognition of two facts which are indisputable.

In the first place it must be recognized that there has never been such as a common Indian culture, that historically there have been three Indias, Brahmanic India, Buddhist India and Hindu India, each with its own culture. Secondly it must be recognized that the history of India before the Muslim invasions is the history of a mortal conflict between Bramhanism and Buddhism. Any one who does not recognize these two facts will never be able to write a true history of India, a history which will disclose the meaning and purpose running through it. It is a corrective to Indian history written as it is and to disclose the meaning and purposes running through it that I was obliged to recast the history of the Brahmanic invasions of Buddhist India and the political triumph of Brahmanism over Buddhism.

We must therefore begin with the recognition of the fact : Pushyamitra's revolution was a political revolution engineered by the Brahmins to overthrow Buddhism.

The curious will naturally ask what did this triumphant Brahmanism do? It is to this question that I will now turn. The deeds or misdeeds of this triumphant Brahmanism may be catalogued under seven heads (1) It established the right of the Brahmin to rule and commit regicide. (2) It made the Bramhins a class of privileged persons. (3) It converted the Varna into caste. (4) It brought about a conflict and anti-social feeling between the different castes. (5) It degraded the Shudras and the women (6) It forged the system of graded inequality and (7) It made legal and rigid the social system which was conventional and flexible.

To begin with the first.

The revolution brought about by Pushyamitra created an initial difficulty in the way of the Brahmins. People could not be easily reconciled to this revolution. The resentment of the public was well expressed by the poet Bana when in referring to this revolution reviles Pushyamitra as being base born and calls his act of regicide as *Anarva*. The act of Pushyamitra was properly described by Bana as *Anarya* i.e. contrary to Aryan law. For on three points the Aryan law at the date of Pushyamitra's revolution was well settled. The then Aryan law declared (1) That Kingship is the right of the Kshatriya only. A Brahmin could never be a king. (2) That no Brahmin shall take to the profession of Arms and (3) That rebellion against the King's authority was a sin. Pushyamitra in fostering the rebellion had committed a crime against each of these three laws. He was Brahmin, and although a Brahmin he rebelled against the King, took to the profession of Arms and became a King. People were not reconciled to this usurption which constituted so flagrant a breach of the law that the Brahmins had to regularize the position created by Pushyamitra. This the

Brahmins did by taking the bold step of changing the law. This change of law is quite manifest from the Manu Smriti. I will quote the appropriate shlokas from the Code :

XII. 100. "The post of the Commander-in-Chief of the Kingdom, the very Headship of Government, the complete empire over every one are deserved by the Brahmin." Here we have one change in the law. This new law declares that the Brahmin has a right to become Senapati (Commander of forces), to conquer a kingdom, and to be the ruler and the Emperor of it.

XI. 31. A Brahmin, who well knows the laws, need not complain to the king of any grievous injury; since, even by his own power, he may chastise those, who injure him.

XI. 32. His (Brahmin's) own power, which depends on himself alone is mightier than the royal power, which depends on other men ; by his own might, therefore may a Brahmin coerce his foes.

XI. 261-62. A Brahmin who has killed even the peoples of the three worlds, is completely freed from all sins on reciting three times the Rig, Yajur or Sama.-Veda with the Upanishadas." Here is the second change in the law. It authorized the Brahmin to kill not only the king but to engage in a general massacre of men if they seek to do injury to his power and position.

VIII. 348. "The twice born man may take arms, when the rightful occupation assigned to each by Dharma is obstructed by force ; and when, in some evil time, a disaster has befallen the twice-born classes."

IX. 320. Of a Kshatriya (Military man or king), who raise his arm violently on all occasions against the Brahmins, Brahmin himself shall be the chastiser; since the soldier originally proceeded from the Brahmin."

This is the third legal change. It recognized the right to rebellion and the right to regicide. The new law is very delicately framed. It gives the right of rebellion to three higher classes. But it is also given to the Brahmins singly by way of providing for a situation when the Kshatriyas and the Vaishyas may not be prepared to join the Brahmin in bringing about a rebellion. The right of rebellion is well circumscribed. It can be exercised only when the king is guilty of upsetting the occupations assigned by Manu to the different Varnas.

These legal changes were as necessary as they were revolutionary. Their object was to legalize and regularize the position created by Pushyamitra by killing the last Maurya King. By virtue of these legal changes, a Brahmin could lawfully become a king, could lawfully take arms, could lawfully depose or murder a king who was opposed to Chaturvarna and could lawfully kill any subject that opposed the authority of the Brahmin. Manu gave the Brahmins a right to commit Barthalomeu if it became necessary to safeguard their interests.

In this way Brahmanism established the right of Brahmana to rule and set at rest whatever doubt and dispute there was regarding the same. But that could hardly be enough for the Brahmins as a whole. It may be a matter of pride but not of any advantage. There can be no special virtue in Brahmin rule if the Brahmin was treated as common man along with the Non-Brahmins having the same rights and same duties. Brahmin rule if it is to justify itself, it must do so by conferring special privileges and immunities on the Brahmins as a class. Indeed Pushyamitra's Revolution would have been an ill wind blowing no good if it had not recognized the superior position of the Brahmins and conferred upon them special advantages. Manu was alive to this and accordingly proceeds to create monopolies for Brahmins and grant them certain immunities and privileges as may be seen from the Code.

First as to monopolies :

1. 88. To Brahmanas he assigned teaching and studying (the Veda) sacrificing for their own benefit and for others, giving and accepting (of alms).

X. 1. Let the three twice-born castes (Varna), discharging their (prescribed) duties, study (the Veda) ; but among them the Brahmana (alone) shall teach it, not the other two; that is an established rule.

X. 2. The Brahmana must know the means of subsistence (prescribed) by law for all, instruct others, and himself live according to (the law).

X. 3. On account of his pre-eminence, on account of the superiority of his origin, on account of his observance of (particular) restrictive rules, and on account of his particular sanctification, the Brahmana is the lord of (all) castes (varna).

X. 74. Brahmanas who are intent on the means (of gaining union with) Brahman and firm in (discharging) their duties, shall live by duly performing the following six acts, (which are enumerated) in their (proper) order.

X. 75. Teaching, studying, sacrificing for himself, sacrificing for others, making gifts and receiving them are the six acts (prescribed) for a Brahamana.

X. 76. But among the six acts (ordained) for him three are his means of subsistence, (viz.) sacrificing for others, teaching, and accepting gifts from pure men.

X. 77. (Passing) from the Brahmana to the Kshatriya, three acts (incumbent) (on the former) are forbidden, (viz.) teaching, sacrificing for others, and, thirdly, the acceptance of gifts.

X. 78. The same are likewise forbidden to a Vaisya, that is a settled rule; for Manu, the lord of creatures (Prajapati), has not prescribed them for (men of) those two (castes).

X. 79. To carry arms for striking and for throwing (is prescribed) for Kshatriyas as a means of subsistence ; to trade, (to rear) cattle, and agriculture for Vaisyas; but their duties are liberality, the study of the Veda, and the performance of sacrifices. Here are three things which Manu made the monopoly of the Brahmin : teaching Vedas, performing Sacrifices and receiving gifts.

The following are the immunities that were granted to the Brahmins. They fall into two classes ; freedom from taxation and exemption from certain forms of punishment for crimes.

VII. 133. Though dying (with want), a king must not levy a tax on Srotriyas, and no Srotriya residing in his kingdom, must perish from hunger.

VIII. 122. They declare that the wise have prescribed these fines for perjury, in order to prevent a failure of justice, and in order to restrain injustice.

VIII. 123. But a just king shall fine and banish (men of) the three (lower) castes (varna) who have given false evidence, but a Brahmana he shall (only) banish.

VIII. 124. Manu, the son of the Self-existent (Svayambhu),

has named ten places on which punishment may be (made to fall) in the cases of the three (lower) castes (varna); but a Brahmana shall depart unhurt (from the country).

VIII. 379. Tonsure (of the head) is ordained for a Brahmana (instead of) capital punishment; but (men of) other castes shall suffer capital punishment.

VIII. 380. Let him never slay a Brahmana, though he have committed all (possible) crimes; let him banish such an (offender), leaving all his property (to him) and (his body) unhurt. Thus Manu places the Brahmin above the ordinary penal law for felony. He is to be allowed to leave the country withdraw a wound on him and with all property in proved offences of capital punishment. He is not to suffer forfeiture of fine nor capital punishment. He suffered only banishment which in the words of Hobbes was only a "Change of air" after having committed the most heinous crimes. Manu gave him also certain privileges. A Judge must be a Brahmin.

VIII. 9. But if the king does not personally investigate the suits, then let him appoint a learned Brahmana to try them.

VIII. 10. That (man) shall enter that most excellent court, accompanied by three assessors, and fully consider (all) causes (brought) before the (king), either sitting down or standing. The other privileges were financial

VIII. 37. When a learned Brahmana has found treasure, deposited in former (times), he may take even the whole (of it) ; for he is master of everything.

VIII. 38. When the king finds treasure of old concealed in the ground, let him give one half to Brahmanas and place the (other) half in his treasury.

IX. 323. But (a king who feels his end drawing nigh) shall bestow all his wealth, accumulated from fines, on Brahmanas, make over his kingdom to his son, and then seek death in battle.

IX. 187. Always to that (relative within three degrees) who is nearest to the (deceased) Sapinda the estate shall belong ; afterwards a Sakulya shall be (the heir, then) the spiritual teacher or the pupil.

IX. 188. But on failure of all (heirs) Brahmanas (shall)

share the estate, (who are) versed in the three Vedas, pure and self-controlled ; thus the law is not violated.

IX. 189. The property of a Brahmana must never be taken by the King, that is a settled rule ; but (the property of men) of other castes the king may take on failure of all (heirs).

These are some of the advantages, immunities and privileges which Manu conferred upon the Brahmins. This was a token of a Brahmin having become a king.

Supporters of Brahmanism—so strong is the belief in the excellence of Brahmanism that there are no appologists for it as yet—never fail to point to the disabilities which Manu has imposed upon the Brahmins. Their object in doing so is to show that the ideal placed by Manu before the Brahmin is poverty and service. That Manu has placed certain disabilities upon the Brahmins is a fact. But to conclude from it that Manu's ideal for a Brahmin is poverty and service is a gross and deliberate concoction for which there is no foundation in Manu.

To understand the real purpose which Manu had in imposing these disabilities, two things must be borne in mind. Firstly the place Manu has assigned to the Brahmins in the general scheme of society and secondly the nature of the disabilities. The place assigned by Manu to the Brahmins is enunciated by him in unequivocal terms. The matter being important I must quote again the Verses already quoted.

1. 93. As the Brahmana sprang from (Brahman's) mouth, as he was the first born, and as he possesses the Veda, he is by right the lord of this whole creation. Consider the nature of the disabilities.

IV. 2. A Brahamana must seek a means of subsistence which either causes no, or at least little pain (to others), and live (by that) except in times of distress.

IV. 3. For the purpose of gaining bare subsistence, let him accumulate property by (following those) irreproachable occupations (which are prescribed for) his (caste), without (unduly) fatiguing his body.

VIII. 337. In (a case of) theft the guilt of a Sudra sha.ll be eightfold, that of a Vaishya sixteenfold, that of a Kshatriya two-and-thirty fold.

VIII. 338. That of a Brahamana sixty-four-fold, or quite a hundred-fold or (even) twice four-and-sixty-fold; (each of them) knowing the nature of the offence.

VIII. 383. A Brahamana shall be compelled to pay a fine of one thousand (panas) if he has intercourse with guarded (females of) those two (castes) ; for (offending with) a (guarded) Sudra female a fine of one thousand (panas) (shall be inflicted) on a Kshatriya or a Vaishya.

VIII. 384. For (intercourse with) an unguarded Kshatriya a fine of five hundred (panas shall fall) on a Vaisya ; but (for the same offence) a Kshatriya shall be shaved with the urine (of a donkey) or (pay) the same fine.

VIII. 385. A Brahamana who approaches unguarded females (of the) Kshatriya or Vaisya (castes), or a Sudra female, shall be fined five hundred (panas); but (for intercourse with) a female (of the) lowest (castes), one thousand.

Examining these disabilities against the background furnished by the place assigned to him by Manu, it is obvious that the object of these disabilities was not to make the Brahmin suffer. On the other hand it becomes clear that the object of Manu was to save the Brahmin from falling from the high pennacle on which he had placed him and incurring the disgrace of the non-Brahmins.

That the object of Manu was not to subject the Brahmins to poverty and destitute is clear from other provisions from Manu-Smriti. In this connection reference should be made to the rule contained in the Manu Smriti regarding the course of conduct a Brahmin should pursue when he is in distres.

X. 80. Among the several occupations the most commendable are, teaching the Veda for a Brahmana, protecting (the people) for a Kshatriya, and trade for a Vaisya.

X. 81. But a Brahmana, unable to subsist by his peculiar occupations just mentioned, may live according to the law applicable to Kshatriyas ; for the latter is next to him in rank.

X. 82. If it be asked, 'How shall it be, if he cannot maintain himself by either (of these occupations?' the answer is), he may adopt a Vaisya's mode of life, employing himself in agriculture and rearing cattle.

X. 83. But a Brahamana, or a Kshatriya, living by a Vaisya's mode of subsistence, shall carefully avoid (the pursuit of) agriculture, (which causes) injury to many beings and depends on others.

X. 84. (Some) declare that agriculture is something excellent, (but) that means of subsistence is blamed by the virtuous ; (for) the wooden (implement) with iron point injures the earth and (the beings) living in the earth.

X. 85. But he who, through a want of means of subsistence, gives up the strictness with respect to his duties, may sell, in order to increase his wealth, the commodities sold by Vaisyas, making (however) the (following) exceptions.

It will be seen that the disabilities imposed upon a Brahmin last as long as he is prospering by the occupations which belong to him as of right. As soon as he is in distress and his disabilities vanish and he is free to do anything that he likes to do in addition to the occupations reserved to him and without ceasing to be a Brahmin. Further whether he is in distress or not is a matter which is left to the Brahmin to be decided in his own discretion. There is therefore no bar to prevent even a prosperous Brahmin to supplement his earnings by following any of the professions open to him in distress by satisfying his conscience.

There are other provisions in Manu Smriti intended to materially benefit the Brahmanas. They are *Dakshina* and *Dana.* Dakshina is the fee which the Brahmin is entitled to charge when he is called to perform a religious ceremony. Brahmanism is full of rites and ceremonies. It is not very difficult to imagine how great must this source of income be to every Brahmin: There was no chance of a priest being cheated of his fees. The religious sense attached to Dakshina was a sufficient sanction for regular payment. But Manu wanted to give the Brahmins the right to recover his fees.

XI. 38. A Brahamana who, though wealthy, does not give, as fee for the performance of an Agnyadheya, a horse sacred to Prajapati, becomes (equal to one) who has not kindled the sacred fires.

XI. 39. Let him who has faith and controls his senses, perform other meritorious acts, but let him on no acount offer sacrifices at which he gives smaller fees (than those prescribed).

XI. 40. The organs (of sense and action), honour, (bliss in) heaven, longevity, fame, offspring, and cattle are destroyed by a sacrifice at which (too) small sacrificial fees are given ; hence a man of small means should not offer a (Srauta) sacrifice. He even goes to the length of excusing a Brahmin by declaring that anything done by him to recover his fees shall not be an offence under the law.

VIII. 349. In their own defence, in a strife for the fees of officiating priests and in order to protect women and Brahmanas ; he who (under such circumstances kills in the cause of right, commits no sin.

But it is the provision of Dana which makes a fruitful source of income to the Brahmins. Manu exhorts the King to make *Dana* to Brahmins.

VII. 79. A King shall offer various (Srauta) sacrifices at which liberal fees (are distributed), and in order to acquire merit, he shall give to Brahmanas enjoyments and wealth.

VII. 82. Let him honour those Brahmanas who have returned from their teacher's house (after studying the Veda) ; for that (money which is given) to Brahmanas is declared to be an imperishable treasure for kings.

VII. 83. Neither thieves nor foes can take it, nor can it be lost; hence an imperishable store must be deposited by kings with Brahmanas.

XI. 4. But a king shall bestow, as is proper, jewels of all sorts, and presents for the sake of sacrifices on Brahmanas learned in the Vedas.

This admonition by Manu to the King did not remain a mere hope for the Brahmin. For as history shows that this exhortation was fully exploited by the Brahmins as the number of *dana patras* discovered by Archialogists indicate. It is astounding how the kings were befooled by the Brahmins to transfer village after village to crafty, lazy and indolent Brahmins. Indeed a large part of the wealth of the present day Brahmins lies in this swindle practised by wily Brahmins upon pious but foolish kings. Manu was not content to let the Brahmin prey upon the King for *dana.* He also allowed the Brahmin to prey upon the public in the mattter of *dana.* This Manu does in three different ways. In the first place he exhorts people to make gifts as a part of the duty owed by the pious to himself at the same time pointing out that the highest dana to a Brahmin.:

VII. 85. A gift to one who is not a Brahmana (yields) the ordinary (reward); a gift to one who calls himself a Brahmana, a double (reward); a gift to a well-read Brahmana, a hundred thousandfold (reward); (a gift) to one who knows the Veda and the Angas (Vedaparanga), (a reward) without end.

VII. 86. For according to the particular qualities of the recipient and according to the faith (of the giver) a small or a great reward will be obtained for a gift in the next world. In the next place Manu declares that in certain circumstances *dana* to a Brahmin is compulsory.

XI. 1. Him who wishes (to marry for the sake of having) offspring, him who wishes to perform a sacrifice, a traveller, him who has given away all his property, him who begs for the sake of his teacher, his father, or his mother, a student of the Veda, and a sick man.

XI. 2 These nine Brahmanas one should consider as Snatakas, begging in order to fulfill the sacred law; to such poor men gifts must be given in proportion to their learning.

XI. 3. To these most excellent among the twice-born, food and presents (of money) must be given ; it is declared that food must be given to others outside the sacrificial enclosure.

XI. 6. One should give, according to one's ability, wealth to Brahmanas learned in the Veda and living alone ; (thus) one obtains after death heavenly bliss.

The third method adopted by Manu to make the rule of Dana become a source of secure and steady income is beyond question the most ingenuous one. Manu linked up *dana* with penance. In the Scheme of Manu, an improper act may be a sin although not an offence or it may be both a sin as well as an offence. As a sin its punishment is a matter for canonical law. As an offence its punishment is a matter of secular law. As sin, the improper act is called Pataka and the punishment for it is called Penance. In the Scheme of Manu every Pataka must be expunged by the performance of a penance.

XI. 44. A man who omits a prescribed act, or performs a

blameable act, or cleaves to sensual enjoyments, must perform a penance.

XI. 45. (All) sages prescribe a penance for a sin unintentionally committed ; some declare, on the evidence of the revealed texts, (that it may be performed) even for an intentional (offences).

XI. 46. A sin unintentionally committed is expiated by the recitation of Vedic texts, but that which (men) in their folly commit intentionally, by various (special) penances.

XI. 53. Thus in consequence of a remnant of (the guilt of former) crimes, are born idiots, dumb, blind, deaf and deformed men, who are (all) despised by the virtuous.

XI. 54. Penances, therefore, must always be performed for the sake of purification, because those whose sins have not been expiated, are born (again) with disgraceful marks.

The penances prescribed by Manu are many and the curious may refer to the Manu Smriti itself for a knowledge of what they are. What is worthy of note is these penances are calculated to materially benefit the Brahmin. Some penances take the form of a simple *dana* to the Brahmin. Others prescribe the performance of some religious rites. But as religious rites cannot be performed by anybody except by a Brahmin and that the performance of religious rite requires the payment of fees the Brahmin alone can be the beneficiary of the *dana* system.

It is therefore absurd to suggest that Manu wanted to place before the Brahmins the ideal of humility, poverty and service. The Brahmins certainly did not understand Manu that way. Indeed they believed that they were made a privileged class. Not only they believed in it but they sought to extend their privileges in other directions a matter which will be discussed later on. They were perfectly justified, in their view. Manu called the Brahmins the 'lords of the earth' and he framed (the law) with such care that they shall remain so.

Having made full provision for Brahmin Rule and Brahmin dominance Manu next launches out to transform society to suit his purposes.

The transformation of Varna into Caste is the most stupendous and selfish task in which Brahmanism after its triumph became primarily engaged. We have no explicit record of the steps that Brahmanism took to bring about this change. On the contrary we have a lot of confused thinking on the relation between Varna and Caste. Some think that Varna and Caste are the same. Those who think that they are different seem to believe that Varna became caste when prohibition on intermarriage became part of the social order. All this, of course, is erroneous and the error is due to the fact that Manu in transforming the Varna into Caste has nowhere explained his ends and how his means are related to those ends. Oscar Wilde has said that to be intelligible is to be found out. Manu did not wish to be found out. He is therefore silent about his ends and means, leaving people to imagine them. For Hindus the subject is important beyond measure. An attempt at clarification is absolutely essential so that the confusion due to different people imagining differently the design of Manu may be removed and light thrown on the way how Brahmanism proceeded to give a wrong and pernicious turn to the original idea of Varna as the basis of society.

As I said Manu's ways are silent and subterranean and we cannot give the detailed and chronological history of this conversion *of* Varna into Caste. But fortunately there are landmarks which are clear enough to indicate how the change was brought about.

Before proceeding to describe how this change was brought about let me clear the confusion between Varna and Caste. This can best be done by noting the similarities and differences between the two. Varna and Caste are identical in their *de jure* connotation. Both connote status and occupation. Status and occupation are the two concepts which are implied both in the notion Varna as well as in the notion of Caste. Varna and Caste however differ in one important particular. Varna is not hereditary either in status or occupation. On the other hand Caste implies a system in which status and occupation are hereditary and descend from father to son.

When I say that Brahmanism converted Varna into Caste what I mean is that it made status and occupation hereditary.

How was this transformation effected? As I said there are no foot prints left of the steps taken by Brahmanism to accomplish this change but there are landmarks which serve to give us a clear view of how the deed came to be done.

The change was accomplished by stages. In the transformation of Varna into Caste three stages are quite well marked. The first stage was the stage in which the duration of Varna i.e. of status and occupation of a person was for a prescrbied period of time only. The second stage was a stage in which the status and occupation involved the Varna of a person ensured during lifetime only. The third stage was a stage in which the status and occupation of the Varna became hereditary. To use legal language the Estate conferred by Varna was at the beginning an Estate for a term only. Thereafter it became a life Estate and finally it became an Estate of inheritance which is tantamount to saying that Varna became Caste.

That these are the stages by which Varna was converted into Caste seems to have ample support from tradition as recorded in the religious literature. There is no reason why this tradition should not be accepted as embodying some thing that is quite genuine. According to this tradition, the task of determining Varna of a person was effected by a body of officers called Manu and Sapta Rishis. From the mass of people Manu selected those who were fit to be Kshatriyas and Vaishas and the Sapta Rishis selected those who were fit to be Brahmanas. After this selection was made by Manu and Sapta Rishis for being Brahmins, Kshatriyas, Vaishas, the rest that were not selected were called Shudras. The Varna arrangement so determined lasts for one *Yug* i.e. a period of four years. Every fourth year a new body of officers known by the same designation Manu and Sapta Rishi were appointed for making a new selection.

It happened that last time some of those who were left to be fit only for being Shudras were selected for being Brahmins, Kshatriyas and Vaishyas while some of those who were, elected last time for being Brahmins, Kshatriyas and Vaishyas were left as being fit only of being Shudras. Thus the personnel of the Varna changed. It was a sort of a periodical shuffling and selection of men to take up according to their mental and physical aptitudes and occupations which were essential to the life of the community. The time when the reshuffling of the

Varnas took place was called *Manwantar* which etymologically means change of Varna made by Manu. The word Manwantar also means the period for which the Varna of an individual was fixed. The word Manwantar is very rich in its contents and expresses the essential elements of the Varna system which were two. First it shows that Varna was determined by an independent body of people called Manu and Saptarshi.

Secondly it shows that the Varna was for a period after which a change was made by Manu. According to ancient tradition as embodied in the Puranas the period for which the Varna of a person was fixed by Manu and Saptarshi was a period of four years and was called *Yug*. At the end of the period of four years there occured the Manwantar whereby every fourth year the list was revised. Under the revision some changed their old Varna, some retained it, some lost it and some gained it.

The original system seems to have in contemplation the determination of the Varna of adults. It was not based on prior training or close scrutiny of bias and aptitude. Manu and Saptarshi was a sort of a Board of Interview which determined the Varna of a person from how he struck them at the interview. The determination of the Varna was done in a rough and tumble manner. This system seems to have gone into abeyance. A new system grew up in its place. It was known as the Gurukul system. The Gurukul was a school maintained by a Guru (teacher) also called Acharya (learned man). All children went to this Gurukul for their education. The period of education extended for twelve years. The child while at Gurukul was known as Bramhachari. After the period of education was over there was the Upanayan ceremony performed at the Gurukul by the Acharya. The Upanayan ceremony was the most important ceremony. It was a ceremony at which the Acharya determined the Varna of the student and sent him out in the world to perform the duties of that Varna. Upanayan by the Acharyas was the new method of determining Varna which came into vogue in place of method of determination by Manu and Saptarshi. The new method was undoubtedly superior to the old method. It retained the true feature of the old method namely that the Varna should be determined by a disinterested and independent body. But it added a new feature namely training as a pre-requisite for assignment of Varna. On the ground that training alone developes individual in the make up of a person and the only safe way to determine the Varna of a person is to know his individuality, the addition of this new feature was undoubtedly a great improvement.

With the introduction of the Acharya Gurukul system, the duration of the Varna came to be altered. Varna instead of being Varna for a period became Varna for life. But it was not hereditary.

Evidently Brahmanism was dissatisfied with this system. The reason for dissatisfaction was quite obvious. Under the system as prevalent there was every chance of the Acharya declaring the child of a Brahmin as fit only to be a Shudra. Brahmanism was naturally most anxious to avoid this result. It wanted the Varna to be hereditary. Only by making the Varna hereditary could it save the children of the Brahmins from being declared Shudra. To achieve this Brahmanism proceeded in the most audacious manner one can think of.

Brahmanism made three most radical changes in the system of determing the Varna of the child. In the first place the system of Gurukul as the place where training to the child was given and its Varna was determined by the Guru at the end of the period of training was abolished. Manu is quite aware of the Gurukul and refers to Guruvas i.e. training and residence in the Gurukul under the Guru.

But does not refer to it at all in connection with the Upanayan. He abolishes the Guru as an authority competent to perform Upanayan by omitting to make even the remotest reference to him in connection with Upanayan. In place of the Guru Manu allows the Upanayan of the child to be performed by its father at home. Secondly Upanayan was made into a Sanskara i.e. a sacrament. In olden times Upanayan was like a convocation ceremony held by the Guru to confer degrees obtained by students in his Gurukul in which certificates of proficiency in the duties of a particular Varna were granted. In Manu's law that Upanayan was a complete change in the meaning and purpose of this most important institution. Thirdly the relation of training to Upanayan was totally reversed. In the olden system training came before Upanayan.

Under the Brahmanism Upanayan came before training. Manu directs that a child be sent to the Guru for training but that is after Upanayan i.e. after his Varna is determined by his father.

The principal change made by Brahmanism was the transfer of authority from the Guru to the father in the matter of performing Upanayan. The result was that the father having the right to perform the Upanayan of his child gave his own Varna to the child and thus made it hereditory. It is by divesting the Guru of his authority to determine the Varna and vesting it in the father that Brahmanism ultimately converted Varna into Caste.

Such is the story of the transformation of Varna into Caste. The story of the transition from one to the other is of course reconstructed. For the reasons already given it may not be quite as accurate as one would wish it to be in all its details. But I have no doubt that the stages and the ways by which Varna ceased to exist and caste came into being must be some such as have been suggested in the foregoing discussion of the subject.

What object Brahmanism could have had in converting Varna into caste it is not difficult to imagine. The object was to make the high status enjoyed by the Brahmins from ancient times the privilege of every Brahmin and his progeny without reference to merits or to qualifications. To put it differently the object was to elevate and ennoble every Brahmin, however mean and worthless he may be, to the high status occupied by some of them on account of the virtue. It was an attempt to ennoble the whole of the Brahmin Community without exception.

That this was the object of Brahmanism is clear from Manu's ordinances. Manu knew that making Varna hereditary, the most ignorant Brahmin will be elevated to the status occupied by the most learned Brahmin. He feared that the former may not be respected as much as the most learned, which was the object of this attempt at the ennoblement of the whole class of Brahmins. Manu is very much concerned about the ignorant Brahmin—a new thing and warns people against being disrespectful to an ignorant and mean Brahmin.

IX. 317. A Brahmin, whether learned or ignornt, is a powerful divinity ; even as fire is powerful divinity, whether consecrated or popular.

IX. 319. Thus although Brahmins employ themselves in all sorts of mean ocupations, they must invariably be honoured ; for they are something transcendently divine.

Such a warning was unnecessary if the object was to ennoble the whole Brahmin class. Here is a case where vice refuses to pay to virtue even the homage of hypocracy. Can there be greater moral degeneracy than what is shown by Manu in insisting upon the worship of the Brahmin even if he is mean and ignorant?

So much for the object of change from Varna to caste. What have been the consequences of this change?

From the spiritual point of view the consequences have been too harmful to be contemplated with equanimity. The harm done may perhaps be better realized by comparing the position of the Brahmin as a priest resulting from the law of Manu with that of the law of the clergy under the Church of England. There the clergy is subject to the criminal law as every citizen is. But in addition to that he is always subject to Church Descipline Act. Under the Criminal Law he would be punished if he officiated as a clergy without being qualified for it. Under the Church Discipline Act he would be lia.ble to be disqualified as a clergy for conduct which would be deemed to be morally wrong although it did not amount to a crime. This double check on the clergy is held justifiable because learning and morality are deemed to be quite essential for the profession of the clergy who are supposed to administer to the spiritual needs of the people. Under Brahmanism the Brahmin who alone can be the clergy need not possess learning or morality. Yet he is in sole charge of the spiritual affairs of the people!! On the value of a creed which permits this, comment is unnecessary.

From the secular point of view, the consequences of this transformation of Varna into Caste has to introduce a most pernicious mentality among the Hindus. It is to disregard merit and have regard only to birth. If one is descended from the high he has respect although he may be utterly devoid of merit or worth. One who is of high birth will be superior to the one who is of low birth although the latter may be superior to the former in point of worth. Under Brahmanism it is birth that always wins, whether it is against birth or against worth. Merit by itself can win no meads. This is entirely due to the dissociation of merits from status which is the work of Brahmanism. Nothing could be better calculated to produce an unprogressive society which sacrifices the rights of intelligence on the altar of aristocratic privilege.

Now the third deed in the catalogue of deeds done by Brahmanism after its triumph over Buddhism. It was to separate the Brahmins from the result of the Non-Brahmin population and to sever the different social strata of the Non-Brahmin population.

Pushyamitra's Brahmanic Revolution was undertaken for the purposes of restoring the ancient social system of Chaturvarna which under the Buddhist regime was put into the melting pot. But when Brahmanism triumphed over Buddhism it did not content itself with merely restoring Charutvarna as it was in its original form. The system of Chaturvarna of the Pre-Buddhist days was a flexible system and was an open to system. This was because the Varna system had no connection with the marriage system. While Chaturvarna recognized the existence of four different classes, it did not prohibit inter-marriage between them. A male of one Varna could lawfully marry a female of another Varna. There are numerous illustrations in support of this view. I give below some instances which refer to well known and respectable individuals which have acquired a name and fame in the sacred lore of the Hindus.

1. Shantanu Kshatriya Ganga Shudra Anamik
2. Shantanu Kshatriya Matsyagandha Shudra Fisher woman
3. Parashara Brahmin Matsyagandha Shudra Fisher woman
4. Vishwamitra Kshatriya Menaka Apsara
5. Yayati Kshatriya Devayani Brahmin
6. Yayati Kshatriya Sharmishta Asuri- Non-Aryan
7. Jaratkaru Brahmin Jaratkari Nag Non-Aryan.

Husband His Varna Wife Her Varna

Should anybody retain doubt on the question that the division of the society into classes did not prohibit intermarriages between the four Varnas let him consider the geneology of the family of the great Brahmin sage Vyas.

Geneology of Vyas

Varuna Mitra = Urvashi

Vashishtha = Akshamala

Shakti =

Parashara = Matsyagandha = Vyas

Brahminism with the ferocity of an outraged brute proceeded to put a stop to these intermarriage between the different Varnas. A new law is proclaimed by Manu. It is in the following terms :—

III. 12. For the first marriage of twice born men (wives) of equal caste are recommended.

III. 13. It is declared that a Sudra woman alone can be the wife of a Shudra.

III. 14. A Shudra woman is not mentioned even in any (ancient) story as the (first) wife of a Brahmana or of a Kshatriya, though they lived in the (greatest) distress.

III. 15. Twice-born men who, in their folly, wed wives of the low (Sudra) caste, soon degrade their families and their children to the state of Sudras.

111.16. According to Atri and to (Gautama) the son of Utathya. he who weds a Sudra woman becomes an outcast, according to Saunaka on the birth of a son, and according to Bhrigu he who has (male) offspring from a (Sudra female, alone).

III. 17. A Brahmana who takes a Sudra wife to his bed, will (after death) sink into hell ; if he begets a child by her, he will lose the rank of a Brahmana.

III. 18. The manes and the gods will not eat the (offerings) of that man who performs the rites in honour of the gods, of the manes, and of guests chiefly with a (Sudra wife's) assistance, and such (a man) will not go to heaven.

III. 19. For him who drinks the moisture of a Sudra's lips, who is tainted by her breath, and who begets a son on her. no expiation is prescribed.

Brahmanism was not satisfied with the prohibition of intermarriage. Brahmanism went further and prohibited interdining.

Manu lays down certain interdicts on food. Some are hygenic. Some are social. Of the social the following are worthy of attention :

IV. 218. Food given by a king, impairs his manly vigour; by one of the servile class, his divine light : by goldsmiths, his life ; by leathercutters, his good name.

IV. 219. Given by cooks and the like mean artizans, it destroys his offsprings : by a washerman, his muscular strength;

IV. 221. That of all others, mentioned in order, whose food must never be tasted, is held equal by the wise to the skin, bones, and hair of the head.

IV. 222. Having unknowingly swallowed the food of any such persons, he must fast during three days; but having eaten it knowingly, he must perform the same harsh penance, as if he had tasted any seminal impurity, ordure, or urine. I said that Brahmanism acted with the ferocity of an outranged brute in undertaking the task of prohibiting intermarriage and interdining. Those who have doubts in this matter ponder over the language of Manu.

Mark the disguest Manu shows with regard to the Shudra woman. Mark what Manu says about the food of the Shudra. He says it is as impure as semen or urine.

These two laws have produced the caste system. Prohibition of intermarriage and prohibition against interdining, are two pillars on which it rests. The caste system and the rules relating to intermarriage and interdining are related to each other as ends to means. Indeed by no other means could the end be realized.

The forging of these means shows that the creation of the caste system was end and aim of Brahmanism. Brahmanism enacted the prohibitions against intemarriage and interdining. But Brahmanism introduced other changes in the social system and if the purposes underlying these changes are those which I suggest them to be, then it must be admitted that Brahmanism was so keen in sustaining the caste system that it did not mind whether ways and means employed were fair or unfair, moral or immoral. I refer to the laws contained in the Code of Manu regarding marriage of girls and the life of widows.

See the law that Manu promulgates regarding the marriage of females.

IX. 4. Reprehensible is the father who gives not (his daughter) in marriage at the proper time.

IX. 88. To a distinguished, handsome suitor of equal caste should a father give his daughter in accordance with the prescribed rule, though she have not attained (the proper age), i.e. although she may not have reached puberty.

By this rule Manu enjoins that a girl should be married even though she may not have reached the age of puberty i.e. even when she is a child. Now with regard to widows Manu promulgates the following rule.

V. 157. At her pleasure let her (i.e. widow) emaciate her body, by living voluntarily on pure flowers, roots and fruits ; but let her not, when her lord is deceased, even pronounce the name of another man.

V. 161. But a widow, who from a wish to bear children, slights her deceased husband by marrying again, brings disgrace on herself here below, and shall be excluded from the seat of her lord (in heaven).

V. 162. Offspring begotten on a woman by any other than her husband, is here declared to be no progeny of hers ; no more than a child, begotten on the wife of another man belongs to the begetter; nor is a second husband any where prescribed for a virtuous woman.

This is the rule of enforced widowhood for a woman. A reference may also be made to Sati or a widow who burns herself on the funeral pyre of her husband and thus puts an end to her life. Manu is silent about it.

Yajnavalkya an authority nearly as great as Manu says, she must not live separately or alone.

86. When deprived of her husband, she must not remain

away from her father, mother, son, brother, mother-in-law or from her maternal uncle; otherwise she might become liable to censure. Here again Yajnavalkya does not suggest that a widow become a Sati. But Vijnaneshwar, the author of Mitakshara a commentary on Yajnavalkya Smriti makes the following observation in commenting on the above Sloka.

"This is in the case of the alternative of leading a celibate life vide the text of Vishnu : "After the death of the husband, either celibacy or ascending the (cremation) pile after him."

Vijnaneshwar3 adds as his opinion that 'There is great merit in ascending the funeral pyre after him.'

From this one can very easily and clearly see how the rule of Sati came to be forged. Manu's rule was that a widow was not to remarry. But it appears from the statement by Vijnaneshwar that from the time of the Vishnu Smriti a different interpretation began to put on the ordinance of Manu. According to this new interpretation Manu's rule was explained to be offering to the widow a choice between two alternatives: (1) Either burn yourself on your husband's funeral pyre or (2) If you don't, remain unmarried. This of course is totally false interpretation quite unwarranted by the clear words of Manu. Somehow it came to be accepted. The date of the Vishnu Smriti is somewhere about the 3rd or 4th Century. It can therefore be said that rule of Sati dates from this period.

One thing is certain, these were new rules. The rule of Manu that girl should be married before she has reached puberty is a new rule. In Pre-Buddhistic Brahmanism marriages were performed not only after puberty but they were performed when girls had reached an age when they could be called grown up. Of this there is ample evidence. Similarly the rule that a woman once she had lost her husband must not remarry is a new rule. In the Pre-Buddhist Brahmanism there was no prohibition on widow remarriage. The fact that the Sanskrit language contains words such as *Punarbhu* (woman who has undergone a second marriage ceremony) and *punarhhav* (second husband) show that such marriages were quite common under the Pre-Buddhist Brahmanism· With regard to Sati the position as to when it arose, there is evidence to suggest that it existed in ancient times. But there is evidence that it had died out and it was revived after Brahmanism under Pushyamitra obtained its victory over Buddhism although it was some time later than Manu.

Question is this, why these changes were made by the triumphant Brahmanism? What did Brahmanism want to achieve by having girls married before they had become pubert, by denying the widow to the right to marry again and by telling her to put herself to death by immolating herself in the funeral pyre of her deceased husband? No explainations are forthcoming for these changes. Mr. C. V. Vaidya who offers an explanation for girl marriage says that girl marriage was introduced to prevent girls from joining the Buddhist order of nuns. This explanation does not satisfy me. Mr. Vaidya omits to take into consideration another rule laid down by Manu—namely the rule relating to suitable age for marriage. According to that rule.

IX. 94. A man aged thirty, shall marry a maiden of twelve who pleases him, or a man of twenty-four a girl eight years of age. The question is not why girl marriage was introduced. The question is why Manu allowed so much discrepancy in the ages of the bride and the bridegroom.

Mr. Kane has attempted an explanation of Sati. His explanation is that there is nothing new in it. It existed in India in ancient times as it did in other parts of the world. This again does not satisfy the world. If it existed outside India, it has not been practised on so enormous a scale as in India. Secondly if traces of it are found in Ancient India in the Kshatriyas, why was it revived, why was it not universalized? There is no satisfactory explanation. Mr. Kane's explanation that the prevalence of Sati by reference to laws of inheritance does not appear to me very convincing. It may be that because under the Hindu Law of inheritance as it prevailed in Bengal, women got a share in property. The relations of the husband of the widow pressed her to be a Sati in order to get rid of a share may explain why Sati was practised on so large a scale in Bengal. But it does not explain how it arose nor how it came to be practised in other parts of India.

Again with regard to the prohibition of widow remarriage, there is no explanation whatsoever. Why was the widow, contrary to established practice, prohibited from marrying? Why was she required to lead a life of misery? Why was she disfigured?

My explanation for girl marriage, enforced widowhood and Sati is quite different and I offer it for what it is worth.

"Thus the superposition of endogamy over exogamy means the creation of Caste. But this is not an easy affair. Let us take an imaginary group that desire to make itself into a caste and analyse what means it will have to adopt to make itself endogamous. If a group desires to make itself endogamous, a formal injunction against intermarriage with outside groups will be of no avail, especially if prior to the introduction of endogamy, exogamy were to be the rule in all matrimonial relations. Again there is a tendency in all groups living in close contact with one another to assimilate and amalgamate, and thus consolidate into a homogeneous society. If this tendency be strongly counteracted in the interest of Caste formation, it is absolutely necessary to circumscribe a circle without which people should not contract marriages."

"Nevertheless this encircling to prevent marriages from without creates problems from within which are not very easy of solution. Roughly speaking in a normal group the two sexes are more or less evenly distributed, and generally speaking there is an equality between those of the same age. But this equality is never quite realised in actual societies.

While to the group that is desirous of making itself into a caste the maintenance of this equality between the sexes becomes the ultimate goal, for without this endogamy can no longer subsist. In other words, if endogamy is to be preserved, conjugal rights from within have to be provided for, else members of the group will be driven out of the circle to take care of themselves in any way they please.

But in order that the conjugal rights be provided for from within, it is absolutely necessary to maintain a numerical equality between the marriageable units of the two sexes within the group desirous of making itself into a Caste. It is only through the maintenance of this equality that the necessary endogamy of the group could be kept intact, and a very large disparity is sure to break it."

"The problem of Caste then ultimately resolves itself into one of repairing the disparity between the marriageable units of the two sexes within it. The much needed parity between the units could be realized only when a couple dies simultaneously. But this is a rare contingency. The husband may die before the wife and create a surplus woman who must be disposed of, else through intermarriage she will violate the endogamy of the group. In like manner the husband may survive his wife and be a surplus man whom the group, while it may sympathise with him for the sad bereavement, has to dispose of, else he will marry outside the Caste and will break the endogamy. Thus both the surplus man and the surplus woman constitute a menace to the Caste if not taken care of, for, not finding suitable partners inside their prescribed circle (and they cannot find any, for there are just enough pairs to go round) very likely they will transgress the boundary, marry outside and import population that is foreign to the Caste. Let us see what our imaginary group is likely *to* do with this surplus man and surplus woman. We will first take up the case of the surplus woman. She can be disposed of in two different ways so as to preserve the endogamy of the Caste."

"First : burn her on the funeral pyre of her deceased husband and get rid of her. This, however, is rather an impracticable way of solving the problem of sex disparity. In some cases it may work, in others it may not. Consequently every surplus woman cannot thus be disposed of, because it is an easy solution but a hard realization. However, the surplus woman (widow) if not disposed of, remains in the group: but in her very existence lies a double danger. She may marry outside the Caste and violate to endogamy or she may marry within the Caste and through competition encroach upon the chances of marriage that must be reserved for the potential brides in the Caste. She therefore is a menace in any case and something must be done to her if she cannot be burned along with her deceased husband."

"The second remedy is to enforce widowhood on her for the rest of her life. So far as the objective results are concerned burning is a better solution than enforcing widowhood. Burning the widow eliminates all the three evils that a surplus woman is fraught with. Being dead and gone she creates no problem of remarriage either inside or outside the Caste. But compulsory widowhood is superior to burning because it is more practicable. Besides being comparatively humane it also guards against the evils of remarriage as does burning ; but it fails to guard the morals of the group. No doubt under compulsory widowhood the woman remains and, just because she is deprived of her natural right of being a legitimate wife in future, the incentive to bad moral conduct is increased. But this is by no means an insuperable difficulty. She can be degraded to a condition where she could no longer be a source of allurement."

"The problem of surplus man (—widower) is much more important and much more difficult than that of the surplus woman in a group that desires to make itself into a Caste. From time immemorial man as compared with woman has had the upper hand. He is a dominant figure in every group and of the two sexes has greater prestige. With this traditional superiority of man over woman his wishes have always been consulted. Woman on the other hand has been an easy prey to all kinds of iniquitous injunctions, religious, social or economic. But man as a maker of injunctions is most often above them all. Such being the case you cannot accord the same kind of treatment to a surplus man as you can to a surplus woman in a Caste."

"The project of burning him with his deceased wife is hazardous in two ways : first of all it cannot be done, simply because he is a man. Secondly, if done, a sturdy soul is lost to the Caste. There remain then only two solutions which can conveniently dispose of him. I say conveniently because he is an asset to the group."

"Important as he is to the group, endogamy is still more important, and the solution must assure both these ends. Under these circumstances he may be forced, or I should say induced, after the manner of the widow to remain a widower for the rest of his life. This solution is not altogether difficult, for without there being any compulsion some are so disposed as to enjoy self-imposed celibacy or may even take a further step of their own accord to renounce the world and its joys. But, given human nature as it is, this solution can hardly be expected to be realized. On the other hand, as is very likely to be the case, if he remains in the group as an active participator in group activities, he is a danger to the morals of the group. Looked at from a different viewpoint, ceilibacy though easy in cases where it succeeds, is not so advantageous even then to the material prospects of the Caste. If he observes genuine celibacy and renounces the world, he would not be a menace to the preservation of Caste endogamy or Caste morals as undoubtedly would be, if he remained a secular person. But as an ascetic celibate he is as good as burned, so far as the material well being of his Caste is concerned. A Caste, in order that it may be large enough to afford a vigorous communal life, must be maintained at a certain numerical strength. But to hope for this and to proclaim celibacy is the same as trying to cure atrophy by bleeding.

"Imposing celibacy on the surplus man in the group therefore fails, both theoretically and practically. It is in the interest of the Caste to keep him as a Grahastha (one who raises a family) to use a Sanskrit technicality. But the problem is to provide him with a wife from within the Caste. At the outset this is not possible, for the ruling ratio in a caste has to be one man to one woman and none can have two chances of marriage, for in a Caste thoroughly self enclosed there are always just enough marriageable women to go round for the marriageable men. Under these circumstances the surplus man can only be provided with a wife by recruiting a bride from the ranks of those not yet marriageable in order to tie him down to the group. This is certainly the best of the possible solutions in the case of the surplus man. By this, he is kept within the Caste. By this, this numerical depletion through constant outflow is guarded against, and by this endogamy and morals are preserved.

"It will now be seen that the four means by which numerical disparity between the two sexes is conveniently maintained are: (1) Burning the widow with her deceased husband ; (2) Compulsory widowhood—a milder form of burning ; (3) Imposing celibacy on the widower ; (4) Wedding him to a girl not yet marriageable. Though as I said above, burning the widow and imposing celibacy on the widower are of doubtful service to the group in its endeavour to preserve its endogamy, all of them operate as means. But means as forces, when liberated or set in motion create an end. What then is the end that these means create? They create and perpetuate endogamy, while caste and endogamy, according to our analysis of the various definitions of caste, are one and the same thing. Thus the existence of these means means caste and caste involves these means."

"This, in my opinion, is the general mechanism of a caste in a system of castes. Let us now turn to the castes in the Hindu Society and inquire into their mechanism. I need hardly promise that there are a great many pitfalls in the path of those who try to unfold the past, and caste in India to be sure is a very ancient institutiion. This is especially true where there exist no authentic or written history or records or where the people, like the Hindus are so constituted that to them Writing history is a folly, for the world is an illusion. But institutions do live, though for a long time they may remain unrecorded and as often as not customs and morals are like fossils that tell their own history. If this is true, our task will be amply rewarded if we scrutinize the solution the Hindus arrived at to meet the problems of the surplus man and surplus woman."

"Complex though it be in its general working the Hindu Society, even to a superficial observer, presents three singular uxorial customs, namely :—

(i) Sati or the burning of the widow on the funeral pyre of her deceased husband.

(ii) Enforced widowhood by which a widow is not allowed to remarry.

(iii) Girl marriage.

In addition to these, one also notes a great hankering after Sannyasa (renunciation) on the part of the widower, but it may in some cases be due purely LO psychic disposition.

"So far as I know, no scientific explanation of the origin of these customs is forth coming even today. We have plenty of philosophy to tell us why these customs were honoured. (Cf. A. K. Coomaraswamy— "Sati : a Defence of the Eastern Woman" in the British Sociological Review Vol. VI 1913) Because it is a" proof of the perfect unity of body and soul" between husband and wife and of "devotion beyond the grave", because it embodied the ideal of wifehood which is well expressed by Uma when she said "Devotion to her Lord is woman's honour, it is her eternal heaven : and O Maheshwara", she adds with a most touching human cry, "I desire not paradise itself if thou art not satisfied with me! " Why compulsory widowhood is honoured I know not nor have I yet met with anyone who sang in praise of it, though there are a great many who adhere to it. The eulogy in honour of girl marriage is reported by Dr. Ketkar to be as follows : "A really faithful man or woman ought not to feel affection for a woman or a man other than the one with whom he or she is united. Such purity is compulsory not only after marriage, but even before marriage, for that is the only correct ideal of chastity. No maiden could be considered pure if she feels love for a man other than to whom she might get married. As she does not know whom she is going to get married to, she must not feel affection for any man at all before marriage. If she does so, it is a sin. So it is better for a girl to know whom she has to love, before any sexual consciousness has been awakened in her". Hence girl marriage.

"This high-flown and ingenious sophistry indicates why these institutions were honoured, but does not tell us why they were practised. My own interpretation is that they were honoured because they were practised. Any one slightly - quainted with rise of individualism in the 18th century will appreciate my remark. At all times, it is the movement that is most important ; and the philosophies grow around it long afterwards to justify it and give it a moral support. In like manner I urge that the very fact that these customs were so highly eulogized proves that they needed eulogy for their prevalence.

Regarding the question as to why they arose, I submit that they were needed to create the structure of caste and the philosophies in honour of them were intended to popularize them or to gild the pill, as we might say, for they must have been so abominable and shocking to the sense of the unsophisticated that they needed a great deal of sweetening. These customs are essentially of the nature of means, though they are represented as ideals.

But this should not blind us from understanding the results that flow from them. One might safely say that idealization of means is necessary and in this particular case was perhaps motivated to endow them with greater efficacy. Calling means an end does not harm except that it disguises its real character, but it does not deprive it of its real nature, that of a means. You may pass a law that all cats are dogs, just as you can call a means an end. But you can no more change the nature of means thereby than you can turn cats into dogs ; consequently I am justified in holding that, regard them as ends or as means. Sati, enforced widowhood and girl marriage are customs that were primarily intended to solve the problem of the surplus man and surplus woman in a caste and to maintain its endogamy. Strict endogamy could not be preserved without these customs, while caste without endogamy is fake." According to my view girl marriage, enforced widowhood and Sati had no other purpose than that of supporting the Caste System which Brahmanism was seeking to establish by prohibiting intermarriage. It is difficult to stop intermarriage. Members of different castes are likely to go out of their Caste either for love or for necessity. It is to provide against necessity that Brahmanism made these rules. This is my explanation of these new rules, made by Brahmanism. That explanation may not be acceptable to all. But there can be no doubt that Brahmanism was taking all means possible to prevent intermarriages between the different classes taking place.

Another illustration of this desire on the part of Brahmanism is to be found in the rule regarding excommunication promulgated by Manu.

Manu says that a person who is excommunicated by his Caste is an outcast. According to Manu an outcast is to be treated as though he was actually dead. Manu ordains that his obsequies should be performed and lays down the mode and manner of performing these obsequies of the outcast.

XI. 183. The Sapindas and Samanodakas of an outcast must offer (a libation of) water (to him, as if he were dead), outside (the village), on an inauspicious day, in the evening and in the presence of the relatives, officiating priests, and teachers.

XI. 184. A female slave shall upset with her foot a pot filled with water, as if it were for a dead person ; (his Sapindas) as well as the Samanodakas shall be impure for a day and a night. Manu however allows the outcast to return to Caste on performing penance as will be seen from the following rules:

XI. 187. But when he has performed his penance, they shall bathe with him in a holy pool and throw down a new pot, filled with water.

XI. 188. But he shall throw that pot into water, enter his house and perform, as before, all the duties incumbent on a relative.

XI. 189. Let him follow the same rule in the case of female outcasts; but clothes, food, and drink shall be given to them, and they shall live close to the (family-) house.

But if the outcast was recalcitrant and impenitent Manu provides for his punishment.

Manu will not allow the outcast to live in the family house. Manu enjoins that

XI. 189. .....Clothes, food, and drink shall be given to them (i.e. the outcast members of the family), and they shall live close to the (family) house.

III. 92. Let him (i.e. the householder) gently place on the ground (some food) for dogs, outcasts, chandals, those aflicted with diseases that are punishments of former sins, crows and insects. Manu declares that having social intercourse with an outcast is a sin. He warns the Snataka

IV. 79. .....not (to) stay together with outcasts. IV. 213. .....Not (to eat food given) by outcasts. To the householder Manu says :—

III. 151. Let him (i.e. the householder) not entertain at a Shradha.

III. 157. (A person) who forsakes his mother, his father, or a teacher without (sufficient) reason, he who has contracted an alliance with outcasts either through the Veda or through a marriage.

Manu ordains a social boycott of the outcast by penalizing those who associate with him.

XI. 181. He who associates himself for one year with an outcast himself becomes an outcast ; not by sacrificing, reading the Veda, or contracting affinity with him, since by those acts he loses his class immediately, but even by using the same carriage or seat, or by taking his food at the same board.

XI. 182. He who associates with any one of those outcasts, must perform, in order to atone for (such) intercourse, the penance prescribed for that (sinner).

Then there are penalties against an outcast who defies his caste and choses to remain an outcast. Manu tells him what will be his penalty in the next world.

XII. 60. He who has associated with outcasts (will) become Brahmarakshas (i.e. an evil spirit). Manu however was not prepared to leave the outcast with this. He proceeds to enact penalty the severity of which cannot be doubted. The following are the penal sections of Manu Smriti against an outcast.

III. 150. .....Those Brahmins who are .....outcasts .... .Athesists are unworthy (to partake) of oblations to the gods and manes.

IX. 201. .....Outcast receive(s) no share (in inheritance). XI. 185. But thenceforward (i.e. after the obsequies of the outcast have been performed) it shall be forbidden to converse with him, to sit with him, to give him a share of the inheritance, and to hold with him such intercourse as is usual among men;

XI. 186. And (if the outcast be the eldest) his right of primogeniture shall be withheld and the additional share, due to the eldest son; and in his stead a younger brother, excelling in virtue (i.e. who observes the rule of caste) shall obtain the share of the eldest.

Such is the law of Manu against an outcast. The severity of the penalties prescribed against him is quite obvious. Its effect is to exclude him from all social intercourse, to suspend him from every civil function, to disqualify him for all offices and to disable him from inheriting any property. Under these pains and penalties the outcaste might as well be dead which indeed Manu considers him to be, directing libations to be offered to the manes as though he was naturally so. This system of privations and mortifications was enforced by prescribing a similar fate to anyone who endeavoured to associate with an outcast. The penalty was not confined to the: outcast. Nor was it restricted to males. Males and females were both subject to the law of the outcast. Even their progeny was subject to penalty. The law was extended to the son of the outcast. Born be son was entitled to inherit immediately, as though his father was dead. Born after excommunication he lost his right to inherit, i.e. he became an outcast along with his father.

The laws of Manu regarding the outcast are of course devoid of justice and humanity. Some might think that there is nothing very strange about them. That is because these laws are very similar to the laws against apostacy and heresy to be found in all religious codes. It is unfortunately a fact All religions—*Except Buddhism*— have used or misued the laws of inheritance for enforcing adhesion and conformity to their codes. The conversion of a Christian to Judaism or paganism or any other religion was punished by the Emperors Constantines and Jul Emperors Theodosius and Valentiniaus added capital punishment, In case the apostle endeavoured to pervert others to the same inequity. This was borrowed by all the European countries' who maintained a similar system of penalities to enforce the Christian faith.

Such a view of the law of the outcast would be quite superficial. First of all the outcast is a creation of Brahmanism. It is a necessary coeffieient of caste. Indeed once Brahmanism was determined to create the caste system the law against the outcast was absolutely essential. For only by punishing the outcast can the caste system be maintained. Secondly there is a difference between the Christian or Mahomedan Law of Apostacy and the Brahmanic law of caste. The disqualification under the Christian or Mahomedan law of apostacy was restricted to want of religious belief or the profession of wrong religious belief. Under the Brahmanic law the disqualification had no connection with belief or want of belief. It was connected with the sanctity of a certain form of social organization namely Caste. It is the act of going out of one's caste that was made punishable. This is a very important difference.

The Brahmanic law of the outcast as compared with the law of apostacy in other religions shows that a belief in God is not essential to Brahmanism; that a belief in life after death is not essential to Brahmanism ; that a belief in salvation either by good deeds or by a belief in a prophet is not essential to Brahmanism; that a belief in the sacredness of the Vedas is essential to Brahmanism. This is only one thing that is essential to Brahmanism. For it is only breach of caste which is penalized. All else is left to violation.

Those who are not blind to these forces of integration will admit that this act of Brahmanism in prohibiting intermarriage and interdining is nothing short of a complete dismemberment of society. It is a deathknell to unity, an effective bar to united action. As will be shown hereafter Brahmanism was keen on preventing united action by Non-Brahmins to overthrow Brahmanism and that is why Brahmanism brought about this segmentation of Indian Society. But the fatal effects of a poison can never be confined to the limits of the original intention of the perpetrator. The same thing has happened in the case of Caste. Brahmanism intended to paralyse the Non-Brahmans for action against Brahmins, it did not design that they as a nation should be paralysed for action against a foreign nation. But the result of the poison of Caste has been they have become stricken for action aga.inst Brahmanism as well as against foreigners. In other words Brahmanism in instituting Caste system has put the greatest impediment against the growth of nationalism.

In spite of what others say the Hindu will not admit that there is any thing evil in the Caste system., and from one point of view he is right. There is love, unity and mutual aid among members of a family. There is honour among thieves. A band of robbers have common interests as respects to its members. Gangs are marked by fraternal feelings and intense loyalty to their own ends however opposed they may be to the other gangs. Following this up one can say that a Caste has got all the praiseworthy characteristics which a society is supposed to have.

It has got the virtues of a family inasmuch as there is love unity and mutual aid. It has got the honour known to prevail among thieves. It has got the loyalty and fraternal feeling we meet with in gangs and it also possesses that sense of common interests which is found among robbers.

A Hindu may take satisfaction in these praiseworthy characteristics of the Caste and deny that there is anything evil in it. But he forgets that his thesis that Caste is an ideal form of social organization is supportable on the supposition that each caste is entitled to regard himself as an independent society, as an end in itself as nations do. But the theory breaks down when the consideration pertains to Hindu Society and to the Caste-System which goes with it.

Even in such a consideration of the subject the Hindu will not admit that the Caste system is an evil. Charge Hinduism with the responsibility for the evils of the Caste-system and the Hindu will at once retort. "What about the Class System in Europe?" Upto a point the retort is good if it means that there exists nowhere that ideal society of the philosophers marked by organic unity, accompanied by praiseworthy community of purpose, mutuality of sympathy, loyalty to public ends and concern for general welfare. Nobody can have much quarrel if the Hindu by way of analogy were *to* say that in every Society there are families and classes marked by exclusiveness suspicion, and jealousy as to those without: bands of robbers, gangs narrow cliques, trade unions. Employees' Associations. Kartels Chambers of Commerce and political parties. Some of these are held together by the interest and plunder and others while aspiring to serve the public do not hesitate to prey upon it.

It may be conceded that everywhere de *facto* society whether in the past or in the present is not a single whole but a collection of small groups devoted to diverse purposes as their immediate and particular objectives. But the Hindu cannot take shelter under this analogy between the Hindu caste system and the Non-Hindu Class system and rest there as though there is nothing more to he said about the subject. The fact is there is a far bigger question which the Hindu has still lo face. He must take note of the fact that although every society consists of groups there are societies in which the groups are only non-social while there are societies in which the groups are anti-social. The difference between a society with the class system and a society with the caste system lies just in this namely the class system is merely nonsocial but the caste system is positively anti-soicial.

It may be important to realize why in some societies the group system produces only non-social feeling and in some societies the group system produces anti-social feeling. No better explanation of this difference can be given than the one given by professor John Dewey. According to him every thing depends upon whether the groups are isolated or associated, whether there is reciprocity of interest between them or whether there is lack of reciprocity of interest. If the groups are associated, if there is a reciprocity of interest between them the feeling between them will be only non-social. If the groups are isolated, if there is no reciprocity between them the feeling between them will be anti-social. To quote Professor Dewey:

"The isolation and exclusiveness of a gang or clique brings its anti-social spirit into relief. But this same spirit is found wherever one group has interests 'of its own' which shut it out from full interaction with other groups, so that its prevailing purpose is the protection of what it has got, instead of reorganization and progress through wider relationships. It marks nations in their isolation from one another; families which seclude their domestic concerns as if they had no connection with a larger life; schools when separated from the interest of home and community; the divisions of rich and poor; learned and unlearned. The essential point is that isolation makes for rigidity and formal institutionalizing of life, for static and selfish ideals within the group."

The question to be asked is not whether there are groups in a Society or whether the Society is one single whole. The question to be asked is what degree of association, cooperative intercourse and interaction exists among the different groups : how numerous and varied are the interests which are consciously shared by them : how full and free is the interplay with other forms of Association? A society is not to be condemned as body because there are groups in it. It is to be condemned if the groups are isolated, each leading an exclusive life of its own. Because it is this isolation which produces the anti-social spirit which makes co-operative effort so impossible of achievement.

I his isolation among the classes is the work of Brahmanism. The principal steps taken by it was to abrogate the system of intermarriage and interdining that was prevalent among the four Varnas in olden times. This has already been discussed in an earlier section of this chapter. There is however one part of the story that remains to be told. I have said the Varna system had nothing to do with marriage. That males and females belonging to the different Varnas could marry and did marry. Law did not come in the way of inter-varna marriage. Social morality was not opposed to such marriages. Savarna marriage was neither required by law nor demanded by Society.

All marriages between different Varnas irrespective of the question whether the bride was of a higher Varna than the bridegroom or whether the bridegroom was of the higher Varna and the bride of the lower Varna were valid. Indeed as Prof. Kane says the distinction between Anuloma and Pratiloma marriage was quite unknown and even the terms Anuloma and Pratiloma were not in existence. They are the creation of Brahmanism. Brahmanism put a stop to Pratiloma marriages i.e. marriages between women of a higher Varna and men of lower Varna. That was a step in the direction of closing the connection between the Varnas and creating in them an exclusive and anti-social spirit regarding one another. But while the inter-connecting gate of the Pratiloma marriage was closed the inter-connecting gate of Anuloma marriage had remained open. That was not closed. As pointed out in the section on graded inequality Anuloma marriage i.e. marriage between a male of the higher Varna and the female of the lower Varna was allowed by Brahmanism to continue. The gate of Anuloma marriage was not very respectable and was a one way gate only still it was an interconnecting gate by which it was possible to prevent a complete isolation of the Varnas. But even here Brahmanism played what cannot but be called a dirty trick. To show how dirty the trick was it is necessary first to state the rules which prevailed for determining the status of the child. Under the rule existing from very ancient times the status of the child was determined by the Varna of the father. I he Varna of the mother was quite unimportant. I he following illustrations will place the point beyond doubt:

Father's Name	Varna of father	Mother's Name	Varna of mother	Child's name	Varna of child
1. Shantanu	Kshatriya (Anamik)	Ganga	Shudra	Bhishma	Kshatriya
2. Shantanu Kshatriya	Kshatriya (Fisher)	Matsyagandha	Shudra	Vichitra	Virya
3. Parashar	Brahmin	Matsyagandha (Fisher)	Shudra	Krishna-Dwaipayana	Brahmin
4. Vishwamitra	Kshtriya	Menaka	(Apsara)	Shakuntala	Kshatriya
5. Yayati	Kshatriya	Devayani	Brahmin	Yadu	Kshatriya
6. Yayati	Kshatriya (Nonaryan)	Sharmishta	Asuri	Druhya	Kshatriya
7. Jaratkaru	Brahmin	Jaratkari	Nag. Asita	Brahmin	(Nonaryan)

The rule was known as the rule *of* Pitra Savarnya. It would he interesting to consider the effect of this rule of Pitra Savarnya on the Anuloma and Pratiloma systems of marriage.

The effect on Pratiloma marriage would be that the children of mothers of the higher Varnas would be dragged down to the level of the lower Varnas represented by their fathers. Its effect on Anuloma marriage would be just the contrary. The children of mothers of the lower Varnas would be raised up and absorbed in the higher Varnas of their fathers.

Manu stopped Pratiloma marriages and thereby prevented the higher from being dragged to the status of the lower. However regrettable, not much damage was done by it so long as the Anuloma marriage and the rule of Pitra Savarnya continued in operation. The two together formed a very useful system. The Anuloma marriage maintained the inter-connection and the Pitra Savarnya rule made the higher classes quite composite in their make up. For they could not but help to he drawn from mothers of different Varnas. Brahmanism did not want to keep this gate of intercommunication between the Varnas open. It was bent on closing it. But it did it in a manner which is disreputable.

The straight and honourable way was to stop Anuloma marriage. But Brahmanism did not do that. It allowed the system of Anuloma marriage to continue. What it did was to alter the rule of determining the status of the child. It replaced the rule of Pitra Savarnya by the rule of Matra Savarnya by which the status of the child came to be determined by the status of the mother. By this change marriage ceased to be that means of intersocial communication which it principally is. It relieved men of the higher Varna from the responsibility to their children simply because they were born of a mother of lower Varna. It made Anuloma marriage mere matter of sex a humiliation and insult to the lower Varnas and a privilege to the higher classes to lawfully commit prostitution with women of the lower classes. And from a larger social point of view it brought the complete isolation among the Varnas which has been the bane of Hindu Society. Notwithstanding all this the Orthodox Hindu still believes that the caste system is an ideal system.

But why talk about the orthodox Hindus. There are among enlightened politicians and historians. There are of course Indians both politicians and historians who vehemently deny that the Caste system comes in the way of nationalism. They presume that India is a nation and feel very much offended if anybody instead of speaking of the Indian Nation speaks of the people of India. This attitude is quite understandable. Most of the politicians and historians are Brahmins and cannot be expected to have the courage to expose the misdeeds of their ancestors or admit the evils perpetrated by them. Ask any one the question, is India a nation, and all in a chorus say, 'yes.' Ask for reasons, they will say that India is a nation firstly because India has a geographical unity of the country and secondly because of the fundamental unity of the culture. All this may be admitted for the sake of argument and yet it is true to say that to draw an inference from these facts that India is a nation is really to cherish a delusion. For what is a nation? A nation is not a country in the physical sense of the country whatever degree of geographical unity it may posses. A nation is not people synthesized by a common culture derived from common language, common religion or common race.

To recall what I have said in another place "Nationality is a subjective psychological feeling. It is a feeling of a corporate sentiment of oneness which makes those who are charged with it feel that they are kith and kin. This national feeling is a double edged feeling. It is at once a feeling of fellowship for one's own kith and an anti-fellowship feeling for those who are not one's own kith. It is a feeling of "consciousness of kind" which binds together those who are within the limits of the kindred and severs them from those who are outside the limits of the kindred. It is a longing to belong to one's own group and a longing not to belong to any other group. This is the essence of what is called a nationality and national feeling. This longing to belong to one's own kindred as I said is a subjective psychological feeling and what is important to bear in mind is that the longing to belong to one's own kindred is quite independent of geography, culture or economic or social conflict.

There may be geographical unity and yet there may be no "longing to belong". There may be no geographical unity and yet the feeling of longing to belong may be very intense. There may be cultural unity and yet there may be no longing to belong. There may be economical conflicts and class divisions and yet there may be an intense feeling of longing to belong. The point is that nationality is not primarily a matter of geography culture or"..........

In the declinging days of the Vedic Regime, the Shudras as well as women had come to occupy a very low position. The rising tide of Buddhism had brought about a great change in the status of both. To put it briefly a Shudra under the Buddhist regime could acquire property, learning and could even become a king. Nay he could even rise to the highest rung of the social ladder occupied by the Brahmin in the Vedic Regime. The Buddhist order of Bhikshus was counterpart of the Vedic order of Brahmins. The two orders, each within its own religious system were on a par in the matter of status and dignity. The Shudra could never aspire to be a Brahmin in the Vedic regime but he could become a Bhikshu and occupy the same status and dignity as did the Brahmin.

For while the Vedic order of Bramhins was closed to the Shudra, the Buddhist order of Bhikshus was open to him and many Shudras who could not become Brahmins under the Vedic Regime had become their peers by becoming Bhikshus under Buddhism. Similar change is noticeable in the case of women. Under the Buddhist regime she became a free person. Marriage did not make her a slave. For marriage under the Buddhist rule was a contract. Under the Buddhist Regime she could acquire property, she could acquire learning and what was unique, she could become a member of the Buddhist order of Nuns and reach the same status and dignity as a Brahmin. The elevation of the status of the Shudras and women was so much the result of the gospel of Buddhism that Buddhism was called by its enemies as the Shudra religion (i.e. the religion of the low classes).

All this of course must have been very galling to the Brahmins. How very galling it must have been to them is shown by the vandallic fury with which Bramhanism after its triumph over Buddhism proceeded to bring about a complete demolition of the high status to which the Shudras and women had been elevated by the revolutionary changes effected by the vivifying gospel of Buddhism.

Starting with this background one shudders at the inhumanity and cruelty of the laws made by Manu against the Shudras. I quote a few of them assembling them under certain general heads.

Manu asks the householders of the Brahmana, Kshatriya and Vaishya Class:

IV. 61. Let him not dwell in a country where the rulers are Shudra.....

This cannot mean that Brarnhana. Kashtriya and Vaishya should leave the country where Shudra is a ruler. It can only mean that if a Shudra becomes a king he should be killed. Not only a Shudra is not to be recognized as fit to be a king, he is not to be deemed as a respectable person. For Manu enacts that:-

XI. 24. A Bramhin shall never beg from a Shudra property for (performing) a sacrifice i.e. for religious purposes. All marriage ties with the Shudra were proscribed. A marriage with a woman belonging to any of the three higher classes was forbidden. A Shudra was not to have any connection with a woman of the higher classes and an act of adultery committed by a Shudra with her was declared by Manu to be an offence involving capital punishment.

VIII. 374. A Shudra who has an intercourse with a woman of the higher caste guarded or unguarded, shall be punished in the following manner if she was unguarded, he loses the offending part. If she was guarded then he should be put to death and his property confiscated.

Manu insists that a Shudra shall be servile, unfit for office, without education, without property and as a contemptible person, his person and property shall always be liable to be conscripted. As to office Manu prescribes.

VIII. 20. A Bramhana who is only a Brahmana by descent i.e. one has neither studied nor performed any other act required by the Vedas may at the king's pleasure, interpret the law to him i.e. act as the judge, but never a Shudra (however learned he may be).

VIII. 21. The Kingdom of that monarch who looks on while a Shudra settles the law will sink low like a cow in a morass.

VIII. 272. If a Shudra arrogantly presumes to preach religion to Bramhins the King shall have poured burning oil in his mouth and ears.

In olden times the study of the Vedas stood for education. Manu declare that the study of the Vedas was not a matter of right but that it was a matter of privilege. Manu deprived the Shudra of the right to study Veda. He made it a privilege of the three higher classes. Not only did he debar the Shudra from the study of the Vedas but he enacted penalties against those who might help the Shudra to acquire knowledge of the Veda. To a person who is previleged to study the Vedas. Manu ordains that :

IV. 99. He must never read the Vedas...in the presence of the Shudras and prescribes that:-

III. 156. He who instructs Shudra pupils and he whose teacher is a Shudra shall become disqualified tor being invited to Shradha. Manu's successor went much beyond him in the cruelty of their punishment of the Shudra for studying the Veda. For instance Katyayana lays down that if a Shudra overheard the Veda or ventured to utter a word of the Veda the King shall cut his tongue in twain and put hot molten lead in his cars.

As to property Manu is both ruthless and shameless. According to the Code of Manu :

X. 129. No superfluous collection of wealth must be made by a Shudra, even though he has power to make it, since a servile man who has amassed riches, becomes proud, and, by his insolence or neglect, gives pain to Bramhans.

The reason for the rule is more revolting than the rule itself. Manu was of course not sure that the prohibitory injunction will be enough to prevent the Shudra from acquiring wealth. To leave no room for the Shudra to give offence to the Bramhins by his accumulation of wealth Manu added another section to his code whereby he declared that :

VIII. 417. A Bramhana may seize without hesitation if he be in distress for his subsistence, the goods of his Shudra. Not only is the property of a Shudra liable to conscription but the labour of the Shudra. Manu declares, is liable to conscription. Compare the following provision in Manu :

VIII. 413. A Bramhana may compel a Shudra, whether bought or unbought to do servile work; for he is created by the creator to be the slave of a Bramhana.

A Shudra was required by Manu to be servile in his speech. How very servile he must be can be seen from the following provisions in Manu :—

VIII. 270. A Shudra who insults a twiceborn man with gross invective, shall have his tongue cut out; for he is of low origin.

VIII. 271. If he mentions the names and castes of the (twiceborn) with contumely, an iron nail, ten fingers long, shall be thrust red hot into his mouth.

Manu's object *was* to make the Shudra not merely a servile person but an altogether contemptible person. Manu will not allow a Shudra the comfort of having a high sounding name. Had Manu not been there to furnish incontrovertible proof it would be difficult to believe that Bramanism could have been so relentless and pitiless in its persecution of the Shudra. Observe Manu's law as to the names that the different classes can give to their children.

II. 31. Let the first part of a Brahman's name denote something auspicious, a Kshatriya's be connected with power, and a Vaishya's with wealth, but a Shudra's express something contemptible.

II. 32. The second part of a Bramhan's name shall be a word implying happiness, of a Kshatrya's a word implying protection, of a Vaisya's a term expressive of thriving and of a Shudra's an expression denoting service.

The basis of all these inhuman laws is the theory enunciated by Manu regarding the Shudra. At the outset of his Code, Manu takes care to assert it emphatically and without blushing. He says :

I. 91. One occupation only, the Lord prescribed to the Shudra, to serve meekly these other three castes (namely Bramhin, Kshatriya and Vaishya).

Holding that the Shudra was born to be servile, Manu made his laws accordingly so as to compel him to remain servile. In the Buddhist regime a Shudra could aspire to be ajudge, a priest and even a King, the highest status that he could ever aspire to. Compare with This the ideal that Manu places before the Shudra and one can get an idea of what fate was to be under Brahmanism :

X. 121. If a Shudra, (unable to subsist by serving Brahmanas), seeks a livelihood, he may serve Kshartiyas, or he may also seek to maintain himself by attending on a wealthy Vaishya.

X. 122. But let a (Shudra) serve Brahmanas, either for the sake of heaven, or with a view to both (this life and the next); for he who is called the servant of a Brahmana thereby gains all his ends.

X. 123. The service of Brahmanas alone is declared (to be) an excellent occupation for a Shudra: for whatever else besides this he may perform will bear him no fruit.

X. 124. They must allot to him out of their own family (property) a suitable maintenance, after considering his ability, his industry, and the number of those whom he is bound to support.

X. 125. The remnants of their food must be given to him, as well as their old household furniture.

Manu can hardly be said to be more tender to women than he was to the Shudra. He starts with a low opinion of women. Manu proclaims :

11.213. It is the nature of women to seduce men in this (world); for that reason the wise are never unguarded in (the company of) females.

II. 214. For women are able to lead astray in (this) world not only a fool, but even a learned man, and (to make) him a slave of desire and anger.

II. 215. One should not sit in a lonely place with one's mother sister or daughter; for the senses are powerful, and master even a learned man.

IX. 14. Women do not care for beauty, nor is their attention fixed on age; (thinking), '(It is enough that) he is a man', they give themselves to the handsome and to the ugly.

IX. 15. Through their passion for men, through their mutable temper, through their natural heartlessness, they become disloyal towards their husbands, however carefully they may be guarded in this (world).

IX. 16. Knowing their disposition, which the Lord of creatures laid in them at the creation, to be such, (every) man should most strenuously exert himself to guard them.

IX. 17. (When creating them) Manu allotted to women (a love of their) bed. (of their) seat and (of) ornament, impure desires, wrath, dishonesty, malice, and bad conduct.

The laws of Manu against women are of a piece with this view. Women are not to be free under any circumstances. In the opinion of Manu :—

IX. 2. Day and night women must be kept in dependence by the males (of) their (families), and, if they attach themselves to sensual enjoyments, they must be kept under one's control.

IX. 3. Her father protects (her) in childhood, her husband protects (her) in youth, and her sons protect (her) in old age: a woman is never fit for independence.

IX. 5. Women must particularly be gurded against evil inclinations, however trifling (they may appear); for, if they are not guarded, they will bring sorrow on two families,

IX. 6. Considering that the highest duty of all castes, even weak husbands (must) strive to guard their wives.

V. 147. By a girl, by a young woman, or even by an aged one, nothing must be done independently, even in her own house.

V. 148. In childhood a female must be subject to her father, in youth to her husband, when her lord is dead to her sons: a woman must never be independent.

V. 149. She must not seek to separate herself from her father, husband, or sons; by leaving them she would make both (her own and her husband's) families contemptible. Woman is not to have a right to divorce.

IX. 45. The husband is declared to be one with the wife, which means that there could be no separation once a woman is married. Many Hindus stop here as though this is the whole story regarding Manu's law of divorce and keep on idolizing it by comforting their conscience by holding out the view that Manu regarded marriage as sacrament and therefore did not allow divorce. This of course is far from the truth. His law against divorce had a very different motive. It was not to tie up a man to a woman but it was to tie up the woman to a man and to leave the man free. For Manu does not prevent a man for giving up his wife. Indeed he not only allows him to abandon his wife but he also permits him to sell her. But what he does is to prevent the wife from becoming free. See what Manu Says:

IX. 46. Neither by sale nor by repudiation is a wife released from her husband.

The meaning is that a wife, sold or repudiated by her husband, can never become the legitimate wife of another who may have bought or received her after she was repudiated. If this is not monstrous nothing can be. But Manu was not worried by considerations of justice or injustice of his laws. He wanted to deprive women of the freedom she had under the Buddhistic regime. He knew, by her misuse of her liberty, by her willingness to marry the Shudra that the system of the gradation of the Varna had been destroyed. Manu was outraged by her license and in putting a stop to it he deprived her of her liberty.

A wife was reduced by Manu to the level of a slave in the matter of property.

IX. 146. A wife, a son, and a slave, these three are declared to have no property, the wealth which they earn is (acquired) for him to whom they belong.

When she becomes a widow Manu allows her maintenance if her husband was joint and a widow's estate in the property of her husband if he was separate from his family. But Manu never allows her to have any dominion over property.

A woman under the laws of Manu is subject to corporal punishment and Manu allows the husband the right to beat his wife.

VIII. 299. A wife, a son, a slave, a pupil, and a younger brother of the full blood, who have committed faults, may be beaten with a rope or a split bamboo.

In other matters woman was reduced by Manu to the same position as the Shudra.

The study of the Veda was forbidden to her by Manu as it was to the Shudra.

II. 66. Even for a woman the performance of the *Sanskaras* are necessary and they should be performed. But they should be performed without uttering the Veda Mantras.

IX. 18. Women have no right to study the Vedas. That is why their Sanskars are performed without Veda Mantras. Women have no knowledge of religion because they have no right to know the Vedas. The uttering of the Veda Mantras is useful for removing sin. As women cannot utter the Veda Mantras they are as unclean as untruth is.

Offering sacrifices according to Bramhanism formed the very soul of religion. Yet Manu will not allow women to perform them. Manu ordains that:—

XI. 36. A woman shall not perform the daily sacrifices prescribed by the Vedas. XI. 37. If she does it she will go to hell.

To disable her from performing such sacrifices Manu prevents her from getting the aid and services of a Bramhin priest.

IV. 205. A Bramhan must never eat food given at a sacrifice performed by a woman.

IV. 206. Sacrifices performed by women are inauspicious and not acceptable to God. They should therefore be avoided. Woman was not to have any intellectual persuits and nor free will nor freedom of thought. She was not to join any heretical sect such as Buddhism. If she continues to adhere to it, till death she is not to be given the libation of water as is done in the case of all dead.

Finally a word regarding the ideal of life, Manu has sought to place before a woman. It had better be stated in his own words :

V. 151. Him to whom her father may give her, or her brother with the father's permission, she shall obey as long as he lives and when he is dead, she must not insult his memory.

V. 154. Though destitute of virtue, or seeking pleasure elsewhere, or devoid of good qualities, yet a husband must be constantly worshipped as a god by a faithful wife.

V. 155. No sacrifice, no vow, no fast must be performed by women, apart from their husbands; if a wife obeys her husband, she will for that reason alone be exalted in heaven. Then comes the choicest texts which forms the pith and the marrow of this ideal which Manu prescribes for the women :

V. 153. The husband who wedded her with sacred Mantras, is always a source of happiness to his wife, both in season and out of season, in this world and in the next.

V. 150. She must always be cheerful, clever in the management of her household affairs, careful in cleaning her utensils, and economical in expenditure.

This the Hindus regard as a very lofty ideal for a woman!!! The severity of these laws against Shudras and women show that the phenomenal rise of these classes during the Buddhist regime had not only offended the Brahmins but had become intolerable to them. It was a complete reversal of their sacred social order from top to bottom. The first had become last and the last had become first. The laws of Manu also explain, the determined way in which the Brahmins proceeded to use their political power to degrade the Shudras and the women to their old status.

The triumphant Bramhanism bega.n its onslaught on both the Shudras and the women in pursuit of the old ideal namely servility and Bramhanism did succeed in making the Shudras and women the servile classes, Shudras the serfs to the three higher classes and women the serfs to their husbands. Of the black deeds committed by Brahmanism after its triumph over Buddhism this one is the blackest. There is no parallel in history for so foul deeds of degradation committed by a class of usurpers in the interest of class domination. The collosal character of this deed of degradation perpetrated by Barahmanism is unfortunately not fully realized. It is concealed by those small monosyllablic words, Stri and Shudra. Let those who wish to get an idea of the enormity of their deed think of the numbers that lie behind these two terms. What part of the population do they apply to? The woman represents one half of the population. Of the balance the Shudra represents not less than two third. The two together make up about 7590 of the total population. It is this huge mass of people that has been doomed by Brahmanism to eternal servility and eternal degradation. It is because of the collosal scale of degradation whereby 75% of her people were deprived of their right to life liberty and persuit of happiness that India became a decaying if not a dead nation.

The principle of graded inequality runs through the whole of the Manu Smriti. There is no department of life in which he has not introduced his principle of graded inequality. For a complete and thorough exposition of it, it would be necessary to reproduce the whole of Manu Smriti. I will take only a few departments to illustrate how in the hands of Manu the principle of graded inequality became embedded in the social life. Take the field of marriage. Observe the rule of Manu :—

III. 13. It is declared that a Shudra woman alone (can be) the wife of a Shudra, she and one of his own caste (the wives) of a Vaishya, those two and one of his own caste the wives of a Kshatriya, those three and one of his own caste (the wives of a Bramhan). Take the rules of Manu regarding the treatment of guests:—

III. 110. But a Kshatriya (who comes) to the house of a Brahmana is not called a guest (atithi), nor a Vaisya, nor a Shudra, nor a personal friend, nor a relative, nor the teacher.

III. 111. But if Kshatriya comes to the house of a Brahmana in the manner of a guest, (the house-holder) may feed him according to his desire, after the above mentioned Brahmanas have eaten.

III. 1 12. Even a Vaisya and a Shudra who have approached his house in the manner of guests, he may allow to eat with his servants, showing (thereby) his compassionate disposition. In the house of a Brahmana nobody except a Brahmin is to have the honour of being a guest. If the Kshatriya comes in the manner of a guest to the house of a Brahmin he is to be fed after all the Brahmins are fed and if the Vaishyas and Shudras come in the manner of guests they are to be fed after everybody is fed and only in the company of servants.

Take the rules of Manu regarding Sanskaras : X. 126. A Shudra has no right to receive the sacraments. X. 68. The law prescribes that neither of the two (that is those who belong to mixed castes) shall receive the sacraments the first being excluded on account of lowness of his origin of his parents was against the order of the castes.

II. 66. The whole series of sacraments must be performed for females also in order to sanctify the body at the proper time and in the proper order, but without the recitaion of sacred Vedic Mantras. Manu further lays down that :

VI. 1. A twice born Snataka, who has thus lived according to the law in the order of householders, may, taking a firm resolution and keeping his organs in subjection, dwell in the forest, duly (observing the rules given below).

VI. 33. But having thus passed the third part of (a man's natural term of) life in the forest, he may live as an ascetic during the fourth part of his existence, after abandoning all attanchment to worldly objects.

Even in law Manu introduces the principle of graded inequality. To take only two illustrations, the law of defamation, abuse and the law of assault :

VIII. 267. A Kshatriya having defamed a Brahmana, shall be fined one hundred (panas); A Vaisya one hundred and fifty or two hundred ; a Shudra shall suffer corporal punishment.

VIII. 268. A Brahamna shall be fined fifty (panas) for defaming a Kshatriya ; in (the case of) a Vaisya the fine shall be twenty five (panas), in (the case of) a Shudra twelve.

VIII. 269. For offences of twice born men against those of equal caste (varna, the fine shall be) also twelve (panas) for speeches which ought not to be uttered, that (and every fine shall be) double.

VIII. 276. (For mutual abuse) by a Brahmana and a Kshatriya a fine must be imposed by a discerning (king), on the Brahmana the lowest amercement, but on the Kshatriya the middlemost.

VIII. 277. A Vaisya and a Shudra must be punished exactly in the same manner according to their respective castes, but the tongue (of the Shudra) shall not be cut out: that is the decision.

VIII. 279. With whatever limb a man of a low caste does hurt to (a man of the three) highest (castes), even that limb shall be cut off: that is the teaching of Manu.

VIII. 280. He who raises his hand or a stick, shall have his hand cut off; he who in anger kicks with his foot, shall have his foot cut off. Everywhere is the principle of graded inequality. So ingrained it had become in the social system that the successors of Manu were careful to introduce it where he had failed to give effect to it. For instance Manu had recognized the system of slavery. But had failed to prescribe whether the system of slavery was or was not subject to the principle of graded order of insubordination.

Lest it should be understood that the law of graded inequality did not apply to slavery and that a Brahmin may be a slave of the Shudra, Yajnavalkya at once proceeds to clear the doubt. He expressly laid down that :-

"Slavery is in the descending order of the Varnas and not in the ascending order" (XIV. 183).

Vijnaneshwar in his commentary on Yajnavalkya makes it concrete by his illustrations when he says :

"Of the Varnas such as the Brahmana and the rest, a state of slavery shall exist *Anulomyena,* in the descending order. Thus, of a Brahmana, a Kshatriya and the rest may become a slave; of a Kshatriya, the Vaishya and the Shudra; and of a Vaishya, Shudra, thus the state of slavery shall operate in the descending order." Stated in the language of equality and inequality, this means that the Brahmin is the highest because he can be the slave of nobody but is entitled to keep a person of any class as his slave. The Shudra is the lowest because everybody can keep him as his slave but he can keep no one as his slave except a Shudra. The place assigned to the Kshatriya and the Vaishya introduces the system of graded inequality. A Kshatriya while he is inferior to the Brahmin he can be the slave of the Brahmin. While he is yet superior to the Vaishyas and the Shudras because he can keep them as his slaves; the Vaishyas and the Shudras have no right to keep a Kshartiya as his slave. Similarly a Vaishya while he is inferior to the Bramhins and the Kshatriyas, because they can keep him as their slave and he cannot keep any one of them as his slave, he is proud that he is at least superior to the Shudra because he can keep the Shudra as his slave while Shudra cannot keep the Vaishya as his slave.

Such is the principle of graded inequality which Bramhanism injected into the bone and the marrow of the people. Nothing worse to paralyze society to overthrow inequity could have been done.

Although its effects have not been clearly noticed there can be no doubt that because of it the Hindus have been stricken with palsy. Students of social organization have been content with noting the difference between equality and inequality. None have realized that in addition to equality and inequality there is such a thing as graded inequality. Yet inequality is not half so dangerous as graded inequality. Inequality carried within itself the seeds of its own destruction. Inequality does not last long. Under pure and simple inequality two things happen. It creates general discontent which forms the seed of revolution. Secondly it makes the sufferers combine against a common foe and on a common grievance. But the nature and circumstances of the system of graded inequality leave no room for either of these two things to happen.

The system of graded inequality prevents the rise of general discontent against inequity. It cannot therefore become the storm centre of revolution. Secondly the sufferers under inequality becoming unequal both in terms of the benefit and the burden there is no possibility of a general combination of all classes to overthrow the inequity. To make the thing concrete the Brahmanic law of marriage is full of inequity. The right of Brahmana to take a woman from the classes below him but not to give a woman to them is in inequity. But the Kshatriya, Vaishya and Shudra will not combine to destroy it. The Kshatriya resents this right of the Brahmana. But he will not combine with Vaishya or the Shudra and that for two reasons. Firstly because he is satisfied that if the Brahman has the right to take the right of three communities, the Kshatriya has the right to appropriate the women of two communities. He does not suffer so much as the other two. Secondly if he joins in a general revolution against this marriage-inequity in one way he will rise to the level of the Bramhins but in another way all will be equal which to him means that the Vaishyas and the Shudras will rise to his level i.e. they will claim Kshatriya women-which means he will fall to their level. Take any other inequity and think of a revolt against it. The same social psychology will show that a general rebellion against it is impossible.

One of the reasons why there has been no revolution against Brahmanism and its inequities is due entirely to the principle of graded inequality. If is a system of permitting a share in the spoils with a view to enlist them to support the spoils system. It is a system full of low cunning which man could have invented to perpetuate inequity and to profit by it. For it is nothing else but inviting people to share in inequity in order that they may all be supporters of inequity.

There now remains to lift the curtain from the last act of this drama of Bramhanism.

Bramhanism inherited from the Vedic past that system of Chaturvarna. The system of Chaturvarna which the Hindus regard as the unique creation of their Aryan ancestors is in no sense unique. There is nothing original about it. The whole ancient world had stumbled into it. The Egyptians had it and the ancient Persians had it. Plato was so convinced about its excellence that hc presented it as ideal form of social organization. The ideal of the Chaturvarna is faulty. The lumping together of individuals into a few sharply marked off classes is a very superficial view of man and his powers. The Ancient Aryans as well as Plato had no conception of the uniqueness *of* every individual, of his incommensurability with others and of each individual forming a class of his own. They had no recognition of the infinite diversity of active tendencies and combination of tendencies of which an individual is capable. To them there were types offaculties or powers in the individual constitution and all that is necessary for social organization is to classify them. All this is demonstrably wrong. Modern science has shown that lumping together of individuals into a few sharply marked off classes each confined to one particular sphere does injustice both to the individual and to Socicty. The stratification of Society by classes and occupations is incompatible with the fullest utilization of the qualities which is so necessary for social advancement and is also incompatible with the safety and security of the individual as well as of Society in general.

There is another mistake which the Ancient Hindus including Plato made. There is probably some truth in saying that there is among human beings a dimorphism or polyformism in human beings as, there is among insects, though in the former it is only psychological while in the latter it is both physical as well as psychlolgical. But assuming that there is a thing psychological dimorphism or polyformism among human beings, it is wrong to separate them into those who are born to do one thing and others to do another, some born *to* command i.e. to be masters and some born to obey i.e. to be slaves. It is wrong to suppose that in a given person some qualities are present and others are absent. On the contrary the truth is that all qualities are present in every person and this truth is not diminished in any way by that, some tendency predominates to the extent of being the only one that is apparent. So well established is this truth that a tendency which may be dominant in a man at one time may be quite different from and even the direct opposite of the tendency that may be dominant at another time. As Prof. Bergson in speaking of the Nietsche's false antithesis of 'men' and 'slaves' observes :

"We have a clear vision of this (falsity) in times of revolution. Unassuming citizens, upto that moment humble and obedient, wake up one fine day with pretentions to be leaders of men". The cases of Mussolini and Hitler are a complete disproof of the theory of the Aryans and of Plato.

This Vedic system of Chaturvarna, far from being an ideal system was made positively worse by the changes which Bramhanism made and which have already been described. Every one of them was mischievous in character is beyond question. The Buddhist order of Bhikshus and the Vedic order of Brahmins were designed to serve the same purpose. They formed the elite of their society whose function was to lead and guide society along the right road. Although designed to discharge the same function the Budhist Bhikshu was better placed to discharged it was the Bramhin. That is because Buddha recognized which nobody either before him or after him has done. Buddna realized that tor a person to give a true lead to Society and he its trustworthy guide he must be intellectually free and further, which is more important, to be intellectually free he must not have private property.

An elite charged with the care of his private property must fail to discharge his duty of leading and guiding Society along the right road. Buddha therefore took care to include in the Code of discipline for the Bhikshus a rule prohibiting a Bhikshu from holding private property. In the Vedic order of Bramhins there was no such prohibition. A Bramhin was free to hold property. This difference produced a profound difference on the character and outlook of the Buddhist Bhikshu and the Vedic Bramhin. The Bhikshus formed an intellectual class. The Bramhins formed on the other hand merely an educated class. There is a great difference between an intellectual class and an ducated class. An intellectual class has no limitations arising out of any affiliations to any class or to any interest. An educated Class on the other hand is not an intellectual class although it has cultivated its intellect. The reason is that its range of vision and its sympathy to a new ideology is circumscribed by its being identified with the interest of the class with which it is affiliated.

The Bramhins from the very beginning therefore were inclined to be a purely educated class, enlightened but selfish. This evil in the Vedic order of Bramhins was extreme by the changes made in the old Vedic System. The right of the Brahmins to rule and the grant of special privileges and immunities made them more selfish, and induced in them the desire to use their education not for the advancement of learning but for the use of their community and against the advancement of society.

All their energy and their education has been spent in maintaining their own privileges against the good of the public. It has been the boast of many Hindu authors that the civilization of India is the most ancient civilization in the world. They will insist that there was no branch of knowledge in which their ancestors were not the pioneers. Open a book like "The Positive Background of Hindu Sociology" by Prof.

Benoy Kumar Sarkar, or a book like "The Positive Sciences of the Ancient Hindus" by Dr. Brajendranath Seal one is overwhelmed with data touching upon the knowledge their ancestors had about various scientific subjects. From these books it would appear that the ancient Indians knew astronomy, astrology, biology, chemistry, mathematics, Medicine, minerology. Physics and in the view of the mass of people even aviation. All this may be very true. The important question is now how the ancient Indians discovered these positive sciences. The important question is why did the ancient Indians cease to make any progress in the sciences in which they were the pioneers? This sudden arrest in the progress of science in ancient India is as astounding as it is deplorable. In the scientific world India occupies a position which even if it be first among the primitive is certainly last among the civilized nation. How did it happen that a people who began the work of scientific progress stopped, halted on the way, left in its incohate and incomplete condition? This is a question that needs to be considered and answered, not what the ancient Indians knew.

There is only one answer to the question and it is a very simple answer. In ancient India the Bramhins were the only educated class. They were also the Class which was claiming to be above all others. Buddha disputed their claim for supremacy and declared a war on the Brahmins. The Brahmins acted as an Educated Class—as distinguished from an intellectual class—would act under the circumstances. It abandoned all pursuits and engaged itself in defending the claim of supremacy and the social, economic and political interests of its class. Instead of writing books on Science, the Brahmins undertook to write Smritis. Here is an explanation why the progress of science in India became arrested. Brahmins found it more important and more imperative to write Smritis to repel the Buddhist doctrine of social equality.

How many Smritis did the Brahmins write? Mr. Kane a great authority on the Smriti literature has computed their number to be 128. And what for? The Smritis are called lawbooks which of course hide their nature. They are really treatises expounding the supremacy of the Brahmins and their rights to special privileges. The defence of Bramhanism was more important than the progress of science. Bramhanism not only defended its previlege:s but set about extending them in a manner that would cover every descent man with shame. The Brahmins started particularly to expand the meaning of certain privileges granted to them by Manu.

Manu had given the Bramhins the right to *dana,* gift. The *dana* was always intended to be money or chattel. But in course of time the concept of *dana* was expanded so as to include the gift of a woman which a Brahmin could keep as his mistress or who could be released by the Bramhin on commutation of money payment. Manu designated the Bramhins as Bhu-devas, lords of the Earth. The Bramhins enlarged the scope of this statement and began to claim the right to sexual intercourse with women of other classes. Even queens were not exempt from this claim. Ludovico Di Varthema who came to India as a traveller in about 1502 A.D. records the following about the Brahmins of Calicut :

"It is a proper, and the same time pleasant thing to know who these Brahmins are. You must know that they are the chief persons of the faith, as priests are among us. And when the King takes a wife, he selects the most worthy and the most honoured of these Brahamins and makes him sleep the first night with his wife, in order that he may deflower her. " Similarly Hamilton another writer says:

"When the Samorin marries, he must not cohabit with his bride till the Nambourie (Nambudari Brahmin), or chief priest, has enjoyed her, and if he pleases, he may have three nights of her company, because the first fruits of her nuptials must be an holy oblation to the god she worships."

In the Bombay Presidency the priests of the Vaishnava sect claimed the right to deflower the women of their sect. This gave rise to the famous Maharaja Libel case brought by the chief priest of the Sect against one Karosondas Mulji in the High Court of Bombay in the year 1869 which shows that the right to claim the benefit of the first night was certainly effective till then.

When such a right to sexual cohabitation for the first night could be extended against the generality of the lower classes the Brahmins did not hesitate to extend it. This they did particularly in Malabar. There, Manu designated the Brahmins as Bhu-devas, lords of the earth. The Brahmins enlarged the scope of this statement and began to claim the right of promiscuous sexual intercourse with the women folk of the other Classes. This happened particularly in Malabar. There

" The Brahman castes follow the Makatyam System that is the system by which the child belongs to its father's family. They contract within their own caste regular marriages, with all the ordinary legal and religious sanctions and incidents. But the Brahmin men are also in the habit of entering into Sambandhan-Unions with women of the lower castes." This is not all. Observe further what the writer has to say:

"Neither party to a Sambadhan Unions becomes thereby a member of the other family; and the offspring of the Union belong to their mothers *tharwad* (family) and have no sort of claim, so far as the law goes, to a share of their father's property or to maintenance there from."

Speaking of the origin of this practice the author of the Gazetteer observes that the origin of this institution :

"Is found in the claim of the Bhu-devas" or "Earth Gods" (that the Brahmanas) and on a lower plain of the Kshatriyas or the ruling classes, to the first fruits of lower Caste Womanhood, a right akin to the medieval droit de Seigneurie."

It is an understatement to say that it is only a right to first fruits as the 'right to the first night' was called in the middle ages in Europe. It is more than that. It is a general right of the Brahmin against the lower caste to claim any woman of that class for mere prostitution, for the mere satisfaction of sexual appetite, without burdening the Brahmin to any of the obligations of marriage.

Such were the rights which the Brahmins the spiritual precepts claimed against the laity!! The Borgese Popes have been run down in history as the most debauched race of spiritual preceptors who ascended the throne of Peter. One wonders whether they were really worse than the Brahmins of India.

A purely intellectual Class, free to consider general good and having no interest of a class to consider, such as the one contemplated by Buddha is not to be had anywhere. For the limitations resulting from property on the freedom of intellect of the elite have not been generally recognized until very recently. But this want of an intellectual class has been made good in other countries by the fact that in those countries each Strata of Society has its educated class. There is safety, if no definite guidance, in the multiplicity of views expressed by different educated classes drawn from different strata of society. In such a multiplicity of views there is no danger of Society being misguided or misdirected by the views of one single educated class drawn from one single class of society and which is naturally bound to place the interest of its class before the interests of the country. By the change made by Brahmanism India ceased to have safe and sure guidance of an intellectual class. But what is worse is that the Hindus lost the safety and security which other peoples have and which arises from the multiplicity of views expressed by various educated classes drawn from different strata of Society.

By the denial of education to the Shudras, by diverting the Kshatriyas to military persuits, and the Vaishyas to trade and by reserving education to themselves the Brahmins alone could become the educated class—free to misdirect and misguide the whole society. By converting Varna into Caste they declared that mere birth was a real and final measure of the worth of a man. Caste and Graded inequality made disunity and discord a matter of course.

All this disfigurement of the original Varna system would have been tolerable if it had remained a mere matter of social practice. But Brahmanism was not content to leave the matter there. It wanted to give the Chaturvarna in its changed and perverted form the force of law. This new Chaturvarna the making of Brahmanism occupies in the Manu Smriti as the Law of Persons and the Law of Family. Nobody can make a mistake about it. Manu made it an offence for a person of a lower Caste to arrogate to himself the status of a higher Caste or to pass off as a member of the higher Caste.

X. 96. A man of low caste who through covetousness lives by the occupations of a higher one, the king shall deprive of his property and banish.

XI. 56. Falsely attributing to oneself high birth, giving information to the king (regarding a crime), and falsely accusing one's teacher, (are offences) equal to slaying a Brahmana. Here there are two offences, General Impersonation (X. 96) and impersonation by the Shudra (XI. 56). Note also the punishments how severe they are. For the first the punishment is confiscation of property and banishment. For the second the punishment is the same as the punishment for causing the death of a Brahmin.

The offence of personation is not unknown in modern jurisprudence and the Indian Penal Code recognizes it in section 419. But what is the punishment the Indian Penal Code prescribes for cheating by personation? Fine, and if imprisonment, then 3 years or both. Manu must be turning in his grave to find the British Government make so light of his law of Caste.

Manu next proceeds to direct the king that he should execute this law. In the first place he appeals to the King in the name of his pious duty :

VIII. 172. By preventing the confusion of Castes . . .. .the power of the King grows, and he prospers in this world and after death. Manu perhaps knows that the law relating to the confusion of Varna may not be quite agreeable to the conscience of the king and he avoids enforcement. Consequently Manu tells the King how in the matter of the execution of the laws the King should act :

VIII. 177. Therefore let the King not heeding his own likes and dislikes behave exactly like Yama. i.e. he should be as impartial as Yama the Judge of the Dead.

Manu however does not wish to leave the matter to the King as a mere matter of pious duty. Manu makes it a matter of obligation upon the King. Accordingly Manu lays down as a matter of obligation that :

VIII. 410. The King should order a Vaishya to trade to lend money, to cultivate the land, or to lend cattle, and the Shudra to serve the twice born Caste. Again Manu reverts to the subject and say:

VIII. 418. The King should carefully compel Vaishyas and Sudras to perform the work (prescribed) for them ; for if these two castes swerved from their duties they would throw this whole world into confusion.

What if the Kings do not act up to this obligation. This law of Chaturvarna is so supreme in the eyes of Manu that Manu will not allow himself to be thwarted by a King who will not keep his obligation to maintain this law. Boldly Manu forges a new law that such a king shall be disposed. One can imagine how dear Chaturvarna was lo Manu and to Brahmanism.

As I have said the Chaturvarna of the Vedic system was better than caste system was not very favourable to the creation of a Society which could be regarded as one single whole possessing the Unity of the ideal society. By its very theory the Chaturvarna has given birth to four classes. These four classes were far from friendly. Often they were quarreling and their quarrels were so bitter that they cannot but be designated as Class wars. All the same this old Chaturvarna had two saving features which Brahminism most selfishly removed. Firstly there was no isolation among the Varnas. Intermarriage and interdining the two strongest bonds for unity had full play. There was no room for the different Varnas to develop that anti-social feeling which destroys the very basis of Society. While the Kshatriyas fought against the Brahmins and the Brahmins fought against the Kshatriyas there were not wanting Kshatriyas who fought against the Kshatriyas for the sake of Brahmins and there were not wanting Brahmins who joined hands with Kshatriyas to put down the Brahmins.

Secondly this old Chaturvarna was conventional. It was the ideal of the Society but it was not the law of the State. Brahmanism isolated the Varnas and sowed the seed of antagonism. Brahmanism made legal what was only conventional. By giving it a legal basis it perpetrated the mischief. The Vedic Chaturvarna if it was an evil would have died out by force of time and circumstances. By giving it the force of Law Brahmanism has made it eternal. This is probably the greatest mischief that Brahmanism has done to Hindu Society.

In considering this question one cannot fail to notice that the obligation imposed upon the King for the maintenance of the law of Chaturvarna which is another name for the system of graded inequality does not require the King to enforce it against the Brahmins and the Kshatriyas. The obligation is limited to the enforcement of the law against the Vaishyas and the Shudras. Having regard to the fact that Brahmanism was so intent on giving the system the force of law the result has been very awkward to say the least about it. Notwithstanding this attempt at legalization the system remained half legal and half conventional, legal as to the Vaishyas and the Shudras and merely conventional as to Brahmins and Kshatriyas.

This difference needs to be accounted for. Was Brahmanism honest in its attempt to give the system the force of law? Did it wish that each of the four Varnas be bound by it? The fact that Brahmanism would not bind the Brahmins and the Kshatriyas by the law it made, shows that in this business

Brahmainsm was far from honest. If it believed in the system as ideal it could not have failed to make it an universal binding force.

But there is more than dishonesty in this foul game. One can quite understand why the Brahmins were left free and untramelled by the shackles of the law. Manu called them Gods on earth and Gods must be above the law. But why were the Kshatriyas left free in the same way as the Brahmins. He knows that the Kshatriyas will not humble themselves before the Brahmins. He then proceeds to warn them, how the Brahmins can punish them if the Kshatriyas show arrogance and plan rebellion.

IX. 320 When the Kshatriyas become in any way overbearing towards the Brahmanas, the Brahmanas themselves shall duly restrain them; for the Kshatriyas sprang from the Brahmanas.

IX. 321. Fire sprang from water, Kshatriya from Brahmanas, iron from stone ; the all-penetrating force of those (three) has no effect on that whence they were produced.

One might think that the reason why Manu does not impose an obligation upon the King to enforce the law against the Kshatriya was because the Brahmins felt themselves quite capable of dealing with Kshatriyas by their own prowess and without the aid of the King and that they meant to put their sanctions against the Kshatriyas when the time came and without fear of consequences. All this could not have been meant by Manu. For after uttering this vows of vengeance, and threats and imprecations Manu suddenly come down and begins to plead with the Kshatriyas for cooperation and common front with the Brahmins. In a verse next after the verse in which he utters the threats and imprecations against the Kshatriyas Manu pleads :

IX. 323. But (a king who feels his end drawing nigh) shall bestow all his wealth, accumulated from fines on Brahmanas, make over his kingdom to his son and then seek death in battle. From imprecations to supplication is a very queer cry. What is the explanation of this anti-climax in the attitude of this strange behaviour of Manu towards the Kshatriyas? What is the object of this cooperation between Brahmins and Kshatriyas? Against whom is this common front to be? Manu does not explain. A whole history of a thousand years must be told before this puzzle is solved and the questions satisfactorily answered.

The history which furnishes the clue to the solution of this puzzle is the history of the class wars between the Brahmins and the Kshatriyas.

Most of the orthdox Hindus are repelled by the doctrine of Class war which was propounded by Karl Marx and would be certainly shocked if they were told that the history of their own ancestors probably furnishes the most cogent evidence that Marx was searching for support of his theory. Indeed there have been numerous class wars between Brahmins and the Kshatriyas and only the most important of them have been recorded in the ancient Hindu literature. We have record of the conflict between the Brahmins and the Kings who were all Kshatriyas. The first of these conflicts was a conflict with King Vena, the second with Pururavas, the third with Nahusha, fourth with Nimi and fifth with Sumukha. There is a record of *a* conflict between Vashishtha a Brahmin and Vishvamitra an ordinary Kshatriya and not a king. Then we have the record of the wholesale massacre of the Brahmins of Bhrigu clan by the Kshatriya decendants of Kratavirya and then we have the record of the whole class of Kshatriyas exterminated by Parashuram acting on behalf of the Brahmanas. The issues that brought them in conflict extended over a wide range and show how bitter and strained must have been the feelings between Brahmins and Kshatriyas. There were conflicts over the question whether the Kshatriya had a right to become a Brahmana. There were conflicts over the question, whether the Brahmins were subject to the authority or not. There were conflicts on the question who should salute first and who should give way to whom. The wars were wars of authority, status and dignity.

The results of these wars could not but be obvious to the Brahmins. Notwithstanding their boastful utterances they must have realized that it was not possible for them to crush the Kshatriyas and that notwithstanding the wars of extermination the Kshatriyas survived in sufficient numbers to plague the Brahmins. One need not pay any attention to the filthy story told by the Brahmins and alluded to by Manu that the

Kshatriyas of the Manu's day were not the original Kshatriyas but a race of new Kshatriyas begotten by the Brahmins upon the widows of the old Kshatriyas who were massacred by Parashuram. Blackmailing is one of the means which Brahmanism is never ashamed of using to advance its own purposes. The fight of Brahmanism against the Kshatriyas was from the very beginning a fight between a fool and a bully. Brahmanas were fighting against the Kshatriyas for the maintenance of the Chaturvarna.

Now it is this very Chaturvarna which allowed bayonets to the Kshatriyas and denied them to the Brahmins. How under this theory could the Brahmin fight with the Kshatriya with any hope of success? It could not have taken long for the Brahmins to realise the truth—which Tallyrand told Napoleon—that it is easy to give bayonets but it is very difficult to sit on them and that as Kshatriyas had bayonets and Brahmins none, war with the Kshatriya was the way to ruin. These were the direct consequences of these wars between the Brahmins and the Kshatriyas. But there were others which could not have escaped the attention of the Brahmins. While the Brahmins and Kshatriyas were fighting among themselves nobody was left to check and keep the Vaishyas and the Shudras under control. They were on the road of social equality almost nearing to the status of the Brahmins and Kshatriyas. To Brahmanism the possibility of suppressing the Kshatriya was very remote and the danger of being overtaken by Vaishyas and Shudras were real and very real.

Should the Brahmana continue to fight the Kshatriya and ignore the danger of the Vaishyas and the Shudras? Or Should the Brahmana give up the hopeless struggle against the Kshatriya and befriend him and make with him a common cause and suppress the growing menace of the Vaishyas and Shudras? Brahmanism after it was exhausted in the wars with the Kshatriyas chose the second alternative. It sought to befriend their worthwhile enemies the Kshatriyas to work for a new ideal namely to enslave and exploit the two classes below them namely the Vaishyas and the Shudras. This new ideal must have taken shape some time when the Satpatha Brahmana came to be composed. It is in the Satpatha Brahmana we find the new ideal expressed it was well established. The language in which it is expressed, and the subject to which it is applied are so telling that I feel it should be quoted in its original terms. Says the author of the Satpatha:

"They then make the beast return (to the Ahavaniya) the he-goat goes first of them, then the ass, then the horse. Now in going away from this (Ahavaniya) the horse goes first, then the ass, then the he-goat—for the horse corresponds to the Kshatra (nobility), the ass to the Vaishya and Shudra, the he-goat to the Brahman and in-as-much as, in going from here, the horse goes first, therefore the Kshatriya, going first, is followed by the three others castes ; and in-as-much as, in returning from here, the he-goat goes first, therefore the Brahman, going first, is followed by the three other castes. And in-as-rnuch as the ass does not go first, either in going back from here, or in coming back from there, therefore the Brahmana and Kshatriya never go behind the Vaishya and Sudra ; hence they walk thus in order to avoid a confusion between good and bad. And, moreover, he thus encloses those two castes (the Vaishyas and Sudra) on both sides by the priesthood and the nobility and makes them submissive."

Here is the explanation of the puzzling attitude of Manu towards the Kshatriyas, attitude of willing to wound but afraid to strike, of wishing to dictate but preferring to befriend.

It is these wars and the compromise that had taught Manu that it was no use trying to coerce the Kshatriyas to submit to the domination of the Brahmin. It may be an ideal to be kept up. But as practical politics it was an impossible ideal. Like Bismark.. Manu knew that politics was the game of the possible. What was possible was to make a common cause and to build up a common front between the Brhamins and the Kshatriyas against the Vaishyas and the Shudras and this is what Manu did. The pity of it is that it was done in the name of religion. This need not shock anybody who has studied the soul and spirit of Brahmanism. With Brahmanism religion is a cloak to cover and hide its acquisitive politics.

The Morals of the House

This is 61 page typed manuscript. This is a second copy hut it is having corrections and modifications by Dr. Ambedkar himself. It is reproduced here taking all the corrections into account. There is one separate file entitled 'Manu Smriti or the Gospel of Counter-Revolution '. In that copy notes on Manu Smriti under various categories have been drawn. However, all these notes have been found to be incorporated in this essay, 'Morals of the House.' It is felt that the printing of these notes would be a mere repetition of this essay. Hence, the said copy is not separately printed:

The morals of the Hindus and their religious creed are prescribed by the *Smritis* which form a part of the Sacred literature of the Hindus. It is to the Smritis that one must go to understand the Ethics and the Religion of the Hindus. The Smritis are by no means few in number. A conservative estimate gives the total number of Smritis to be 108. The large number of *Smritis* cannot however make our problem difficult. For though the Smritis are numerous they do not differ in essentials. Indeed they repeat one another so closely that reading the Smritis creates a most monotonous task. They are all derived from one common source. That source is the Smriti of Manu otherwise known as Manava Dharma Shastra. The other Smritis are faithful repetitions of the Manu Smriti. A study of the Manu Smriti is therefore quite sufficient to obtain an adequate conception of the moral standards and Religious notions of the Hindus.

It may be said that Manu Smriti—and the same is true of the other Smritis—is a Code of Laws. It is not a book of Ethics nor is it a book of Religion and to take a book of Laws and to treat it as though it is a book of Ethics and Religion is to confound Ethics, Religion and Law.

In the first place it is only in modern times that Law has been separated from Religion. In all ancient Society, Law and Religion were one. As Prof. Max Muller points out that though:—

"Law seems naturally to be the foundation of society, and the bond that binds a nation together. Those who look below the surface have quickly perceived that law itself, at least ancient law, derives its authority, its force, its very life from religion. . . .. The belief that the lawgiver enjoyed some closer intimacy with the Deity than ordinary mortals, pervades the ancient traditions of many nations. According to a well known passage in Diodorus Siculus, the Egyptians believed their laws to have been communicated to Menvis by Hermes; the Cretaus held that Minos received his laws from Zeus, the Lacedaemonians that Lykurgus received his laws from Apollon. According to the Arians, their lawgiver Zarathustras had received his Laws from the Good Spirit; According to the Stoe, Zamolixis received his laws from the goddess Hestia; and according to the Jews, Moses received his laws from the God las."

No one has pointed out more forcibly than Sir Henry Mains that in ancient times religion as a divine influence was underlying and supporting every relation of life and every social institution when he says of Religion as:

"A supernatural presidency (which) is supposed to consecrate and keep together all the cardinal institutions of those times, the state, the Race, and the Family ".

From this superntural presidency of Reigion, Law had not succeded in finding an escape until at a later time when law finally breaks away from religion but not without leaving many traces to show the link it had with Religion at the very beginning of human history.

Again it is only in modern times that a difference is being made between Religion and Ethics. Religion and Ethics are inextricably and indissolubly bound together. Morality and Ethics are essentially practical. As Prof. Jacks insists that the problem of Ethics is not merely getting the Good understood but *realised,* not merely getting the Right placed on scientific basis but *done.* Morality is a mere matter of defining what is good and what is right. Prof. Jacks: rightly says :

"Whenver we embark on the study of morality without interest in its application I cannot but think that it is not morality we are studying. Morality does not arise till the point of application is reached. The effect of a moral theory launched upon the world is next to nothing unless the application of it can be reinforced by powerful motives. The good life, as Aristotle pointed out is a very difficult affair; difficult even when it goes no further than conformity to existing conventions. But when the good life demands that existing standards must be transcended how can this be effected without an immense liberation of power? Mere information as to why men should do right has no effect against their natural tendencies to do wrong-it is no match for the difficulties that beset good life. "

Unless some motive force comes to its aid morality remains inert. There can be no doubt that what gives motive force to morality is Religion. It is a propelling force which creates, to use again the language of Principal Jacks :

"Motives which are strong enough to overcome the enormous difficulties involved in living the good life, even in its simpler forms, and adequate to maintain that continuous improvement of the moral ideal."

Religion as a motive force reinforces the moral will in various ways. Sometimes it takes the form of sanctions by laying down a scheme of rewards and punishments after death; some times it makes rules of morality as the commandments of God; some times it invests these rules with sanctity which evokes willing obedience. But these are only different ways in which motive power generated by Religion helps to sustain moral life in action. Religion is the dynamics which moves the wheels of morality.

If Ethics and Morality are duties then there can be no doubt that Manu Smriti is a book of Ethics. Any one who takes the trouble to read the Smriti of Manu will have to admit that if there is any subject which figures prominently in the book it is that of duties. Manu was the first to syatematise and codify the duties to which a Hindu was bound. He distinguishes between *Varnashramadharmas* and *Sadharandharmas.* The Varnashramdharmas are the specific duties relating to one's station in life i.e. one's station as determined by one's Varna or caste and one's Ashram or particular stage of life. The Sadharandharmas are duties irrespective of one's age, caste or creed i.e. duties obligatory on man as man and not as a member of a particular community or social class or as being at a particular stage or period of life. The whole book deals with duties and with nothing else.

Manu Smriti is thus a book of Law, Religion and Ethics rolled into one. It is Ethics because it deals with duties of men. It is religion because it deals with Caste which is the soul of Hinduism. It is Law because it prescribes penalties for breach of duties. In this view there is nothing wrong in going to Manu Smriti to ascertain the moral standards and religious notions of the Hindus.

That Manu Smriti is a book of Religion may not be quite obvious. That is because Hinduism is a very illusive term. Different writers have defined it in various ways. Sir D. lbbetson defines Hinduism as :

"A hereditary sacerdotalism with Brahmins for its devices, the vitality of which is preserved by the social institution of caste and which include all shades and diversities of religion native to India, as distinct from foreign importations of Christianity and Islam, and from the later outgrowths of Buddhism, more doubtfully of Sikhism and still more doubtfully of Jainism ". Sir J. A. Baines defined Hinduism as :—

"The large residium that is not Sikh, or Jain, or Buddhist or professedly Animistic, or included in one of the foreign religions such as Islam, Mazdaism, Christianity, or Hebraism." To Sir Edward Gait Hinduism :—

"is a complex congenies of creeds and doctrines. It shelters within its portals monotheists, polytheists, and pantheists; Worshippers of the great God Siva and Vishnu, or of their female counterparts, as well as worshippers of the divine mothers, of the spirits of trees,rocks and streams and of the tutelary village deities; persons who propitate their deity by all matter of bloody sacrifices, and persons who will not only kill no living creature, but who must not even use the word "cut"; those whose ritual consists mainly of prayers and hymns, and those who indulge in unspeakable orgies in the name of religion".

This discription of complexity is full but is still incomplete. To the list must be added those who revere the cow and those who eat it, those who worship natural forces, and those who worship a single God; those who are worshippers of idols, demons, ghosts, ancestors, saints and heroes.

Such are the answers given by the three Census Commissioners to the simple question what is Hinduism. Others have not found it less difficult to answer the question. Consider how Sir A. Lyall has fared in answering the question. In his "Rede Lecture" delivered at Cambridge in 1891 he said:

"And if I were asked for a definition of Hinduism I could give no precise answer, I could not define it concisely by giving its central doctrines and its essential articles of faith; as I might do in describing of the great historical Religions. For the word Hindu is not exclusively a religious denomination; it denotes also a country, and to certain degree a race. When we speak of Christian, a Mahomedan, or a Buddhist, we mean a particular religious community, in the widest sense, without distinction of race or place. When we talk of a Russian or a Persian, we indicate country or parentage without distinction of creed. But when a person tells me that he is a Hindu, I know that he means all three things together— Religion. Parentage and Country." Speaking of Hinduism as a Religion Sir Alfred Lyall said that:

"Hindism was a tangled mugle of disorderly superstitions, the collection of rights, worships, beliefs, traditions and mythologies, that are sanctioned by the sacred books and ordinances of the Brahmins and are propogated by Brahmanic teachings." Lastly I will quote the defintion given by a Hindu Mr. G. P. Sen who not merely a Hindu but is a student of Hinduism. In his book called 'Introduction to the study of Hinduism' Mr. Sen says :—

"Hinduism is what the Hindus, or a major portion of them in a Hindu Community do."

Is there then no principle in Hinduism which all Hindus no matter what their other differences are, feel bound to render willing obedience? It seems to me there is and that principle is the principle of Caste. There may be a difference of opinion as to which matters constitute matters of essence so far as Hinduism is concerned. But there can be no doubt that Caste is one and an essential and integral part of Hinduism. Every Hindu—if he is not merely a statutory Hindu-believes in Caste and every Hindu-even one who prides himself on being a statutory Hindu—has a Caste. A Hindu is as much born into caste as he is born in Hinduism. Indeed a person connot be born in Hinduism unless he is born in a Caste. Caste and Hinduism are inseparable. As Prof. Max Muller observes :

"Modern Hinduism rests on the system of Caste as on a rock which no arguments can shake."

It therefore follows that in so far as Manu lays down the creed of the Caste and in so far as Hinduism at its core is the creed of Caste the Manu Smriti must be accepted as the Book of Religion.

What are the Ethical and Religious norms prescribed by Manu for Hindus to observe and follow?

To begin with, Manu divides Hindus into four varnas or social orders. He not only divides Hindus into four orders he also grades them. The dollowing is his scheme of gradation.

X. 3. On account of his pre-eminence, on account of the superiority of his origin, on account of his observance of(particular) restrictive rules, and on account of his particular sanctification the Brahman is the Lord of (all) Varnas.

He procceds to amplify his reasons and does so in the following characteristic manner :—

1. 93. As the Brahmana sprang from (Prajapati's i.e.Gods) mouth, as he was first-born, and as he possesses the Veda, he is by right the lord of this whole creation.

1. 94. For the self existent (Svayambhu i.e. God), having performed austerities, produced him first from his own mouth, in order that the offerings might be conveyed to the Gods and Manes and that this universe might be preserved.

1. 95. What created being can surpass him, through whose mouth the Gods continually consume the sacrificial viands and the manes the offerings to the dead.

1. 96. Of created beings the most excellent are said to be those which are animated; of the animated, those who subsist by intelligence: of the inteligent, mankind; and of the men, the Brahmans.

Besides the reason given by Manu the Brahmin is first in rank because he was produced by God from his mouth, in order that the offerings might be conveyed to the Gods and manes. Manu gives another reason for the supremacy of the Brahmins. He says :—

1. 98. The very birth of a Brahmana is an eternal incarnation of the sacred Law (Veda); for he is born to (fulfil) the sacred law, and become one with Brahman (God).

1. 99. A Brahamana, coming into existence, is born as the

highest on earth, the lord of all created beings, for the protection of the treasury of the Law. Manu concludes by saying that :

1. 101. The Brahmana eats but his own food, wears but his own apparel, bestows but his own alms; other mortals subsist through the benevolence of the Brahmana." Because according to Manu :

1. 100. Whatever exists in the world is the property of the Brahmana; on account of the excellence of his origin the Brahmana is, indeed, entitled to it all.

It is really an understatement to say that according to Manu the Brahman is a lord of all creation. For Manu gives a warning to the effect that :-

IX. 317. A Brahmana, be he ignorant or learned, is a great divinity, just as the fire, whether carried forth (for the performance of a burnt oblation) or not carried forth, is a great divinity.

IX. 319. Thus, though the Brahmans employ themselves in all (sorts) of mean occupations, they must be honoured in every way; (for each of) them is a very great deity.

Being a deity the Brahmin is above law and above the King. Manu directs :-

VII. 37. Let the King, after rising early in the morning, worship Brahmans who are well versed in the threefold sacred science and learned (in polity), and follow their advice VII. 38. Let him daily worship aged Brahmans who know the Veda and are pure...... Finally Manu says :

XI. 35. The Brahman is (hereby) declared (to be) the creator (of the world), the punisher, the teacher, (and hence) a benefactor (of all created beings); to him let no man say anything unpropitions, nor use any harsh words.

In the Code of Manu there are rules regarding the different occupations which the different orders are required to follow:

I. 88. To Brahmens he (Swayambhu Manu) assigned the duties of reading the Veda, of teaching it, of sacrificing, of assisting others to sacrifice, of giving alms, if they the rich, and if indiquent, of receiving of gifts.

I. 89. To defend the people, to give alms, to sacrifice, to read the Veda, to shun the allurements of sensual gratifiction, are, in a few words, the duties of a Kshatriya.

I. 90. To keep herds of cattle, to bestow largeness, to sacrifice, to read the scriptures, to carry on trade, to lend at interest, and to cultivate land are prescribed or permitted to a Vaisya.

1. 91. One principal duty the supreme Ruler assigns to a Sudra; namely, to serve the before mentioned classes, without depreciating their worth.

X. 74. Let such Brahmans as are intent on the means of attaining the supreme Godhead, and firm in their own duties, completely perform, in order, the six following acts:

X. 75. Reading the Vedas, the teaching others to read them, sacrificing, and assisting others, to sacrifice, giving to the poor if themselves have enough, and accepting gifts from the virtuous if themselves are poor, are the six prescribed acts of the first born class;

X. 76. But, among those six acts of a Brahmin, three are his means of susbsistence; assisting to sacrifice, teaching the Vedas, and receiving gifts from a pure handed giver.

X. 77. Three acts of duty cease with the Brahman, and belong not to the Kshatriya; teaching the Vedas, officiating at a sacrifice, and, thirdly, receiving presents.

X. 78. Those three are also (by the fixed rule of law) forbidden to the Vaisya; since Manu, the Lord of all men, prescribed not those acts to the two classes, military and commercial.

X. 79. The means of subsistence, peculiar to the Kshatriya, are bearing arms, either held for striking or missile, to the Vaisya, merchandize, attending on cattle, and agriculture but with a view to the next life, the duties of both are almsgiving, reading, sacrificing." Besides prescribing rank and occupation Manu grants privileges to certain orders and imposes penalties on certain orders. As to privileges those relating to marriage may be referred to first. Manu says :

III. 12. For the first marriage of the twice born classes, a woman of the same class is recommended but for such as are impelled by inclination to marry again, women in the direct order of the classes are to be preferred :

III. 13. A Sudra woman only must be the wife of a Sudra;

she and a Vaisya, of a Vaisya; they two and a Kshatriya, of a Kshatriya; those three and a Brahmani of a Brahman. Then there are privileges relating to occupations. These privileges stand out quite prominently when Manu deals with the question as to what a person is to do when he is in distress :

X. 81. Yet a Brahmen, unable to subsist by his duties just mentioned, may live by the duty of a soldier; for that is the next in rank.

X. 82. If it be asked, how he must live, should he be unable to get a subsistence by either of those employments; the answer is, he may subsist as a mercantile man, applying himself in person to tillage and attendance on cattle.

X. 83. But a Brahman and a Kshatriya, obliged to subsist by the acts of a Vaisya, must avoid with care, if they can live by keeping herds, the business of tillage, which gives great pain to sentient creatures, and is dependent on the labour of others, as bulls and so forth.

X. 84. Some are of opinion, that agriculture is excellent, but it is a mode of subsistence which the benevolent greatly blame, for the iron mouthed pieces of wood not only wound the earth, but the creatures dwelling in it.

85. If through want of a virtuous livelihood, they cannot follow laudable occupations,they may then gain a competence of wealth by selling commodities usually sold by merchants, avoiding what ought to be avoided.

X. 86. They must avoid selling liquids of all sorts, dressed grain, seeds of tila, stones, salt, cattle, and human creatures.

X. 87. All woven cloth dyed red, cloth made of sana, of cshuma-bark, and of wool, even though not red; fruit, roots, and medicinal plants.

X. 88. Water, iron, poison, flesh-meat, the moon-plant, and perfumes of any sort; milk, honey, butter milk, clarified butter, oil of tila, wax sugar, and blades of cusa grass;

X. 89. All beasts of the forest, as deer and the like, ravenous beasts, birds, and fish; spirituous liquors, nili, or indigo, and lascha, or lac; and all beasts with uncloven hoofs.

X. 90. But the brahmen-husbandman may at pleasure sell pure tila-seeds for the purpose of holy rites, if he keep them not long with a hope of more gain, and shall have produced them by his own culture.;

X. 91. If he apply seeds of tila to any purpose but food, anoiting, and sacred oblations, he shall be plunged, in the shape of a worm, together with his parents, into the ordure of dogs.

X. 92. By selling flesh-meat, lac or salt, a Brahmen immediately sinks low; by selling milk three days, he falls to a level with a Sudra.

X. 93. And by selling the other forbidden commodities with his own free will, he assumes in this world, after seven nights, the nature of a mere Vaisya.

X. 94. Fluid things may, however, be bartered for other fluids, but not salt for anything liquid; so may dressed grain for grain undressed, and tila-seeds for grain in the husk, equal weights or measures being given and taken.

X. 102. The Brahmen having fallen into distress, may receive gifts from any person whatever; for by no sacred rule can it be shown, that absolute purity can be sullied.

X. 103. From interpreting the Veda, from officiating at sacrifices, or from taking presents, though in modes generally disapproved, no sin is committed by priests in distress; lor they are as pure as fire or water.

Compare with this what Manu has to say with regard, to what the other Varnas can do in an emergency, Manu says :

X. 96. A man of lowest class, who, through covetousness, lives by the acts of the highest, let the king strip of all his wealth and instantly banish.

X. 97. His own office, though defectively performed, is preferable to that of another, though performed completely; for he, who without necessity discharges the duties of another class, immediately forfeits his own.

X. 98. A mercantile man, unable to subsist by his own duties, may descend even to the servile acts of a Sudra, taking care never to do what ought never to be done; but, when he has gained a competence, let him depart from service.

X. 99. A man of fourth class, not finding employment by waiting on the twice born, while his wife and son are tormented with hunger, may subsist by handicrafts.

X. 121. If a Sudra want a subsistence and cannot attend priest, he may serve a Kshatriya; or, if he cannot wait on a soldier by birth, he may gain his livelihood by serving an opulent Vaisya.

X. 122. To him, who serves Brahmens, with a view to a heavenly reward, or even with view to both this life and the next, the union of the word Brahmen with his name of servant will assuredly bring success.

X. 123. Attendance on Brahmens is pronounced the best work of Sudra; whatever else he may perform will comparatively avail him nothing.

X. 124. They must allot him a fit maintenance according to their own circumstances, after considering his ability, his exertions, and the number of those, whom he must provide with nourishment.

X. 125. What remains of their dressed rice must be given to him, and apparel which they have worn, and the refuse of their grain, and their old household furniture.

X. 126. There is no guilt in a man of the servile class who eats leeks and other forbidden vegetables; he must not have the sacred investiture; he has no business with the duty of making oblations to fire and the like, but there is no prohibition against his offering dressed grain as a sacrifice, by way of discharging his own duty.

X. 127. Even Sudras, who were anxious to perform their entire duty, and, knowing what they should perform, imitate the practice of good men in the household sacraments, but without any holy text, except those containing praise and salutations, are so far from sinning, that they acquire just applause.

X. 128. As a Sudra, without injuring another man, performs the lawful acts of the twice-born, even thus, without being censured, he gains exaltation in this world and in the next.

X. 129. No superfluous collection of wealth must be made by a Sudra, even though he has power to make it, since a servile man, who has amassed riches, becomes proud, and, by his insolence or neglect, gives pain even to Brahmens. He concludes:—

X. 130. Such, as have been fully declared, are the several duties of the four classes in distress for subsistence, and, if they perform them exactly, they shall attain the highest beatitude. The privileges to some were not merely social they were also financial, Says Manu :—

VIII. 35. From the man, who shall say with truth, 'This property, which has been kept, belongs to me', the king may take a sixth or twelfth part, for having secured it.

VIII. 36. But he, who shall say so falsely, may be fined either an eighth part of his own property, or else in some small proportion to the value of the goods falsely claimed, a just calcultion having been made.

VIII. 37. A learned Brahmen, having found a treasure formerly hidden, may take it without any deduction; since he is the lord of all.

VIII. 38. But of a treasure anciently deposited under ground, which any other subject or the king has discovered, the king may lay up half in his treasury having given half to the Brahmens.

IX. 323. Should the king be near his end through some incurable disease, he must bestow on the priests all his riches, accumulated his kingdom to his son, let him seek death in battle, or if there be no war, by abstaining from food.

VII. 127. Having ascertained the rates of purchase and sale, the length of the way, the expenses of food and of condiments the charges of securing the goods carried, and the net profits of trade, let the king oblige traders to pay taxes on their saleable commodities.

VII. 128. After full consideration, let a king so levy those taxes continually in his dominions, that both he and the merchant may receive a just compensation for their several acts.

VII. 129. As the leech, the suckling calf, and the bee, take their natural food by little and little, thus must a king draw from his dominions an annual revenue.

VII. 130. Of cattle, of gems, of gold and silver, added each year to the capital stock, a fiftieth part may be taken by the king; of grain, an eighth part, a sixth, or a twelfth, according to the difference of the soil, and the labour necessary to cultivate it.

VII. 131. He may also take a sixth part of the clear annual increase of trees, fleshmeat, honey, clarified butter, perfumes, medical substances, liquids, flowers, roots, and fruit.

VII. 132. Of gathered leaves, pot-herbs, grass, utencils made with leather or cane, earthen pots, and all things made of stone.

VII. 133. A king, even though dying with want, must not receive any tax from a Brahman learned in the Vedas, nor suffer such a Brahmen, residing in his territories, to be afflicted with hunger.

VII. 134. Of that king, in whose dominion a learned Brahmen is afflicted with hunger, the whole kingdom will in a short time be afflicted with famine.

VII. 137. Let the king order a mere trifle to be paid, in the name of the annual tax, by the meaner inhabitants of his realm, who subsist by petty traffic.

VII. 138. By low handicraftsmen, artificers, and servile men, who support themselves by labour, the king may cause work to be done for a day in each month.

VIII. 394. Neither a blind man, nor an idiot, nor a cripple, nor a man full seventy years old, nor one who confers great benefits on priests of eminent learning, shall be compelled by any king to pay taxes.

X. 118. A military king, who takes even a fourth part of the crops of his realm at a time of urgent necessity, as of war or invasion, and protects his people to the utmost of his power, commits no sin :

X. 119. His peculiar duty is conquest, and he must not recede from battle; so that, while he defends by his arms the merchant and husbandman, he may levy the legal tax as the price of protection.

X. 120. The tax on the mercantile class, which in times of prosperity must be only a twelfth part of their crops, and a fiftieth of their personal profits, may be an eighth of their crops in a time of distress, or a sixth, which is the medium, or even a fourth in great public adversity ; but a twentieth of their gains on money, and other moveables, is the highest tax ; serving men, artisans, and mechanics must assist by their labour, but at no time pay taxes.

X. 187. To the nearest sapinda, male or female, after him in the third degree, the inheritance next belongs ; then, on failure of sapindas and of their issue the samanodaca, or distant kinsman, shall be the heir ; or the spiritual preceptor, or the pupil, or the fellow student, of the deceased.

IX. 188. On failure of all those, the lawful heirs are such Brahmens, as have read the three Vedas, as are pure in body and mind, as have subdued their passions ; and they must consequently offer the cake; thus the rites of obsequies cannot fail.

IX. 189. The property of a Brahmen shall never be taken as an escheat by the king; this is a fixed law; but the wealth of the other classes, on failure of all heirs, the king may take. The terms on which the different social orders should carry on their associated life has been defined by Manu in a set of rules which form a very important part of the morals of the Hindu House. Manu ordains that :

X. 3. From priority of birth, from superiority of origin, from a more exact knowledge of scripture, and from a distinction in the sacrificial thread, the Brahmen is the lord of all classes.

IX. 317. A Brahmen, whether learned or ignorant, is a powerful divinity ; even as fire is powerful divinity, whether consecrated or popular.

IX. 319. Thus, although Brahmens employ themselves in all sorts of mean occupations, they must invariably be honoured ; for they are something transcendently divine.

VII. 35. A king was created as the protector of all those classes and orders, who, from the first to the last, discharge their several duties.

VII. 36. And all, that must be done by him, for the protection of his people, with the assistance of good ministers, I will declare to you, as the law directs, in due order.

VII. 37. Let the king, having risen at early dawn, respectfully attend to Brahmen, learned in the three Vedas, and in the science of ethics, and by their decision let him abide.

VII. 38. Constantly must he show respect to Brahmens, who have grown old, both in years and in piety, who know the scriptures, who in body and mind are pure ; for he, who honours the aged, will perpetually be honoured even by cruel demons:

IX. 313. Let him not, although in the greatest distress for money, provoke Brahmens to anger by taking their prosperty ; for they, once enraged, could immediately by sacrifices and imprecations destroy him with his troops, elephants, horses and cars.

Such was to be the relationship in the field of political life. For ordinary social intercourse between the different Varnas Manu lays down the following rules :—

III. 68. A house-keeper has five places of slaughter, or where small living creatures may be slain ; his kitchen-hearth, his grindstone, his broom, his pestle and mortar, his water-pot; by using which, he becomes in bondage to sin :

III. 69. For the sake of expiating offences committed ignorantly in those places mentioned in order, the five great sacraments were appointed by eminent sages to be performed each day by such as keep house.

III. 70. Teaching and studying the scripture is the sacrament of the Veda ; offering cakes and water, the sacrament of the Manes, an oblation to fire, the sacrament of the Deities ; giving rice or other food to living creatures, the sacrament of spirits ; receiving guests with honour, the sacrament of men.

III. 71. Whoever omits not those five great ceremonies, if he have ability to perform them, is untainted by the sons of the five slaughtering places, even though he constantly reside at home ;

111.84. In his domestic fire for dressing the food of all the Gods, after the prescribed ceremony, let a Brahmen make an oblation each day to these following divinities. After it is offered to the deities Manu directs :—

III. 92. The share of dogs, of outcasts, of dog-feeders, of sinful men, punished with elephantiasis or consumption, of crows, and of reptiles, let him drop on the ground by little and little. With regard to the rules of hospitality Manu directs the householder:

III. 102. A Brahmen, staying but one night as a guest, is called an atithi, since continuing so short a time, he is not even a sojourner for a whole tithi, or day of the moon.

III. 98. But an offering in the fire of a sacerdotal mouth, which richly blazes with true knowledge and piety, will release the giver from distress and even from deadly sin.

III. 107. To the highest guests in the best form, to the lowest in the worst, to the equal equally, let him offer seats, resting places, couches; giving them proportionable attendance when they depart; and honour, as long as they stay.

III. 110. A military man is not denominated a guest in the house of a Brahman; nor a man of the commercial or servile class ; nor his familiar friend, nor his paternal kinsmen ; nor his preceptor.

III. 111. But if a warrior come to his house in the form of a guest, let food be prepared for him, according to his desire, after the beforementioned Brahmens have eaten.

III. 112. Even to a merchant or a labourer, approaching his house in the manner of guests, let him give food, showing marks of benevolence at the same time with his domestics. On social bearing of one class towards another Manu has laid down some very interesting ordinances. He has an equation for social status :

II. 135. The student must consider a Brahmen, though but ten years old, and a Kshatriya, though aged a hundred years, as father and son ; as between those two, the young Brahmen is to be respected as the father.

II. 136. Wealth, kindred, age, moral conduct, and, fifthly divine knowledge, entitle men to respect ; but that which is last mentioned in order, is the most respectable.

II. 137. Whatever man of the three highest classes possesses the most of those five, both in number and degree that man is entitled to most respect ; even a Sudra, if he have entered the tenth decade of his age.

II. 138. Way must be made for a man in a wheeled carriage, or above ninety years old, or afflicted with disease, or carrying a burthen ; for a woman ; for a priest just returned from the mansion of his preceptor; for a prince, and for a bridegroom.

II. 139. Among all those, if they be met at one time, the priest just returned home and the prince are most to be honoured; and of those two, the priest just returned, should be treated with more respect than the prince.

As illustrating the rules of social bearing a reference may be made to rules regarding salutation:

II. 121. A youth who habitually greets and constantly reverses the aged, obtains an increase of four things; life, knowledge, fame, strength.

II. 122. After the word of salutation, a Brahman must address an elder; saying, "I am such an one," pronouncing his own name.

II. 123. If any persons, through ignorance of the Sanskrit language, understand not the import of his name, to them should a learned man say, " It is I "; and in that manner he should address all classes of women.

II. 124. In the salutation he should pronounce, after his own name, the vocative particle 'bhoh'; for the particle 'bhoh' is held by the wise to have the same property with names fully expressed.

II. 125. A Brahmen should thus be saluted in return; "May'st thou live long, excellent man", and at the end of his name, the vowel and preceding consonant should be lengthened, with an acute accent, to three syllabic moments or short vowels.

II. 126. That Brahmen, who knows not the form of returning a salutation, must not be saluted by a man of learning; as a Shudra, even so is he.

II. 127. Let a learned man ask a priest, when he meets him, if his devotion prospers, a warrior, if he is unhurt; a merchant, if his wealth is secure; and one of the servile classes, if he enjoys good health; using respectively the words, cusalam, anamayam, ksheman and anarogyam.

The provisions laid down by Manu in relation to Religion and Religious Sacraments and Sacrifice are worthy of note.

The ordinances of Manu relating to Sacraments and sacrifices are as follows :

III. 68. A house-keeper has five places of slaughter, or where small living creatures may be slain; his kitchen-hearth, his grindstone, his broom, his pastle and mortar, his water-pot; by using which, he become in bondage to sin.

III. 69. For the sake of expiating offences committed ignorantly in those places mentioned in order, the five great sacraments were appointed by eminent sages to be performed each day by such as keep house.

III. 70. Teaching and studying the scriptures is the sacrament of the Veda; offering cakes and water, the sacrament of the Manes, an oblation to fire, the sacrament of the Deities; giving rice or other food to living creatures, the sacraments of spirits; receiving guests with honour, the sacrament of men.

III. 71. Whoever omits not those five great ceremonies, if he have ability to perform them, is untainted by the sons of the five slaughtering places, even though he constantly reside at home. Manu then proceeds to lay down that all are not entitled to the benefit of the sacraments and all have not the same right to perform the sacrifices.

He defines the position of women and Shudras in the matter of Sacraments and sacrifices. As to women Manu says :—

II. 66. The same ceremonies, except that of the sacrificial thread, must be duly performed for women at the same age and in the same order, that the body may be made perfect; but without any text from the Veda." As to Shudras, Manu says:—

X. 127. Even Shudras, who were anxious to perform their entire duty, and, knowing what they should perform initate the practice of good men in the household sacraments, but without any holy text, except those containing praise and salutation, are so far from sinning, that they acquire just applause.

The investiture of a person with the sacred thread is a very important sacrament.

II. 36. In the eighth year from the conception of a Brahman., in the eleventh from that of a Kshatriya, and in the twelfth from that of a Vaisya, let the father invest the child with the mark of his class.

II. 37. Should a Brahman, or his father for him, be desirous of his advancement in sacred knowledge; a Kshatriya, of extending his power; or a Vaisya of engaging in mercantile business; the investiture may be made in the fifth, sixth, or eighth years respectively.

II. 38. The ceremony of investiture hallowed by the Gayatri must not be delayed, in the case of a priest, beyond the sixteenth year; nor in that of a soldier, beyond the twenty second; nor in that of a merchant, beyond the twenty fourth.

II. 39. After that, all youths of these three classes, who have not been invested at the proper time, become vratyas, or outcasts, degraded from the Gayatri, and condemned by the virtuous. As to the *Gayatri* it is a *mantra* and this is how Manu explains its importance :—

II. 76. Brahma milked out, as it were, from the three Vedas, the letter A, the letter U, and the letter M which form by their coalition the triliteral monosyllable, together with three mysterious words bhur, bhuvah, svah or earth, sky, heaven.

II. 77. From the three Vedas, also, the Lord of creatures, incomprehensibly exalted, successively milked out the three measures of that ineffable text,beginning with the word tad, and entitled Savitri or Gayatri.

II. 78. A priest who shall know the Veda, and shall pronounce to himself, both morning and evening, that syllable, and that holy text preceded by the three words, shall attain the sanctity which the Veda confers :

II. 79. And a twice born man, who shall a thousand times repeat those three (om, the vyahritis, and the gayatri), apart from the multitude, shall be released in a month even from a great offence, as a snake from his slough.

II. 80. The priest, the soldier, and the merchant, who shall neglect this mysterious text, and fail to perform in due season his peculiar acts of piety, shall meet with contempt among the virtuous.

II. 81. The great immutable words, preceded by the triliteral syllable, and followed by the gayatri which consists of three measures, must be considered as the mouth, or principal part of the Veda;

II. 82. Whoever shall repeat, day by day, for three years, without negligence, that sacred text, shall hereafter approach the divine essence, move as freely as air, and assume an ethereal form. II. 83. The triliteral monosyllable is an emblem of the Supreme, the suppressions of breath with a mind fixed on God are the highest devotion; but nothing is more exalted than the Gayatri; a declaration of truth is more excellant than silence.

II. 84. All rites ordained in the Veda, oblations to fire, and solemn sacrifices pass away ; but that which passes not away, is declared to be the syllable om, thence called acshara ; since it is a symbol of God, the Lord of created beings.

II. 85. The act of repeating his Holy Name is ten times better than the appointed sacrifice; an hundred times better when it is heard by no man ; and a thousand times better when it is purely mental.

II. 86. The four domestic sacraments which are accompanied with the appointed sacrifice, are not equal though all be united, to a sixteenth part of the sacrifice performed by a repetition of the gayatri. This investiture is equivalent to a new birth.

II. 147. Let a man consider that as a mere human birth, which his parents gave him for their mutual gratification, and which he receives after lying in the womb.

II. 148. But that birth which his principal acharya, who knows the whole Veda, procures for him by his divine mother the gayatri, is a true birth ; that birth is exempt from age and from death.

II. 169. The first birth is from a natural mother: the second, from the ligation of the zone ; the third from the due performance of the sacrifice ; such are the births of him who is usually called twice-born, according to a text of the Veda.

II. 170. Among them his divine birth is that, which is distinguished by the ligation of the zone, and sacrificial cord ; and in that birth the Gayatri is his mother, and the Acharya, his father. This sacrament is not permitted by Manu to Shudras and to women.

II. 103. But he who stands not repeating it in the morning and sits not repeating it in the evening, must be precluded, like a Sudra, from every sacred observance of the twice born class. Manu has not forgotten to mention rules relating to education and learning. Manu has nothing to say about mass education. He does not see the utility of it and he does not see the necessity of imposing any obligation upon the king or the state. He was merely concerned with the learning of the sacred and Religious literature namely the Vedas.

Veda must be learned from a preceptor and with his assent. No one can read and study the Vedas by himself. He will be guilty of theft if he did it.

II. 116. He who shall acquire knowledge of the Veda without the assent of his preceptor, incurs the guilt of stealing the scripture and shall sink to the region of torment. But others cannot study at all.

IX. 18. Women have no business with the texts of the Veda; thus is the law fully settled ; having, therefore, no evidence of law, and no knowledge of expiatory texts, sinful women must be as foul as falsehood itself; and this is a fixed rule.

IV. 99. He must never read the Veda without accents and letters well pronounced ; nor even in the presence of Sudras ; nor, having begun to read it in the last watch of the night, must he, though fatigued, sleep again.

This prohibition applies to *Vratyas* or outcasts from the three higher classes. For Manu says :

II. 40. With such impure men, let no Brahmen, even in distress for subsistence, ever form a connexion in law, either by the study of the Veda, or by affinity.

Teaching Veda or performing of sacrifices for disqualified persons was prohibited by Manu.

IV. 205. Never let a priest eat part of a sacrifice not begun with texts of the Veda, nor of one performed by a common sacrificer, by a woman, or by an eunuch :

IV. 206. When those persons offer the clarified butter, it brings misfortune to good men, and raises aversion in the deities, such oblations, therefore, he must carefully shun.

XI. 198. He, who has officiated at a sacrifice for outcasts, or burned the corpse of a stranger, or performed rites to destroy the innocent, or made the impure sacrifice, called Ahimsa, may expiate his guilt by three prajapatya penances. Take equality before Law.

When they come as witnesses—according to Manu they are to be sworn as follows :

VIII. 87. In the forenoon let the judge, being purified, severally call on the twice-born, being purified also, to declare the truth, in the presence of some image, a symbol of the divinity, and of Brahmens, while the witnesses turn their faces either to the north or to the east.

VIII. 88. To a Brahmen he must begin with saying, "Declare;" to a Kshatriya, with saying, " Declare the truth"; to a Vaisya, with comparing perjury to the crime of stealing kine, grain, or gold; to a Sudra, with comparing it in some or all of the following sentences, to every crime that men can commit.

VIII. 1 13. Let the judge cause a priest to swear by his veracity ; a soldier, by his horse, or elephant, and his weapons; a merchant, by his kine, grain, and gold; a mechanic or servile man, by imprecating on his own head, if he speak falsely, all possible crime; Manu also deals with cases of witnesses giving false evidence. According to Manu giving false evidence is a crime. Says Manu:

VIII. 122. Learned men have specified these punishments, which were ordained by sage legislators for perjured witnesses, with a view to prevent a failure of justice and to restrain iniquity.

VIII. 123. Let a just prince banish men of the three lower classes, if they give false evidence having first levied the fine ; but a Brahmen let him only banish." But Manu made one exception:

VIII. 1 12. To women, however, at a time of dalliance, or on a proposal of marriage, in the case of grass or fruit eaten by a cow, of wood taken for a sacrifice, or of a promise made for the preservation of a Brahmen, it is deadly sin to take a light oath. As parties to proceedings—Their position can be illustrated by quoting the ordinances of Manu relating to a few of the importa.nt criminal offences dealt with by Manu. Take the offence of Defamation. Manu says :

VIII. 267. A soldier, defaming a priest, shall be fined ahundred panas a merchant, thus offending, an hundred and fifty, or two hundred : but, for such an offence, a mechanic or servile man shall be whipped.

VIII. 268. A priest shall be fined fifty, if he slander a soldier; twenty five, if a merchant ; and twelve, if he slander a man of the servile class. Take the offence of Insult—Manu says:

VIII. 270. A once-born man, who insults the twice-born with gross invectives, ought to have his tongue slit ; for he sprang from the lowest part of Brahma.

VIII. 271. If he mention their names and classes with contumely as, if he say, "Oh Devadatta, thou refuse of Brahmen", an iron style, ten fingers long, shall be thrust red into his mouth.

VIII. 272. Should he, through pride, give instruction to priests concerning their duty, let the king order some hot oil to be dropped into his mouth and his ear. Take the offence of Abuse—Manu says:

VIII. 276. For mutual abuse by a priest and a soldier, this fine must be imposed by a learned king; the lowest amercement on the priest, and the middle-most on the soldier.

VIII. 277. Such exactly, as before mentioned, must be the punishment for a merchant and a mechanic, in respect of their several classes, except the slitting of the tongue; this is a fixed rule of punishment. Take the offence of Assault—Manu propounds:

VIII. 279. With whatever member of a low-born man shall assault or hurt a superior, even that member of his must be slit, or cut more or less in proportion to the injury; this an ordinance of Manu.

VIII. 280. He who raises his hand or a staff against another, shall have his hand cut ; and he, who kicks another in wrath, shall have an incision made in his foot. Take the offence of Arrogance—According to Manu :

VIII. 281. A man of the lowest class, who shall insolently place himself on the same seat with one of the highest, shall either be banished with a mark on his hinder parts, or the king shall cause a gash to be made on his buttock.

VIII. 282. Should he spit on him through pride, the king shall order both his lips to be gashed; should he urine on him, his penis; should he break wind against him, his anus.

VIII. 283. If he seize the Brahmen by the locks, or by the feet, or by the beard, or by the throat, or by the scrotum, let the king without hesitation cause incisions to be made in his hands. Take the offence of Adultery. Says Manu:

VIII. 359. A man of the servile class, who commits actual adultery with the wife of a priest, ought to suffer death ; the wives, indeed, of all the four classes must ever be most especially guarded.

VIII. 366. A low man, who makes love to a damsel of high birth, ought to be punished corporally; but he who addresses a maid of equal rank, shall give the nuptial present and marry her, if her father please.

VIII. 374. A mechanic or servile man, having an adulterious connection with a woman of a twice-born class, whether guarded at home or unguarded, shall thus be punished ; if she was unguarded, he shall lose the part offending, and his whole substance ; if guarded, and a priestless, every thing, even his life.

VIII. 375. For adultery with a guarded priestess, a merchant shall forfeit all his wealth after imprisonment for a year; a soldier shall be fined a thousand panas, and be shaved with the urine of an ass.

VIII. 376. But, if a merchant or soldier commit adultery with a woman of the sacerdotal class, whom her husband guards not at home, the king shall only fine the merchant five hundred, and the soldier a thousand ;

VIII. 377. Both of them, however, if they commit that offence with a priestess not only guarded but eminent for good qualities, shall be punished like men of the servile class, or be burned in a fire of dry grass or reeds.

VIII. 382. If a merchant converse criminally with a guarded woman of the military, or a soldier with one of the mercantile class, they both deserve the same punishment as in the case of a priestess unguarded.

VIII. 383. But a Brahmen, who shall commit dultery with a guarded woman of those two classes, must be fined a thousand panas ; and for the like offence with a guarded woman of the servile class, the fine of a soldier or a merchant shall be also one thousand.

VIII. 384. For adultery with a woman of the military class, if unguarded, the fine of a merchant is five hundred ; but a soldier, for the converse of that offence, must be shaved with urine, or pay the fine just mentioned.

VIII. 385. A priest shall pay five hundred panas if he connect himself criminally with an unguarded woman of the military, commercial, or servile class, and a thousand, for such a connexion with a woman of vile mixed breed.

Turning to the system of punishment for offences Manu's Scheme throws an interesting light on the subject. Consider the following ordinances :

VIII. 379. Ignominious tonsure is ordained, instead of capital punishment, for an adulterer of the priestly class, where the punishment of other classes may extend to loss of life.

VIII. 380. Never shall the king slay a Brahmen, though convicted of all possible crimes: let him banish the offender from his realm, but with all his property secure, and his body unhurt.

XI. 127. For killing intentionally a virtuous man of the military class, the penance must a fourth part of that ordained for killing a priest ; for killing a Vaisya, only an eighth ; for killing a Sudra, who had been constant in discharging his duties, a sixteenth part.

XI. 128. But, if a Brahmen kill a Kshatriya without malice, he must, after a full performance of his religious rites, give the priests one bull together with a thousand cows.

XI. 129. Or he may perform for three years the penance for slaying a Brahmen, mortifying his organs of sensation and action, letting his hair grow long, and living remote from the town, with the root of a tree for his mansion.

XI. 130. If he kill without malice a Vaisya, who had a good moral character, he may perform the same penance for one year, or give the priests a hundred cows and a bull.

XI. 131. For six months must he perform this whole penance, if without intention he kill a Sudra ; or he may give ten white cows and a bull to the priests.

VIII. 381. No greater crime is known on earth than slaying a Brahmen ; and the king, therefore, must not even form in his mind an idea of killing a priest.

VIII. 126. Let the king having considered and ascertained the frequency of a similar offence, the place and time, the ability of the criminal to pay or suffer and the crime itself, cause punishment to fall on those alone, who deserve it.

VIII. 124. Manu, son of the Self-existent, has named ten places of punishment, which are appropriate to the three lower classes, but a Brahmen must depart from the realm unhurt in any one f them.

VIII. 125. The part of generation, the belly, the tongue, the two hands, and, fifthly, the two feet, the eye, the nose, both ears, the property, and, in a capital case, the whole body. On the point of rights and duties relating to religious Sacraments and Sacrifices the views of Manu are noteworthy :

II. 28. By studying the Veda, by religious observances, by oblations to fire, by the ceremony of Traividya, by offering to the Gods and Manes, by the procreation of children, by the five great sacraments, and by solemn sacrifices, this human body is rendered fit for a divine state.

III. 69. For the sake of expiating offences committed ignorantly in those places mentioned in order, the five great sacrements were appointed by eminent sages to be performed each day by such as keep house.

III. 70. Teaching and studying the scripture is the sacrament of the Veda; offering cakes and water, the sacrament of the Manes; an oblation to fire, the sacrament of the Deities ; giving rice or other food to living creatures, the sacrament of spirits ; receiving guests with honour, the sacrament of men.

III. 71. Whoever omits not those five great ceremonies, if he have ability to perform them, is untained by the sins of the five slaughtering places, even though he constantly reside at home. Such are the ordinances of Manu. Laws are never complete enough to cover every point. There are always moot questions. Manu was conscious of this and provides for such contingencies.

XII. 108. If it be asked, how the law shall be ascertained, when particular cases are not comprised under any of the general rules, the answer is this : "That which well instructed Brahmens propound, shall be held incontestible law."

XII. 109. Well instructed Brahmens are they, who can adduce occular proof from the scripture itself, having studied, as the law ordains, the Vedas and their extended branches, or Vedangas, Mimansa, Nyaya, Dharma, Shastra, Puranas.

XII. 113. Even the decision of one priest, if more cannot be assembled, who perfectly knows the principles of the Vedas, must be considered as law of the highest authority ; not the opinion of myriads, who have no sacred knowledge.

The Laws of Manu are eternal. Therefore there is no question of considering how changes could be effected in them. The only question Manu had to consider was the upholding and maintaining the system. Manu has laid down several provisions with this purpose in view.

As to the preservation of the Social Code, Manu has made it the duty of the King to uphold and maintain:

VIII. 410. The king should order each man of the mercantile class to practice trade, or money lending, or agriculture and attendance on cattle ; and each man of the servile class to act in the service of the twice-born.

VIII. 418. With vigilant care should the king exert himself in compelling merchants and mechanics to perform their respective duties ; for, when such men swerve from their duty, they throw this world into confusion.

Failure to maintain was made an offence in the King punishable at Law.

VIII. 335. Neither a father, nor a preceptor, nor a friend, nor a mother, nor a wife, nor a son, nor a domestic priest must be left unpunished by the king, if they adhere not with firmness to their duty.

VIII. 336. Where another man of lower birth would be fined one pana, the king shall be fined a thousand, and he shall give the fine to the priests, or cast it into the river, this is a sacred rule.

Failure to uphold and maintain the system on the part of the king involved a forfeiture of his right to rule. For Manu allows a right to rebel against such a King.

VIII. 348. The twice-born may take arms, when their duty is obstructed by force: and when, in some evil time a disaster has befallen the twice-born classes.

The right of rebellion is given to the three higher classes and not to the Shudra. This is very natural. Because it is only the three upper classes who would benefit by the maintenance of this system. But supposing the Kshatriyas joined the King in destroying the system what is to be done? Manu gives the authority to the Brahmins to punish all and particularly the Kshatriyas.

XI. 31. A priest, who well knows the laws, need not complain to the king of any grievious injury; since, even by his own power, he may chastise those, who injure him.

XI. 32. His own power, which depends on himself alone, is mightier than the royal power, which depends on other men ; by his own might, therefore, may a Brahman coerce his foes.

XI. 33. He may use, without hesitation, the powerful charms revealed to Atharvan, and by him to Angiras ; for speech is the weapon of a Brahmen ; with that he may destroy his oppressors.

IX. 320. Of a military man, who raises his arm violently on all occasions against the priestly class, the priest himself shall be the chastiser; since the soldier originally proceeded from the Brahmen." How can the Brahmins punish the Kshatriyas unless they can take arms? Manu knows this and therefore allows the Brahmins to arm themselves to punish the Kshatriyas.

XII. 100. Command of armies, royal authority, power of inflicting punishment, and sovereign dominion over all nations, he only well deserves, who perfectly understands the Veda Shastra. So intent is Manu on the maintenance of the system of Chaturvarna that he did not hesitate to make this fundamental change in it. For to ask a Brahman to take up arms is a fundamental change as compared with the rule that was prevalent before Manu. The prohibition against Brahmin handling arms was very strict. In the Apastamba Dharma Sutras which is prior to Manu the rule is laid down in the following terms :

1.10, 29,6. A Brahmin shall not take up a weapon in his hand though he be only desirous of examining it." Successor of Manu—Baudhayana—improved upon him, and laid down in his Code of Laws :

II. 24, 18. For the protection of the Cows, Brahmins, or in the case of the confusion of Varnas, Brahmins and Vaisyas (also) should take up arms, out of consideration for the Dharma. and maintain the system at any cost.

5

Essays on the Bhagwat Gita : Philosophic Defence of Counter-Revolution: Krishna and His Gita

The first page of 'Essays on the Bhagvat Gita' is autographed by Dr. Ambedkar. Next 42 pages consist of analytical notes on Virat Parva and Uddyog Parva including the table of contents on this subject. The table of contents is printed in the schemes. This file contains two typed copies of an essay entitled 'Philosophic Defence of Counter-Revolution—Krishna and His Gita '. The last sentence of this essay is left incomplete. The total number of typed pages of this essay is 40 only. The notes on Viral Parva & Udyog Parva are printed in the next chapters.—Editors.

What is the place of the Bhagwat Gita in the literature of ancient India? Is it a gospel of the Hindu Religion in the same way as the Bible is of the Christian Religion? The Hindus have come to regard it as their gospel. If it is a gospel, what does it really teach? What is the doctrine it stands for? The variety of answers given to this question by students competent to speak on the subject is really bewildering. Bohtlingk says:

" The Gita contains by the side of many high and beautiful thoughts, not only a few weak points ; contradictions (which the commentators have tried to pass over as excusable), repetitions, exaggerations, absurdities and loathsome points.'"

" Hopkins speaks of the Bhagvat Gita as a charactaristic work of the Hindu Literature in its sublimity as in its puerilities, in its logic as in its want of it; ..... an ill-assorted cabinet of primitive philosophical opinions." In his judgment:

"Despite its occasional power and music exaltation, the Divine song in its present state as a poetical production is unsatisfactory. The same thing is said over again, and the contradictions in phraseology and in meaning are as numerous as the repetitions, so that one is not surprised to find it described as "the wonderful song, which causes the hair to stand on end."

Holtzrnan says:

"We have before us (in the Bhagvat Gita) a Vishnuite revision of a pantheistic poem."

Garbe observes :

"The whole character of the poem in its design and execution is preponderatingly theistic. A personal God Krishna stands forth in the form of a human hero, expounds his doctrine, enjoins, above all things, on his listener, along with the performance of his duties, loving faith in Him and self-surrender:...... And by the side of this God—(who is) delineated as personally as possible, and who dominates the whole poem—stands out frequently the impersonal neutral Brahman, the Absolute, as the highest principle.

At one time Krishna says that He is the sole Highest God who has created the world and all beings and rules over it all ; at another time, he expounds the Vedantic doctrine of Brahman and *maya-the* Cosmic Illusion, and expounds as the highest goal of human being that he be freed from the World-Illusion and become Brahman. These two doctrines—the theistic and the pantheistic—are mixed up with each other, and follow each other, sometimes quite unconnected and sometimes loosely connected. And it is not the case that the one is represented as a lower, exoteric. (Text p. 9) and, (p.) as the higher esoteric doctrine. It is nowhere taught that the Theism is a preliminary step to the knowledge of the reality or that it is its symbol, and that the pantheism of the Vedanta is the (ultimate) reality itself ; but the two beliefs are treated of almost throughout as though there was indeed no difference between them, either verbal or real." Mr. Telang says :

"There are several passages in the Gita which it is not very easy to reconcile with one another ; and no attempt is made to harmonise them. Thus, for example, in stanza 16 of Chapter VI I, Krishna divides his devotees into four classes, one of which consists of `men of knowledge', whom, Krishna says, he considers 'as his own self'. It would probably be difficult to imagine any expression which could indicate higher esteem. Yet in stanza 46 of chapter VI, we have it laid down, that the devotee is superior not only to the mere performer of penances, but even to the men of knowledge.

The commentators betray their gnostic bias by interpreting 'men of knowledge' in this latter passage to mean those who have acquired erudition in the Shastras and their significations. This is not an interpretation to be necessarily rejected. But there is in it a certain twisting of words, which, under the circumstances here, I am not inclined to accept. And on the other hand, it must not be forgotten, that the implications fairly derivable from Chapter IV, stanza 39 (pp. 62, 63), would seem to be rather than knowledge is superior to devotion—is the higher stage to be reached by means of devotion as the stepping stone. In another passage again at Gita, Chapter XII, stanza 12, concentration is preferred to knowledge, which also seems to me to be irreconcileable with Chapter VII, stanza 16. Take still another instance.

At Gita, Chapter B stanza 15, it is said, that 'Lord receives the sin or merit of none.' Yet at Chapter V, stanza 24 Krishna calls himself the Lord and enjoyer," of all sacrifices and penances. How, it may be well asked, can the Supreme Being 'enjoy that which he does not even receive?'

Once more at Chapter X, stanza 29, Krishna declares that 'none is hateful to me, none dear.' And yet the remarkable verse at the close of Chapter XII seem to stand in pointblank contradiction to that declaration. There through a most elaborate series of stanzas, the burden of Krishna's eloquent sermon is 'such a one is dear to me.' And again in those fine verses, where Krishna winds up his Divine Law, he similarly tells Arjuna, that he, Arjuna, is 'dear' to Krishna. And Krishna also speaks of that devotee as 'dear' to him, who may publish the mystery of the Gita among those who references Supreme Being.

And yet again, how are we to reconcile the same passage about none being 'hateful or dear' to Krishna, with his own words at Chapter XVI, stanza 18 and following stanzas? The language used in describing the 'demoniac' people there mentioned is not remarkable for sweetness towards them, while Krishna says positively, ' I hurl down such people into demoniac wombs, whereby they go down into misery and the vilest condition.' These persons are scarcely characterized with accuracy 'as neither hateful nor dear' to Krishna. It seems to me, that all these are real inconsistencies in the Gita, not such, perhaps, as might not be explained away, but such, I think, as indicate a mind making guesses at truth, as Professor Max Muller puts it, rather than a mind elaborating a complete and organized system of philosophy. There is not even a trace of consciousness on the part of the author that these inconsistencies exist. And the contexts of the various pasages indicate, in my judgment, that a half-truth is struck out here and another half-truth there, with special reference to the special subject then under discussion; but no attempt is made to organize the various half-truths which are apparently incompatible, into a symmeterical whole, where the apparent inconsistencies might possibly vanish altogether in the higher synthesis."

These are the views of what might be called modern scholars. Turning to the view of the orthodox Pandits, we again find a variety of views. One view is that the Bhagvat is not a sectarian book it pays equal respect to the three ways of salvation (1) Karma marge or the path of works (2) Bhakti marga or the path of devotion and (3) Jnana marga or the path of knowledge and preaches the efficacy of all three as means of salvation. In support of their contention that the Gita respects all the three ways of salvation and accepts the efficacy of each one of them, the Pandits point out that of the 18 Chapters of the Bhagvat Gita, Chapters I to 6 are devoted to the preaching of the Jnana marga, Chapters 7 to 12 to the preaching of Karma marga and Chapters 12 to 18 to the preaching of Bhakti marga and say that this equal distribution of its Chapters shows that the Gita upholds all the three modes of salvation.

Quite contrary to the view of the Pandits is the view of Shankaracharya and Mr. Tilak, both of whom must be classed amongst orthodox writers. Shankaracharya held the view that the Bhagvat Gita preached that the Jnana marga was the only true way of salvation. Mr. Tilak does not agree with the views of any of the other scholars. He repudiates the view that the Gita is a bundle of inconsistencies. He does not agree with the Pandits who say that the Bhagvat Gita recognizes all the three ways of salvation. Like Shankaracharya he insists that the Bhagvat Gita has a definite doctrine to preach. But he differs from Shankaracharya and holds that the Gita teaches Karma Yoga and not Jnana Yoga.

It cannot but be a matter of great surprise to find such a variety of opinion as to the message which the Bhagvat Gita preaches. One is forced to ask why there should be such divergence of opinion among scholars? My answer to this question is that scholars have gone on a false errand. They have gone on a search for the message of the Bhagvat Gita on the assumption that it is a gospel as the Koran, the Bible or the Dhammapada is. In my opinion this assumption is quite a false assumption. The Bhagvat Gita is not a gospel and it can therefore have no message and it is futile to search for one. The question will no doubt be asked : What is the Bhagvat Gita if it is not a gospel? My answer is that the Bhagvat Gita is neither a book of religion nor a treatise on philosophy. What the Bhagvat Gita does is to defend certain dogmas of religion on philosphic grounds. If on that account anybody wants to call it a book of religion or a book of philosophy he may please himself. But essentially it is neither. It uses philosophy to defend religion. My opponents will not be satisfied with a bare statement of view. They would insist on my proving my thesis by reference to specific instances. It is not at all difficult. Indeed it is the easiest task.

The first instance one comes across in reading the Bhagvat Gita is the justification of war. Arjuna had declared himself against the war, against killing people for the sake of property. Krishna offers a philosophic defence of war and killing in war. This philosophic defence of war will be found in Chapter II verses II to 28. The philosophic defence of war offered by the Bhagvat Gita proceeds along two lines of argument. One line of argument is that anyhow the world is perishable and man is mortal. Things are bound to come to an end. Man is bound to die. Why should it make any difference to the wise whether man dies a natural death or whether he is done to death as a result of violence? Life is unreal, why shed tears because it has ceased to be? Death is inevitable, why bother how if has resulted ? The second line of argument in justification of war is that it is a mistake to think that the body and the soul are one. They are separate. Not only are the two quite distinct but they differ in-as-much as the body is perishable while the soul is eternal and imperishable. When death occurs it is the body that dies. The soul never dies. Not only does it never die but air cannot dry it, fire cannot burn it, and a weapon cannot cut it. It is therefore wrong to say that when a man is killed his soul is killed. What happens is that his body dies. His soul discards the dead body as a person discards his old clothes—wears a new ones and carries on. As the soul is never killed, killing a person can never be a matter of any movement. War and killing need therefore give no ground to remorse or to shame, so argues the Bhagvat Gita.

Another dogma to which the Bhagvat Gita comes forward to offer a philosophic defence is Chaturvarnya. The Bhagvat Gita, no doubt, mentions that the Chaturvarnya is created by God and therefore sacrosanct. But it does not make its validity dependent on it. It offers a philosophic basis to the theory of Chaturvarnya by linking it to the theory of innate, inborn qualities in men. The fixing of the Varna of man is not an arbitrary act says the Bhagvat Gita. But it is fixed according to his innate, inborn qualities.

The third dogma for which the Bhagvat Gita offers a philosphic defence is the Karma marga. By Karma marga the Bhagvat Gita means the performance of the observances, such as Yajnas as a way to salvation. The Bhagvat Gita most stands out for the Karma marga throughout and is a great upholder of it. The line it takes to defend Karma yoga is by removing the excrescences which had grown upon it and which had made it appear quite ugly. The first excrescence was blind faith. The Gita tries to remove it by introducing the principle of Buddhi yoga as a necessary condition for Karma yoga. Become Stihtaprajna i.e., 'Befitted with Buddhi' there is nothing wrong in the performance of Karma kanda. The second excrescence on the Karma kanda was the selfishness which was the motive behind the performance of the Karmas. The Bhagvat Gita attempts to remove it by introducing the principle of *Anasakti* i.e., performance of karma without any attachment for the fruits of the *Karma*· Founded in Buddhi yoga and dissociated from selfish attachment to the fruits of Karma what is wrong with the dogma of Karma kand? this is how the Bhagvat Gita defends the Karma marga. It would be quite possible to continue in this strain, to pick up other dogmas and show how the Gita comes forward to offer a philosophic defence in their support where none existed before. But this could be done only if one were to write a treatise on the Bhagvat Gita it is beyond the scope of a chapter the main purpose of which is to assign to the Bhagvat Gita its proper place in the ancient Indian literature. I have therefore selected the most important dogmas just to illustrate my thesis.

Two other questions are sure to be asked in relation to my thesis. Whose are the Dogmas for which the Bhagvat Gita offers this philosophical defence? Why did it become necessary for the Bhagvat Gita to defend these Dogmas?

To begin with the first question, the dogmas which the Gita defends are the dogmas of counter-revolution as put forth in the Bible of counter-revolution namely Jaimini's Purvamimamsa. There ought to be no difficulty in accepting this proposition. If there is any it is largely due to wrong meaning attached to the word Karma yoga. Most writers on the Bhagvat Gita translate the word Karma yoga as 'action' and the word Janga yoga, as 'knowledge' and proceed to discuss the Bhagvat Gita as though it was engaged in comparing and contrasting knowledge versus action in a generlized form. This is quite wrong. The Bhagvat Gita is not concerned with any general, philosophical discussion of action versus knowledge. As a matter of fact, the Gita is concerned with the particular and not with the general. By Karma yoga or action Gita means the dogmas contained in Jaimini's Karma kanda and by Jnana yoga or knowledge it means the dogmas contained in Badarayana's Brahma Sutras. That the Gita in speaking of Karma is not speaking of activity or inactivity, quieticism or energism, in general terms but religious acts and observances cannot be denied by anyone who has read the Bhagvat Gita. It is to life the Gita from the position of a party pamphlet engaged in a controversy on small petty points and make it appear as though it was a general treatise on matters of high philosophy that this attempt is made to inflate the meaning of the words Karma and Jnana and make them words of general import. Mr. Tilak is largely to be blamed for this trick of patriotic Indians. The result has been that these false meanings have misled people into believing that the Bhagvat Gita is an independent self-contained book and has no relation to the literature that has preceded it. But if one were to keep to the meaning of the word Karma yoga as one finds it in the Bhagvat Gita itself one would be convinced that in speaking of Karma yoga the Bhagvat Gita is referring to nothing but the dogmas of Karma kanda as propounded by Jaimini which it tries to renovate and strengthen.

To take up the second question : Why did the Bhagvat Gita feel it necessary to defend the dogmas of counter-revolution? To my mind the answer is very clear. It was to save them from the attack of Buddhism that the Bhagvat Gita came into being. Buddha preached non-violence. He not only preached it but the people at large—except the Brahmins—had acepted it as the way of life. They had acquired a repugnance to violence. Buddha preached against Chaturvarnya. He used some of the most offensive similes in attacking the theory of Chaturvarnya. The frame work of Chaturvarnya had been broken. The order of Chaturvarnya had been turned upside down. Shudras and women could become sannyasis, a status which counter-revolution had denied them. Buddha had condemned the Karma kanda and the Yajnas he condemned them on the ground of *Himsa* or violence. He condemned them also on the ground that the motive behind them was a selfish desire to obtain bonus. What was the reply of the counter revolutionaries to this attack? Only this. These things were ordained by the Vedas, the Vedas were infallible, therefore the dogmas were not to be questioned. In the Buddhist age, which was the most enlightened and the most rationalistic age India has known, dogmas resting on such silly, arbitrary, unrationalistic and fragile foundations could hardly stand. People who had come to believe in non-violence as a principle of life and had gone so far as to make it a rule of life—How could they be expected to accept the dogma that the Kshatriya may kill without sinning because the Vedas say that it is his duty to kill? People who had accepted the gospel of social equality and who were remaking society on the basis of each one according to his merits—how could they accept the chaturvarnya theory of gradation, and separation of man based on birth simply because the Vedas say so? People who had accepted the doctrine of Buddha that all misery in society is due to Tanha or what Tawny calls acquisitive instinct—how could they accept the religion which deliberatly invited people to obtain boons by sacrifices merely because there is behind it the authority of the Vedas? There is no doubt that under the furious attack of Buddhism, Jaimini's counter-revolutionary dogmas were tottering and would have collapsed had they not received the support which the Bhagvat Gita gave them. The philosophic defence of the counter-revolutiona.ry doctrines given by the Bhagwat Gita is by no means impregnable. The philosophic defence offered by the Bhagvat Gita of the Kshtriya's duty to kill is to say the least puerile. To say that killing is no killing because what is killed is the body and not the soul is an unheard of defence of murder. This is one of the doctrines which make some people say that the doctrines make one's hair stand on their end. If Krishna were to appear as a lawyer acting for a client who is being tried for murder and pleaded the defence set out by him in the Bhagvat Gita there is not the slightest doubt that he would be sent to the lunatic asylum. Similarly childish is the defence of the Bhagvat Gita of the dogma of chaturvarnya.

Krishna defends it on the basis of the Guna theory of the Sankhya. But Krishna does not seem to have realized what a fool he has made of himself. In the chaturvarnya there are four Varnas. But the gunas according to the Sankhyas are only three. How can a system of four varnas be defended on the basis of a philosophy which does not recognise more than three varnas? The whole attempt of the Bhagvat Gita to offer a philosophic defence of the dogmas of counterrevolution is childish—and does not deserve a moment's serious thought. None-the-less there is not the slightest doubt that without the help of the Bhagvat Gita the counter-revolution would have died out, out of sheer stupidity of its dogmas. Mischievous as it may seem, to the revolutionaries the part played by the Bhagvat Gita, there is no doubt that it resuscitated counter-revolution and if the counterrevolution lives even today, it is entirely due to the plausibility of the philosophic defence which it received from the Bhagvat Gita— anti-Veda and anti-Yajna. Nothing can be a greater mistake than this. As will appear from other portions of the Bhagvat Gita that it is not against the authority of the vedas and shastras (XVI, 23, 24: XVII, I I, 13, 24). Nor is it against the sanctity of the yajnas (III. 9-15). It upholds the virtue of both.

There is therefore no difference between Jaimini's Purva Mimansa and the Bhagvat Gita. If anything, the Bhagvat Gita is a more formidable supporter of counter-revolution than Jaimini's Purva Mirnansa could have ever been. It is formidable because it seeks to give to the doctrines of counter-revolution that philosophic and therefore permanent basis which they never had before and without which they would never have survived. Particularly formidable than Jaimini's Purva Mimansa is the philosophic support which the Bhagvat Gita gives to the central doctrine of counterrevolution—namely Chaturvarnya. The soul of the Bhagvat Gita seems to be the defence of Chaturvarnya and securing its observance in practice, Krishna does not merely rest content with saying that Chaturvarnya is based on Guna-karma but he goes further and issues two positive injunctions.

The first injunction is contained in Chapter III verse 26. In this Krishna says: that a wise man should not by counter propaganda create a doubt in the mind of an ignorant person who is follower of Karma kand which of course includes the observance of the rules of Chaturvarnya. In other words, you must not agitate or excite people to rise in rebellion against the theory of Karma kand and all that it includes. The second injunction is laid down in Chapter XVIII verses 41-48. In this Krishna tells that every one do the duty prescribed for his Varna and no other and warns those who worship him and are his devotees that they will not obtain salvation by mere devotion but by devotion accompanied by observance of duty laid down for his Varna. In short, a Shudra however great he may be as a devotee will not get salvation if he has transgressed the duty of the Shudra—namely to live and die in the service of the higher classes. The second part of my thesis is that the essential function of the Bhagvat gita to give new support to Jaimini at least those portions of it which offer philosophic defence of

Jaimini's doctrines—has become to be written after Jaimini's Purva Mimansa had been promulgated. The third part of my thesis is that this philosophic defence of the Bhagvat Gita, of the doctrines of couter-revolution became necessary because of the attack to which they were subjected by the revolutionary and rationalistic thought of Buddhism.

I must now turn to the objections that are likely to be raised against the validity of my thesis. I see one looming large before me. I shall be told that I am assuming that the Bhagvat Gita is posterior in time to Buddhism and to Jaimini's Purva Mimansa and that this asumption has no warrant behind it. I am aware of the fact that my thesis runs counter to the most cherished view of Indian scholars all of whom, seem to be more concerned in fixing a very ancient date to the compositon of the Bhagvat Gita far anterior to Buddhism and to Jaimini than in finding out what is the message of the Bhagvat Gita and what value it has as a guide to man's life. This is particularly the case with Mr.Telang and Mr.Tilak. But as Garbe observes "To Telang, as to every Hindu—how much so ever enlightened—it is an article of faith *to* believe in so high an antiquity of the Bhagvat Gita and where such necessities are powerful criticism indeed comes to an end." In the words of Prof. Garbe : -

"The task of assigning a date to the Gita has been recognized by every one who has earnestly tried to solve the problem, as being very difficult ; and the difficulties grow (all the more) if the problem is presented two fold, viz., to determine as well the age of the original Gita as also of its revision. I am afraid that generally speaking, we shall succeed in arriving, not at any certainties, but only at probabilities in this matter."

What are the probabilities? I have no doubt that the probabilities are in favour of my thesis. Indeed so far as I can see there is nothing against it. In examining this question, I propose first to advance direct evidence from the Gita itself showing that it has been composed after Jaimini's Purva Mimansa and after Buddhism.

Chapter III verses 9-13 of the Bhagvat Gita have a special significance. In this connection it is true that the Bhagvat Gita does not refer to Jaimini by name: nor does it mention Mimansa by name. But is there any doubt that in Chapter III verses 9-

18 the Bhagvat Gita is dealing with the doctrines formulated by Jaimini in his Purva Mimansa? Even Mr. Tilak who believes in the antiquity of the Bhagvat Gita has to admit that here the Gita is engaged in the examination of the Purva Mimansa doctrines. There is another way of presenting this argument. Jaimini preaches pure and simple Karma yoga. The Bhagvat Gita on the other hand preaches *anasakti* karma. Thus the Guta preaches a doctrine which is fundamentally modified Not only the Bhagvat Gita modifies the Karma yoga but attacks the upholders of pure and simple Karma yoga in somewhat severe terms. If the Gita is prior to Jaimini one would expect Jaimini to take note of this attack of the Bhagvat Gita and reply to it. But we do not find any reference in Jaimini to this *anasakti* karma yoga of the Bhagvat Gita.

Why? The only answer is that this modification came after Jaimini and not before—which is simply another way of saying that the Bhagvat Gita was composed after Jaimini's Purva Mimansa.

If the Bhagvat Gita does not mention Purva Mimansa it does mention by name the Brahma Sutras of Badarayana. This reference to Brahma Sutras is a matter of great significance for it furnishes direct evidence for the conclusion that the Gita is later than the Brahma Sutras.

Mr. Tilak admits that the reference to the Brahma Sutras is a clear and defniite reference to the treatise of that name which we now have. It may be pointed out that Mr. Telang discusses the subject in a somewhat cavalier fashion by saying that the treatise "Brahma Sutras" referred to in the Bhagvat Gita is different from the present treatise which goes by that name. He gives no evidence for so extraordinary a proposition but relies on the conjectural statement of Mr. Weber—given in a foot-note of his Treatise in Indian Literature, again without any evidence—that the mention of Brhma Sutras in the Bhagvat Gita "may be taken as an appellative rather than as a proper name." It would not be fair to attribute any particular motives to Mr. Telang for the view he has taken on this point. But there is nothing unfair in saying that Mr. Telang shied at admitting the reference to Brahma Sutra because he saw that Weber had on the authority of Winternitz assigned 500 A.D. to the composition of the Brahma Sutras, which would have destroyed his cherished theory regarding the antiquity of the Bhagvat Gita. There is thus ample internal evidence to support the conclusion that the Gita was composed after Jaimini's Purva Mimansa and Badarayana's Brahma Sutras.

Is the Bhagvat Gita anterior to Buddhism? the question was raised by Mr. Telang:

"We come now to another point. What is the position of the Gita in regard to the great reform of Sakya Muni? The question is one of much interest, having regard particularly to the remarkable coincidences between Buddhistic doctrines and the doctrines of the Gita to which we have drawn attention in the footnotes to our translation. But the materials for deciding the question are unhappily not forth coming. Professor Wilson, indeed, thought that there was an allusion to Buddhism in the Gita. But his idea was based on a confusion between the Buddhists and the Charvakas or materialists. Failing that allusion, we have nothing very tangible but the unsatisfactory 'negative argument' based on mere non-mention of Buddhism in the Gita. That argument is not quite satisfactory to my own mind, although, as I have elsewhere pointed out, some of the ground occupied by the Gita is common to it with Buddhism, and although various previous thinkers are alluded to directly or indirectly in the Gita. There is, however, one view of the facts of this question, which appears to me to corroborate the conclusion deducible by means of the negative argument here referred to. The main points on which Budddha's protest against Brahmanism rests, seem to be the true authority of the Vedas and the true view of the differences of caste. On most points of doctrinal speculation, Buddhism is still but one aspect of the older Brahmanism. The various coincidences to which we have drawn attention show that, if there is need to show it. Well now, on both these points, the Gita, while it does not go the whole length which Buddha goes, itself embodies a protest against the views current about the time of its composition. The Gita does not, like Buddhism, absolutely reject the Vedas, but it shelves them. The Gita does not totally root out caste. It places caste on a less untenable basis. One of two hypothesis therefore presents itself as a rational theory of these facts. Either the Gita and Buddhism were alike the outward manifestation of one and the same spiritual upheaval which shook to its centre the current religion, the Gita being the earlier and less thorough going form of it ; or Buddhism having already begun to tell on Brahmanism, the Gita was an attempt to bolster it up, so to say, at its least weak points, the weaker ones being altogether abandoned. I do not accept the latter alternative, because I cannot see any indication in the Gita of an attempt to compromise with a powerful attack on the old Hindu system while the fact that, though strictly orthodox, the author of the Gita still undermines the authority, as unwisely venerated, of the Vedic revelation; and the further fact, that in doing this, he is doing what others also had done before him or about his time ; go, in my opinion, a considerable way towards fortifying the results of the negative argument already set forth. To me Buddhism is perfectly intelligible as one outcome of that play of thought on high spiritual topics, which in its other, and as we may say, less thorough going, manifestation we see in the Upanishads and the Gita."

I have quoted this passage in full because it is typical of all Hindu scholars. Everyone of them is most reluctant to admit that the Bhagvat Gita is anyway influenced by Buddhism and is ever ready to deny that the Gita has borrowed anything from Buddhism. It is the attitude of Prof. Radhakrishnan and also of Tilak. Where there is any similarity in thought between the Bhagvat Gita and Buddhism too strong and too close to be denied, the argument is that it is borrowed from the Upanishads. It is typical of the mean mentality of the counter revolutionaries not to allow any credit to Buddhism on any account.

The absurdity of these views must shock all those who have made a comparative study of the Bhagvat Gita and the Buddhist Suttas. For if it is true to say that Gita is saturated with Sankhya philosophy it is far more true to say that the Gita is full of Buddhist ideas. The similarity between the two is not merely in ideas but also in language. A few illustrations will show how true it is.

The Bhagvat Gita discusses Bramha-Nirvana. The steps by which one reaches Bramha. Nirvana are stated by the Bhagvat Gita to be (1) Shraddha (Faith in oneself); (2) Vyavasaya (Firm determination): (3) Smriti (Rememberance of the goal); (4) Samadhi (Earnest contemplation) and (5) Prajna (Insight or True Knowledge). From where has the Gita borrowed this

Nirvana theory? Surely it is not borrowed from the Upanishads. For no Upanishad even mentions the word Nirvana. The whole idea is peculiarly Buddhist and is borrowed from Buddhism. Anyone who has any doubt on the point may compare this Bramha-Nirvana of the Bhagvat Gita with the Buddhist conception of Nirvana as set out in the Mahapari-nibbana Sutta, It will be found that they are the same which the Gita has laid down for Bramha-Nirvana. Is it not a fact that the Bhagvat Gita has borrowed the entire conception of Brmhma Nirvana instead of Nirvana for no other reason except to conceal the fact of its having stolen it from Buddhism?

Take another illustration. In Chapter VII verses 13-20 there is a discussion as to who is dear to Krishna; one who has knowledge, or one who performs karma or one who is adevotee. Krishna says that the Devotees is dear to him but adds that he must have the true marks of a Devotee. What is the charcter of a true Devotee? According to Krishna the true devotee is one who practices (1) Maitri; (loving Kindness); (2) Karuna (compassion): (3) Mudita (sympathizing joy) and (4) Upeksa (unconcernedness). From where has the Bhagvate Gita borrowed these qualifications of a perfect Devotee? Here again, the source is Buddhism. Those who want proof may compare the Mahapadana Sutta, and the Tevijja Sutta where Buddha has preached what Bhavanas (mental attitude) are necessary for one to cherish for the training of the heart. This comparison will show that the whole ideology is borrowed from Buddhism and that too word for word.

Take a third illustration. In chapter XIII the Bhagvat Gita descusses the subject of Kshetra-Kshetrajna. In verses 7-11 Krishna points out what is knowledge and what is ignorance in the following language:

"Pridelessness (Humility), Unpretentiousness, Non-injury or Harmlessness, Forgiveness, Straight-forwardness, (uprightness), Devotion to Preceptor, Purity, Steadiness, Self-restraint, Desirelessness towards objects of sense, absence of Egoism, Reflection on the suffering and evil of Birth, Death, decrepitude and disease, Non-attachment, Non-identification of oneself with regard to son, wife and home and the rest, Constant even-mindedness on approach of both (what is) agreeable and (what is) disagreeable unswerving devotion to

Me with undivided meditation of Me, Resort to sequestered spots (contemplation, concentration, in solitude), Distaste for the society of worldly men, Incessant application to the knowledge relating to self, Perception or realisation of the true purport of the knowledge of the Tattvas (Samkhya Philosophy), all this is called 'knowledge'; what is Ajnana (Ignorance) which is the reverse thereof." Can anyone who knows anything of the Gospel of Buddha deny that the Bhagvat Gita has not in these stanzas reproduced word for word the main doctrines of Buddhism?

In chapter XIII verses 5, 6, 18, 19, the Bhagvat Gita gives a new metaphorical interpretation of karmas under various heads (1) Yajnas (sacrifices); (2) Dana (Gifts); (3) Tapas (penances); (4) Food and (5) Svadhyaya (Vedic study). What is the source of this new interpretation of old ideas ? Compare with this what Buddha is reported to have said in the Majjhina Nikaya 1, 286 Sutta XVI. Can anyone doubt that what Krishna says in verses 5,6, 18, 19 of chapter XVII is a verbatim reproduction of the words of Buddha?

These are only a few illustrations I have selected those of major doctrinal importance. Those who are interested in pursuing the subject may take up the reference to similarities between Gita and Buddhism given by Telang in the footnotes to his edition of the Bhagvat Gita and satisfy their curiosity. But the illustrations I have given will be enough to show how greatly the Bhagvat Gita is permeated by Buddhistic ideology and how much the Gita has borrowed from Buddhism. To sum up the Bhagvat Gita seems to be deliberately modelled on Buddhists Suttas. The Buddhists Suttas are dialogues. So is the Bhagvat Gita. Buddha's religion offered salvation to women and Shudras. Krishna also comes forward to offer salvation to women and Shudras. Buddhists say, "I surrender to Buddha, to Dhamma and to Sangha." So Krishna says, "Give up all religions and surrender unto Me." No parallel can be closer than what exists between Buddhism and Bhagvat Gita.

I have shown that Gita is later than Purva Mimansa and also later than Buddhism. I could well stop here. But I feel I cannot. For there still remains one argument against my thesis which requires to be answered. It is the argument of Mr. Tilak. It is an ingenious argument. Mr. Tilak realizes that there are many similarities in ideas and in words between the Bhagvat Gita and Buddhism. Buddhism being earlier than the Bhagvat Gita, the obvious conclusion is that the Bhagvat Gita is the debtor and Buddhism is the creditor. This obvious conclusion is not palatable to Mr. Tilak or for the matter of that to all upholders of counter-revolution. With them it is a question of honour that counter-revolution should not be shown to be indebted to Revolution. To get over this difficulty Mr. Tilak has struck a new line. He points out the distinction between Hinayana Buddhism and Mahayana Buddhism and say, that Mahayana Buddhism was later than Bhagvat Gita and if there are any similarities between the Buddhism and Bhagvat Gita it is due to the borrowing by the Mahayanist from the Bhagvat Gita. This raises two questions. What is the date of the origin of the Mahayana Buddhism? What is the date of the composition of the Bhagvat Gita? The argument of Mr. Tilak is ingenious and clever. But it has no substance. In the first place, it is not original. It is based on certain casual remarks made by Winternitz and by Kern in foot-notes that there are certain similarties between the Bhagvat Gita and the Mahayan Buddhism and that there similarities are the result of Mahayana Buddhism borrowing its ideas from the Bhagvat Gita. Behind these remarks there is no evidence of special research either on the part of Winternitz, Kern or Mr. Tilak. All of them seem to be led away by the assumption that the Bhagvat Gita is earlier than Mahayana Buddhism.

This leads me to examine the question of the date of the Bhagvat Gita particularly with reference to the theory as put forth by Mr. Tilak. Mr. Tilak is of opinion that the Gita is part of the Mahabharata and that both have been written by one and the same author named Vyasa and consequently the date of the Mahabharata must be the date of the Bhagvat Gita. The Mahabharata, Mr. Tilak argues, must have been written at least 500 years before the Shaka Era on the groung that the stories contained in the Mahabharata were known to Megasthenes who was in India about 300 B.C. as a Greek ambassador to the court of Chandragupta Maurya. The Shaka Era began in 78 A.D. On this basis it follows that the Bhagvat Gita must have been composed before 422 B.C. This is his view about the date of the composition of the present Gita. According to him, the original Gita must have been some centuries older than Mahabharata If reliance be placed on the tradition referred to in the Bhagvat Gita that the religion of the Bhagvat Gita was taught by Nara to Narayan in very ancient times. Mr. Tilak's theory as to the date of the composition of the Mahabharata is untenable. In the first place, it assumes that the whole of the Bhagvat Gita and the whole of Mahabharat have been written at one stretch, at one time and by one hand. There is no warrant for such an assumption, either in tradition, or in the internal evidence of these two treatises. Confining the discussion to the Mahabharata the assumption made by Mr. Tilak is quite opposed to well-known Indian traditions. This tradition divides the compostion of the Mahabharata into three stages; (1) Jaya (2) Bharata and (3) Mahabharata and assigns to each part a different author.

According to this tradition Vyasa was the author of the 1st edition so to say of the Mahabharata called 'Jaya'. Of the Second Edition called 'Bharata' tradition assigns the authorship to Vaishampayana and that of the Third Edition called Mahabharata to `Sauti'. That this tradition is well-founded has been confirmed by the researches of Prof. Hopkins based on the examination of internal evidence furnished by the Mahabharata. According to Prof. Hopkins there have been several stages in the composition of the Mahabharata. As has been pointed out by Prof. Hopkins in the first stage it was just a Pandu Epic consisting of plays and legends about heroes who took part in the Mahabharata war without the masses of didactic material. Such a Mahabharata, says Prof. Hopkins, may have come into existence between 400-200 B.C.

The second stage was the remaking of the epic by the inclusion of didactic matter and the addition of Puranic material. This was between 200 B.C. and 200 A.D. The third stage is marked when (1) the last books were added to the composition as it stood at the end of the second stage with the introduction of the first book and (2) the swollen Anushasana Parva was separated from Shanti Parva and recognized as a separate book. This happened between 200 to 400 A.D. To these three stages Prof. Hopkins adds a fourth or a final stage of occasional amplification which started from 400 A.D. onwards. In coming to this conclusion Prof. Hopkins has anticipated and dealt with all the arguments advanced by Mr. Tilak such as the mention of Mahabharata in Panini and in the Grihyasutras. The only new pieces of evidence produced by Mr. Tilak which has not been considered by Prof. Hopkins are two. One such piece of evidence consists of the statements which are reported to have been recorded by Megasthenes· the Greek Ambassador to the court of Chandra Gupta Maurya, and the other is the astronomical evidence, in the Adi Parva which refers to the Uttarayana starting with the Shravana constellation. The facts adduced by Mr. Tilak as coming from Megasthenes may not be denied and may go to prove that at the time of Megasthenes i.e., about 300 B.C. a cult of Krishna worship had come into existence among the Sauraseni community. But how can this prove that the Mahabharata had then come into existence? It cannot. Nor can it prove that the legends and stories mentioned by Megasthenes were taken by him from the Mahabharata. For there is nothing to militate against the view that these legends and stories were a floating mass of Saga and that it served as a reservoir both to the writer of the Mahabharata as well as to Greek Ambassador.

Mr. Tilak's astronomical evidence may be quite sound. He is right in sayingthat "it is stated in the Anugita that Visvamitra started the enumeration of the constellation with Shravana (Ma.Bha.Asva.44.2, and Adi.71.34). That has been interpreted by commentators as showing that the Uttarayana then started with the Shravana constellation, and no other interpretation is proper. At the date of the Vedanga-Jyotisa, the Uttarayana used to start with the Sun in the Dhanistha constellation. According to astronomical calculations, the date when the Uttarayana should start with the Sun in the Dhanistha constellation to about 1,500 years before the Saka era; and according to astronomical calculations, it takes about a thousand years for the Uttarayana to start one constellation earlier. According to this calculation, the date when the Uttarayana ought to start with the Sun in the Shravana constellation comes to about 500 years before the Saka era. This conculsion would have been proper if it was true that the Mahabharata was one whole piece, written at one time by one author. It has, however, been shown that there is no warrant for such an assumption. In view of this Mr. Tilak's astroncomical evidence cannot be used to determine the date of the Mahabharata. It cam be used only to determine the date of that part of the Mahabharata which is affected by it—in this case the Adi Parva of the Mahabharata. For these reasons Mr. Tilak's theory as to the date of the composition of the Mahabharata must fall to the ground. Indeed any attempt to fix a single date for a work like the Mahabharata which is a serial story produced in parts at long intervals must be regarded as futile. All that one can say is that the Mahabharata was composed between 400B.C. to 400A.D. a conclusion too broad to be used for the purpose which Mr. Tilak has in view. Even this span seems to some scholars to be too narrow. It is contended that the reference to *Edukas* in the 190th Adhyaya of the Vanaparva has been wrongly interpreted to mean Buddhist Stupas when, as a matter of fact, it refers to the I*dgahas* created by the Muslim invaders for Muslim converts. If this interpretation is correct it would show that parts of the Mahabharata were written about or after the invasions of Mohammed Ghori.

Let me now turn to examine Mr. Tilak's theory as to the date of the composition of the Bhagvat Gita. There are really two propositions underlying his theory. First is that the Gita is part of the Mahabharata, both are written at one time and are the handiwork of one man. His second proposition is that the Bhagvat Gita has been the same what it is today from the very beginning when it first came to be written. To avoid confusion I propose to take them separately.

Mr. Tilak's object in linking the Gita with the Mahabharata in the matter of its composition is quite obvious. It is to have the date of the Mahabharata which he thinks is known to derermine the date of the Bhagvat Gita which is unknown. The basis on which Mr. Tilak has tried to establish an integral connection between the Mahabharata and the Bhagvat Gita is unfortunately the weakest part of his theory. To accept that the Gita is a part of the Mahabharata because the author of both is Vyasa- and this is the argument of Mr. Tilak—is to accept a fiction for a fact. It assumes that Vyasa is the name of some particular individual capable of being identified. This is evident from the fact that we have Vyasa as the author of the Mahabharata, Vyasa as the author of the Puranas, Vyasa as the author of Bhagvat Gita and Vyasa as the author of the

Bramha Sutras. It cannot therefore be accepted as true that the same Vyasa is the author of all these works separated as they are by a long span of time extending to several centuries. It is well-known how orthodox writers wishing to hide their identity get better authority for their works by the use of a revered name were in the habit of using Vyasa as a nom-de-plume or pen name. If the author of the Gita is a Vyasa he must be a different Vyasa. There is another argument which seems to militate against Mr. Tilak's theory of synchroniety between the composition of the Bhagvat Gita and the Mahabharata. The Mahabharata consists of 18 Parvas. There are also 18 Puranas. It is curious to find that Bhagvat Gita has also 18 Adhyayas. The question is : Why should there be this parallelism? The answer is that the ancient Indian writers regarded certain names and certain numbers as invested with great sanctity. The name Vyasa and the number 18 are illustrations of this fact. But there is more in the fixation of 18 as the chapters of the Bhagvat Gita than is apparent on the face of it. Who set 18 as the sacred number, the Mahabharata or the Gita? If the Mahabharata, then Gita must have been written after the Mahabharata. If it is the Bhagvat Gita, then the Mahabharata must have been written after the Gita. In any case, the two could not have been written at one and the same time.

These considerations may not be accepted as decisive against Mr. Tilak's first proposition. But there is one which I think is decisive. I refer to the relative position of Krishna in the Mahabharata and in the Bhagvat Gita. In the Mahabharata, Krishna is nowhere represented as a God accepted by all. The Mahabharata itself shows the people were not prepared even to give him the first place. When at the time of the Rajasuya Yajna, Dharma offered to give Krishna priority in the matter of honouring the guest, Shishupala—the near relation of Krishna—protested and abused Krishna. He not only charged him with low origin, but also with loose morals, an intriguer who violated rules of war for the sake of victory. So abhorent but so true was this record of Krishna's foul deeds that when Duryodhan flung them in the face of Krishna, the Mahabharata itself in the Gada Parva records that the Gods in heaven came out to listen to the charges made by Duryodhan against Krishna and after listening showered flowers as a token of their view that the charges contained the whole truth and nothing but the truth. On the other hand, the Bhagvat Gita presented Krishna as God omnipotent, omniscient, omnipresent, pure, loving, essence of goodness. Two such works containing two quite contradictory estimates about one and the same personality could not have been written at one and the same time by one and the same author. It is a pity that Mr. Tilak in his anxiety to give a pre-Buddhist date to the composition of the Bhagvat Gita should have completely failed to take note of these important considerations.

The second proposition of Mr. Tilak is equally unsound. The attempt to fix a date for the composition of the Bhagvat Gita is nothing but the pursuit of a mirage. It is doomed to failure. The reason is that the Bhagvat Gita is not a single book written by a single author. It consists of different parts written at different times by different authors.

Prof. Garbe is the only scholar who has seen the necessity of following this line of inquiry. Prof. Garbe hold that there are two parts of the Bhagvat Gita one original and one added. I am not satisfied with this statement. My reading of the Bhagvat Gita leads me to the conclusion that there have been four separate parts of Bhagvat Gita. They are so distinct that taking even the present treatise as it stands they can be easily marked off.

(i) The original Gita was nothing more than a heroic tale told or a ballad recited by the bards of how Arjuna was not prepared to fight and how Krishna forced him to engage in battle, how Arjuna yielded and so on. It may have been a romantic story but there was nothing religious or philosophical in it.

This original Gita will be found embedded in Chapter I, Chapter II, verses.. . .. and Chapter XI verses 32-33 in which Krishna is reported to have ended the argument:

" Be my tool, carry out my will, don't worry about sin and evil resulting from fighting, do as I tell you, don't be impudent.". This is the argument which Krishna used to compel Arjuna to fight. And this argument of coercion and compulsion made Arjuna yield. Krishna probably threatened Arjuna with brute force if he did not actually use it. The assumption of Vishva-rupa by Krishna is only different way of describing the use of brute force. On that theory it is possible that the chapter in the present Bhagvat Gita dealing with Vishva-rupa is also a part of the original Bhagvat Gita.

(ii) The first patch on the original Bhagvat Gita is the part in which Krishna is spoken of as Ishvara the God of the Bhagvat religion. This part of the Gita is embedded in those verses of the present Bhagvat Gita which are devoted to Bhakti Yoga.

(iii) The second patch on the original Bhagvat Gita is the part which introduces the Sankhya and the Vedanta philosophy as a defence to the doctrines of Purva Mimansa which they did not have before. The Gita was originally only a historical Saga with the cult of Krishna came to be interwoven. The Philosophy portion of the Bhagvat Gita was a later intrusion can be proved quite easily from the nature of the original dialogue and the sequence of it.

In chapter I verses 20-47 Arjuna mentions those difficulties. In chapter II Krishna attempts to meet the difficulties mentioned by Arjuna. There are arguments and counter arguments. Krishna's first argument is contained in verse 2 and 3 in which Krishna tells Arjuna that his conduct is infamous, unbecoming an Arya and that he should not play the part of an effeminate which was unworthy of him. To this, Arjuna gives a reply which is embodied in verses 4 to 8. In verses 4 to 5 he says, "how can I kill Bhishma and Drona who are entitled to highest reverence: it would be better to live by begging than kill them. I do not wish to live to enjoy a kindom won by killing old revered elders. " In verses 6 to 8 Arjuna says: "I do not know which of the two is more meritorious, whether we should vanquish the Kauravas or whether we should be vanquished by them. "Krishna's reply to this is contained in verses 11 to 39 in which he propounds (i) that grief is unjustified because things are imperishable, (ii) that it is a false view that a man is killed when the atman is eternal and (iii) that he must fight because it is the duty of the Kshatriya to fight. Any one who reads the dialogue will notice the following points:

(1) The questions put by Arjuna are *not* philosophical questions. They are natural questions put by a worldly man faced with worldly problems.

(2) Upto a point Krishna treats them as natural questions and returns to them quite natural replies.

(3) The dialogue takes a new turn. Arjuna after having informed Krishna positively and definitely that he will not fight, suddenly takes a new turn and expresses a doubt whether it is agood to kill the Kauravas or be killed by them.This is a deliberate departure designed to give Krishna a philosophical defence of war, uncalled for by anything said by Arjuna.

(4) Again there is a drop in the tone of Krishna from verses 31 to 38. He treats the question as natural and tells him to fight because it is the duty of the Kshatriya to fight.

Anyone can see from this that the introduction of the Vedanta philosophy is quite unnatural and therefore a later intrusion. With regard to the introduction of the Sankhya philosophy the case is quite obvious. Often it is expounded without any question by Arjuna and whenever it has been propounded in answer to a question that question has nothing to do with the war. This shows that the philosophic parts of the Bhagvat Gita are not parts of the original Gita but have been added later on and in order to find a place for them, new, appropriate and leading questions have been put in the mouth of Arjuna which have nothing to do with the mundane problems of war.

(iv) The third patch on the oriinal Bhagvat Gita consists of verses in which Krishna is elevated from the position of Ishwara to that of Parmeshwara. This patch can be easily detected as being chapters X and XV where Krishna says: (Quotation not mentioned) .... As I said, to go in for a precise date for the composition of the Bhagvat Gita is to go on a fool's errand and that if an attempt in that direction is to be of any value, effort must be directed to determine the date of each patch separately. Proceeding in this way it is possible that what I have called the original unphilosophic Bhagvat Gita was part of the first edition of the Mahabharata called Jaya. The first patch on the original Bhagvat Gita in which Krishna is depicted as Ishvara must be placed in point of date sometimes later than Megasthenes when Krishna was only a tribal God. How much later it is not possible to say. But it must be considerably later. For it must be remembered that the

Brahmins were not friendly to Krishnaism in the beginning. In fact they were opposed to it. It must have taken some time before the Brahmins could have become reconciled to Krishna worship. The second patch on the original Bhavat Gita having reference to Sankhya and Vedanta must for reason already given be placed later than the Sutras of Jaimini and Badarayana. The question of the date of these Sutras has carefully been examined by Prof. Jacobi· His conclusion is that these Sutras were composed sometime between 200 and 450 A.D.

The third patch on the original Bhagvat Gita in which Krishna is raised into Parmeshvara must be placed during the reign of the Gupta Kings. The reason is obvious. Gupta kings made Krishna-Vas.udev their family deity as their opponents the Shaka kings had made Mahadeo their family deity. The Brahmins to whom religion has been a trade, who were never devoted to one God but came forward to worship the deity of the ruling race thought of pleasing their masters by making their family deity into a high and mighty Parmeshvar. If this is correct explanation then this patch on the original Bhagvat Gita must be placed between 400 and 464 A.D.

All this goes to confirm the view that the attempt to place the Bhagvat Gita prior in point of time to Buddhism cannot succeed. It is the result of wishful thinking on the part of those who have inherited a positive dislike to Buddha and his revolutionary gospel. History does not support it. History proves quite abnormally that at any rate those portions of the Bhagvat Gita which have any doctrinal value are considerably later in point of time to the Buddhist canon and the Sutras of Jaimini and Badarayana.

The discussion of the dates not only proves that the Bhagvat Gita is later than Hinayana Buddhism but is also later than Mahayana Buddhism. The impression prevails that Mahayana Buddhism is later in origin. It is supposed to have come into being after A.D. 100 when Kanishka held the third Buddhist Council to settle the dissension in the Buddhist Church. This is absolutely a mistake. It is not true that after the Council a new creed of Buddhism came into existence. What happened is that new names of abuse came into existence for parties which were very old. As Mr. Kimura has shown the Mahayanist is simply another name for the sect of Buddhists known as

Mahasanghikas. The sect of Mahasanghikas had come into being very much earlier than is supposed to be the case. If tradition be believed the sect had come into being at the time of the First Buddhist Council held at Pataliputra 236 years after the death of Buddha i.e., 307 B.C or settling the Buddhist canon and is said to have led the opposition to the Theravad sect of Buddhism which later on came to be stigmatized as Hinayana (which means those holding to the low path). There could hardly be any trace of Bhagvat Gita when the Mahasanghikas later known as Mahayanists came into being.

Apart from this what have the Mahayanists borrowed from the Bhagvat Gita? Indeed what can they borrow from the Bhagvat Gita? As Mr. Kimura points out the doctrine of every school of Buddhism is mainly concerned at least with three doctrines: (1) Those which deal with cosmic existence; (2) Those which deal with Buddhology; and (3) Those which deal with conception of human life. Mahayana is no exception to this. Except probably on Buddhology the Mahayanists could hardly use the Bhagvat Gita to draw upon So different is the aproach of the two on the other doctrines and even this possibility is excluded by the factor of time.

The foregoing discussion completely destroys the only argument that could be urged against my thesis—namely that the Bhagvat Gita is very ancient, pre-Buddhistic in origin and therefore could not be related to Jaimini's Purva Mimansa and treated as an attempt to give a philosophic defence of his counter-revolutionary doctrines. To sum up, my thesis is three-fold. In other words it has three parts. First is that the Bhagvat Gita is fundamentally a counter-revolutionary treatise of the same class as Jamini's Purva Mimansa—the official Bible of counter-revolution. Some writers relying on verses 40-46 of Chapter II hold the view that the Bhagvat Gita is,

{In all the copies available with us, the essay has been left here incomplete, as is seen from the above sentence—Editors.)

Analytical Notes of Virat Parva & Udyog Parva

Virat Parva

1. The spies sent by Kauravas to search for the existence of the Pandavas return to Duryodhan and tell him that they

are unable to discover them. They ask his permission as to what to do Virat Parva, Adhya. 25.

2. Duryodhan asks for advice from his advisers. Kama said send other spies. Dushasan said they might have gone beyond the sea. But search for them.—*Ibid.* —Adhya. 26.

3. Drona said the Pandavas are not likely to be defeated or destroyed. They may be living as Tapasis. therefore send Siddhas and Brahamins as spies— *Ibid.* Adhya 27.

4. Bhishma supports Drona—*Ibid* Adhya. 28.

5. Kripacharya supported Bhishma and added—Pandavas are great enemies. But wise man does not neglect even small enemies. While they are in *Agnyatavasa* you should go on collecting armies from now.— *Ibid* Adhya. 29.

6. Then Susharma King of Trigarth raised quite a different subject. He said that *Kichaka* who was the *Senapati* of King Virat I hear dead, King Virat is to give us great trouble. Kichaka having been dead Virat must have become very weak. Why not invade the Kingdom of Virat? This is the most opportune time. Kama also supported Susharma. Why worry about the Pandavas, these Pandavas are without wealth, without army and fallen. Why bother with them? They might have even been dead by now. Give up the search and let undertake the project of Susharma—*Ibid* Adhya. 30.

7. Susharma's invasion of Vairat. Susharma carries away the cows of Virat. The cow herds go and inform Virat of this and ask him to pursue Susharma and rescue the cows.—*Ibid* Adhya. 31.

8. Virat became ready for war. In the meanwhile *Shatanik* the younger brother of Virat suggested that instead of going alone he

might take with him Kank (Sahadeo) Ballava (Yudhishtira) Santipal (Bhima) and Granthik (Nakula) to help him to fight Susharma. Virat agreed and they all went—*Ibid.* Adhya. 31.

9. War between Shusharma and Virat—*Ibid* Adhya. 32.

10. Yudhishthira rescues Virat.—*Ibid.* Adhya. 33.

11. Announcement in the Virat Nagari that their King is safe.— *Ibid* Adhya. 34.

Entry in Virat Nagari by Kaurvas

12. While King Virat went after Susharman Duryodhan with *Bhishma, Drona, Kama, Krapa, Ashvashthama, Shakuni, Dushashana, Vivinshati, Vikarna, Chitrasen, Durmukha, Dushala* and other warriers entered the Virat Nagari and captured the cows of Virat and were going away. The cowherds came to the palace of King Virat and gave the news. They need not find the King but they found his son *Uttar* so they gave him the news.—*Ibid* Adhya. 35.

13. *Uttar* began to boast saying he was superior to Arjuna and would do the job. But his complaint was that there was no one to act his *Sarathi. Draupadi went and told him that Brahannada* was at one time the Sarathi of Arjuna. Why not ask him? He said he had no courage and requested Draupadi to make the request. Why not ask your younger sister *Manorama.* So he told Manorama to bring Brahannada—*Ibid* Adhya. 36.

14. Manorama takes Brahannada to his brothers and Uttara persuades him to be his Sarathi. Brahannada agreed and took the Rath of Uttara in front of the Kauravas—*Ibid.* Adhya. 37.

15. On seeing the army of the Kauravas Uttara left the Rath and started running away. Arjuna stopped him. The Kauravas seeing this began to suspect that the man might be Arjuna. Arjuna told him not to be afraid—*Ibid* Adhya. 38.

16. Arjuna took his Ratha to the Shami tree. Seeing this Drona said he must be Arjuna. Hearing this the Kauravas were greatly upset. But Duryodhana said if Drona is right it is good for us. Because it is before the thirteenth year that the Pandavas will have been discovered and they will have to suffer Vanavas again for 12 years.—*Ibid* Adhya. 39.

17. Arjuna asks Uttara to climb the Shami tree and to take down the weapons.—*Ibid* Adhya. 40.

18. Uttara's doubts about the corpse on the Shami *Tree—Ibid* Adhya. 41.

19. Uttara's excitement after seeing the weapons—*Ibid* Adhya. 42.

20. Arjuna's description of the weapons.—*Ibid* Adhya. 43.

21. Uttara's Inquiry regarding the whereabouts about the Pandavas.—*Ibid* Adhya. 44.

22. Climbing down of Uttara from the tree—*Ibid* Adhya. 45.

23. The Rath with Vanar Symbol. Drona becomes sure that he is Arjuna. Bad omens seen by the army of the Kauravas.—*Ibid* Adhya. 46.

24. Duryodhan encourages the soldiers who were frightened by Drona's saying that it was Arjuna. Kama's slander of Drona and proposal to Duryodhan to remove Drona as a Commander-in-Chief.— *Ibid* Adhya. 47.

25. Boasting by Kama and Pratijna to defeat Arjuna— *Ibid* Adhya. 48.

26. Krapacharya's admonition to Kama not to brag and boast. War is regarded as bad by the Shastras—*Ibid* Adhya. 49.

27. Ashvasthama abuses Kama and Duryodhan because of their slander of Drona—*Ibid* Adhya. 50.

28. Ashavashthama abused Kama and Duryodhan for speaking ill of Drona. Kama replied, 'after all I am only a Suta.,' But Arjuna has behaved as bad as Rama behaved towards Vali—*Ibid* Adhya. 50.

29. Ashvashthama was quieted by Bhisma, Drona and Krapa, Duryodhan and Kama tendered apology to Drona— - *Ibid* Adhya. 51. 30. Bhishma's decision that the Pandavas have completed 13 years.— *ibid* Adhya. 52.

31. Arjuna has defeated the army of the Kauravas.— *Ibid* Adhya. 53.

32. Arjuna defeats Kama's *Bhrata.* Arjuna defeats Kama and Kama runs away— *Ibid* Adhya. 54.

33. Arjuna destroys the army of the Kauravas and breaks the Rath of Kripacharya—Ibid Adhya. 55.

34. Gods came out in heaven to witness the fight between Arjuna and the army of the Kauravas—*Ibid* Adhya. 56.

35. Battle between Krapa and Arjuna and the running away of Krapa.—*Ibid* Adhya. 57.

36. Battle between Drona and Arjuna and running away of Drona.—*Ibid* Adhya. 58.

37. Battle between Ashavashthama and Arjuna—*Ibid* Adhya. 59.

38. Battle between Kama and Arjuna, defeat of Kama—Adhya. 60.

39. Attack on Bhishma by Arjuna—*Ibid* Adhya. 61.

40. Arjuna kills the Kauravas soldiers—*Ibid* Adhya. 62.

41. Defeat of Bhishma and his running away from the Battle-field— *Ibid* Adhya. 64.

42. Fainting of the soldiers of the Kauravas. Bhishmas telling them to return home.—*Ibid* Adhya. 66.

43. Kaurava soldiers surrendering to Arjuna from *Abhay*. Uttar and Arjuna return to Virat Nagari— I*bid* Adhya. 67.

44. Virat enters his capital and his people honouring him.—*Ibid* Adhya. 68.

45. The Pandavas enter the King's Assembly.—Ibid Adhya. 69.

46. Arjuna introduces his other brothers in Virat.— *Ibid* Adhya. 71.

47. Marriage between Arjuna's son and the daughter of Virat.— -*lbid* Adhya. 72.

48. Thereafter the Pandavas leave Virat Nagari and live in Upaplowya Nagari— Ibid Adhya. 72.

49. Arjuna thereafter brought his son Abhimanyu, Vasudev, and Yadav from Anrut Desh—*lbid* Adhya. 72.

50. Friends of Yudhisthir such as Kings Kashiraj and Shalya came with two Akshauhini army. Similarly Yagyasen Drupadraj came with one Akshauhini. Draupadi's all sons Ajinkya, Shikhandi, Drustadumna also came .—*Ibid* 72.

Udyogaparva

1. After the marriage of Abhimanyu the Yadavas and the Pandavas met in the Sabha of King Virat. Krishna addresses them as to what is to be done about the future. We must do what is good both Kauravas and Pandavas. Dharma will accept anything—even one villaga—by *Dharma*. Even if he is given the whole kingdom by Duryodhana he will not accept it. Upto now the Pandavas have observed *Niti*. But if the Kauravas

observe *Aniti* the Pandavas will not hesitate to kill the Kauravas. Let nobody be afraid on account of the fact that the Pandavas are a minority. They have many friends who will come to their rescue. We must try to know the wishes of the Kauravas. I suggest that we should send a messanger to Duryodhan and ask him to give part of the Kingdom to the Pandavas.—Udyog Parva, Adhya. 1.

2. Balaram supports the proposal of Krishna but added that it was the fault of Dharma knowing that he was losing at the hands of Shakuni. Therefore instead of fighting with the Kauravas get what you can by negotiation.— *lhid,* Adhya. 2.

3. Satyaki got up and condemned Balaram for his attitude—*Ibid,* Adhya. 3.

4. Drupad supports Satyaki. Drupad agrees to send his Purohit as a messanger—*Ibid,* Adhya. 4.

5. Krishna supports Drupad and goes to Dwarka. Kings invited by Drupad and Virat arrive. Similarly Kings invited by Duryodhan arrive.— *lhid.* Adhva. 5.

6. Drupada instructs his purohit how to speak in the assembly and deal with the issue.—*Ibid* Adhya. 6.

7. Arjuna and Duryodhana both go to Dwarka to ask for his aid in the war. He said I will help you both. I can give my army to one and I can join one singly. Choose what you want. Duryodhan chose the army. Arjuna choose Krishna.—*Ibid* Adhya. 7.

8. Coming of Shalya to the Pandavas with alarge army. Duryodhan thinks him lower. Meeting of Shalya and Pandavas. Pandavas request Shalya to discourage Kama in the war. Agreement of Shalya.— *Ibid.* Adhya. 8.

9. Adhya. 9—Irrelevant. 1

10. Adhya. 10—Irrelevant.

11. Adhya. II—Irrelevant.

12. Adhya. 12—Irrelevant.

13. Adhya. 13—Irrelevant.

14. Adhya. 14—Irrelevant.

15. Adhya. 15—Irrelevant.

16. Adhya. 16—Irrelevant.

17. Adhya. 17—Irrelevant.

18. Adhya. 18—Irrelevant.

19. Adhya—Satyaki comes to Pandvas with his army and Bhagadatta went to Duryodhana.

20. Adhya. 20—The Purohit of Drupada enters the Kauravas Sabha. The Purohit said that the Pandvas are prepared to part evil deeds of the Kauravas and make a compromise with them. He told them that the Pandavas have a large army yet they wish to compromise.

21. Adhya. 21—Bhishma supports the Purohit. Kama objects. Dispute between Bhishma and Kama. Dhratrarashtra suggests that Sanjaya be sent for negotiation on their behalf.

22. Adhya. 22—Dhratrarashtra sends Sanjaya to go to the Pandvas and give his blessings and say what you think best for the occasion and which will not advance enmity between the two.

23. Adhya. 23—Sanjaya's going to the Pandvas.

24. Adhya. 24—Conversation betwen Sanjaya and Yudhistira.

25. Adhya. 25—Sanjaya condemns war.

26. Adhya. 26—Dharma says 'I am prepared to compromise if the Kauravas give us our Kingdom of Indraprastha.

27. Adhya. 27—It is *Adharma* to kill *Gurujan* and obtain a Kingdom. If the Kauravas refuse to give you any kingdom without war you had better live by begging in the Kingdom of Vrishni and Andhakas.

28. Adhya. 28—Says, Dharma Blame us Sanjaya if you think we have acted or acting against Dharma. Sanjaya says I want Swadharma or Sama.

29. Adhya. 29—Krishna's address to Sanjaya why war is legitimate and asks him to go and tell his views to Dhratarashtra.

30. Adhya. 30—Sanjaya returns to Kauravas and tells Duryodhana to war. Duryodhan either to return Indraprastha to the Pandavas or be ready for war.

31. Adhya. 30—Sanjaya tells Duryodhan to live and let live. If he cannot give Indraprastha let him give us five villages.

32. Adhya. 31—Sanjaya reaches Dratrarashtra at night and tells him I will give you the message of Dharma in the morning.

33. Adhya. 32—Dhratarashtra is uneasy and wants to know the message Sanjaya brought. So he sends for Sanjaya immediately. Sanjaya gives him the message and says settle the dispute by g:iving them their share of the Kingdom.

34. Adhya. 34—Dhratarashtra calls for Vidura and asks his advice. His advice is, give the Pandavas their portion of the Kingdom.

35. Adhya. 35—Irrelevant.

36. Adhya. 36—Irrelevant. Vidur says make the two sides friends.

37. Adhya. 37—Irrelevant.

38. Adhya 38—Irrelevant.

39. Adhya. 39—Dhratarashtra tells Vidura I cannot give up Duryodhan although he is bad.

40. Adhya. 40—Vidura describes Chaturvarna.

41. Adhya. 41—Dhratarashtra asks Vidur about Brahma. He says I can't because I am a Shudra. Then comes Sanat-Sujata.

42. Adhya. 42—Conversation between Dhratarashtra & Sanat Sujata on Brahma Vidya.

43. Adhya. 43—Dialogue between Sanat Sujat and Dhratarashtra on the same subject.

44. Adhya. 44—Sanat Sujata on Brahma Vidya.

45. Adhya. 45—Sanat Sujata preaches yoga.

46. Adhya. 46—Sanat Sujat on Atma.

47. Adhya. 47—Kauravas come to the Sabha to hear the message brought by Sanjaya.

48. Adhya. 48—Sanjaya delivers the message. (Particularly that part which was given by Arjuna?)

49. Adhya. 49—Praise of Arjuna & Krishna by Bhishma. Kama gets angry. Drona supports Bhisma and advices compromise.

50. Adhya. 50—Dhratarashtra asks Sanjaya who are the

allies of the Pandvas & their strength. Sanjaya taunts, gets up answers.

51. Adhya. 51—Dhratarashtra thinks of the prowess of Bhismna and sighs.

52. Adhya. 52—Dhratarashtra thinks of the prowess of Arjuna and sighs.

53. Adhya. 53—Dhratarashtra thinks of the prowess of Dharma and his friends. He tells his sons to compromise with the Pandavas.

54. Adhya. 54—Sanjaya predicts the defeat of the Kauravas.

55. Adhya. 55—Duryodhan says Pandavas cannot defeat us because our forces are greater.

56. Adhya. 56—Sanjaya describes the disposition of the army made by the Pandavas.

57. Adhya. 57—Sanjaya describes how Pandavas have designed to kill the warriors of the Kauravas. Duryodhan says he is not affraid of the Pandvas defeating the Kauravas who have a larger army.

58. Adhya. 58—Dhratarashtra tells Duryodhan not to fight. Duryodhan takes oath not to swerve from battle. Dhratarashtra weeps.

59. Adhya. 59—Dhratarashtra tells Sanjaya to tell him what conversation took place between Krishna & Arjuna.

60. Adhya. 60—Dhratarashtra tells Duryodhan that the Devas will help the Pandavas and will ruin the Kauravas.

61. Adhya. 61—Duryodhan says he is not afraid of that.

62. Adhya. 62—Kama says he alone is capable of killing Arjuna.

63. Adhya. 63—Duryodhan says he is fighting relying on Kama & not on Bhishma, Drona etc.

64. Adhya. 64—Vidura tells Duryodhan give up enmity.

65. Adhya. 65—Dratarashtra admonishes Duryodhan.

66. Adhya. 66—Sanjaya tells Dratarashtra the message of Arjuna.

67. Adhya. 67—The kings who had assembled in the hall of the Kauravas return to their homes. Vyas and Gandhari

come with Vidur. Vyas told Sanjaya to tell Dhratarashtra every thing he knows about the real Swarup of Krishna & Arjuna.

68. Adhya. 68—Sanjaya tells Dhratarashtra about Krishna.

69. Adhya. 69—Dhratarashtra tells Duryodhan to surrender to Krishna. Refusal of Duryodhan. Gandhari abuses Duryodhan.

70. Adhya 70—Different names of Krishna & their origin.

71. Adhya 71—Dhratarashtra surrenders to Krishna.

72. Adhya. 72—Conversation between Yudhistira and Krishna. Yudhistir says Sanjaya told him not to rely on Dhratarashtra. Yudhistir stresses the importance of property Speaks of (Kshatradharma) & the necessity of observing it Krishna proposes to go to the Kauravas. Yudhistir does not like the idea but says to what you think is the best.

73. Adhya. 73—Krishna tells Dharma the secret which has in mind. Don't use soft speech with the Pandvas tells Krishna to Dharma. There are plenty of reasons why you should not make any compromise with the Kauravas. Emphasizes how the Kauravas disgraced Draupadi. Therefore Oh ; Dharma do not hesitate to kill them.

74. Adhya. 74—Bhishma tells Krishna to use soft speech with the Kauravas.

75. Adhya. 75—Krishna redicules Bhima.

76. Adhya. 76—Bhima makes up his mind to fight.

77. Adhya. 77—Krishna tells Bhima the difference between *Daiva* and *Paurush.*

78. Adhya. 78—Arjuna tells Krishna to adopt Shama—failing war can be considered.

79. Adhya. 79—Krishna's talk to Arjun. I will try to bring about a settlement by peace. If that is not possible be ready for war. I will not communicate to Duryodhan Dharma's willingness to accept five villages.

80. Adhya. 80—Nakul tells Krishna to do the best.

81. Adhya. 81—Sahadev meets Krishna and tells him to bring about a war with the Kauravas. Satyaki said that all warriors assembled here agree with the view of Sahadeo.

82. Adhya. 82—Draupadi meets Krishna & tells him that

she will not be satisfied unless Duryodhan is punished. Krishna gives her assurance.

83. Adhya. 83—Last meeting between Arjuna and Krishna. Arjuna makes the best effort for *Shama*. Yudhishtir tells Krishna to give assurances to Kunti. Krishna starts on his mission.

84. Adhya. 84—Good & Bad omens to Krishna on his way to Hastinapura.

85. Adhya. 85—Duryodhana creates Resting places for Krishna's journey to Hastinapur. Krishna arrives in Hastinapura.

86. Adhya. 86—Dhratarashtra tells Vidura what gifts are to be offered to krishna.

87. Adhya. 87—Vidur tells Dhratarashtra that he cannot separate Krishna from the Pandavas.

88. Adhya. 88—Duryodhan says Krishna is worship. But this is not the time to worship him. Bhishma tells Duryodhan to make a compromise with Pandavas. Duryodhan desires to look up Krishna. Bhishma's strong opposition to Duryodhana.

89. Adhya. 89—Krishna's entry into Hastinapur. Meeting with Dhratarashtra. His stay with Vidura.

90. Adhya. 90—Meeting between Kunti and Krishna—Kunti's sorrow. Krishna consoles her. Kunti tells Krishna— (1) Tell my sons to fight for their kingdom. (2) I am sorry for Draupadi.

91. Adhya. 91—Kauravas invite Krishna to dinner. Krishna's refusal. Krishna goes for meal to Vidur.

92. Adhya. 92—Vidur tells Krishna that he does not like his going among the Kauravas.

93. Adhya. 93—Krishna tells Vidura not all the Kauravas can hurt him. I have come only because *Shama* is Punnyakarak.

94. Adhya. 94—Krishna enters the assembly Hall of the Kauravas.

95. Adhya. 95—Krishna's address to the Assembly. He told them pandavas are ready for both peace as well as war. Give them half their kingdom.

96. Adhya. 96—Jamadgni tells a story against arrogance.

97. Adhya. 97-105—Matali Akhyan.

98. Adhya. 106—Narada's advice to Duryodhana.

99. Adhya. 106-123— Galava Akhyan.

100. Adhya. 124—Dratarashtra tells Krishna to advise Duryodhana.

101. Adhya. 125—Bhishma's advice to Duryodhan.Drona's support. Vidura's condemnation of Duryodhana. Dhratarashtra's advice.

102. Adhya. 126—Bhishma & Drona advice Duryodhana a second time.

103. Adhya. 127—Duryodhana announces not to give anything to the Pandavas.

104. Adhya. 128—Krishna condemns Duryodhana. Duryodhan leaves the Assembly. Dushyasana's speech. Krishna warns Bhishma.

104. Adhya. 129—Dhratarashtra asks Vidur to bring Gandhari to the Assembly. Duryodhan comes back—Gandhari asks him to give half the Kingdom to Pandavas.

104. Adhya. 130—Duryodhana leaves the assembly. His intention to kill Krishna. Satyaki informs Dhratarashtra of this secret plot. Srikrishna's speech. Dhratarashtra calls back Duryodhana to the assembly, warns him. Vidur's condemnation.

105. Adhya. 131—*Bhagwana's Vishwarup Darshan* Dhratarashtra gets *Divya Chakshu?* Krishna leaves the assembly and goes to. Kunti.

106. Adhya. 132—Krishna tells Kunti what happened in the assembly. Kunti tells Krishna war is natural to Kshatriyas. There is no better Dharma than that.

107. Adhya. 133—Kunti tells Krishna the story of Vidula to reinforce her point.

108. Adhya. 134—Vidula's story.

109. Adhya. 135—Vidula's story.

110. Adhya. 136—Vidula's story.

III. Adhya. 137—Kunti's advice to her sons. Krishna's advice to Kama and his departure to *Upapalavya Nagari.*

112. Adhya. 138—Advice to Duryodhana by Bhishma & Drona.

113. Adhya. 139—Bhishma's sorrow. Drona again advises Duryodhana.

114. Adhya. 140—Conversation between Dhratarashtra and Sanjaya. Krishna advices Kama.

115. Adhya. 141—Kama's reply to Krishna.

116. Adhya. 142—Krishna's assurance to Kama that the Pandava's will win.

117. Adhya. 143—Kama sees bad omens. His determination to finish Pandavas. His going home.

118. Adhya. 144—Conversation between Vidura and Pratha. Knows Duryodhana is determined to fight. Kunti's sorrow. Her wish to tell Kama his origin. Kunti goes to the bank of the river.

119. Adhya. 145—Kunti meets Kama and tells him his origin and request him to join the Pandavas.

120. Adhya. 146—Surya supports the proposal of Kunti. Kama rejects it. Promises to save all the Pandavas except Arjuna.

121. Adhya. 147—Krishna goes to Pandavas. Yudhistir asks what happened in the Kaurava Sabha.

122. Adhya. 147, 148, 149, 150—Krishna relates the whole story.

123. Adhya. 151—Appointment of Senapati for the Pandavas Army. Entry of Pandava's Army in Kurushetra.

124. Adhya. 152—Description of Pandavas arrangement for supply to the Army.

125. Adhya. 153—Arrangement on Kaurava's side. Our army must enter Kurushetra tomorrow early morning.

126. Adhya. 154—Dharma's fear of fall from his moral rectitude by going to war. Krishna satisfied him. Arjuna said you must fight.

127. Adhya. 155—Description of Duryodhan's army.

128. Adhya. 156—Bhishma is made Senapati of the Kaurava's army. Kama is offended. His decision not to take command till Bhishma is dead. Kaurava's *Army enters Kurushetra.*

129. Adhya. 157—Krishna becomes commander of Pandava's Army.

130. Balrarn goes on Pilgrimage saying I do not like the Kauravas destroyed.

131. Adhya. 158—Rukmi neither wanted by Arjuna nor by Duryodhana goes home.

132. Adhya. 159—Conversation between Sanjaya and Dhratarashtra. He blames Dhratarashtra.

133. Adhya. 160—Pandava's Army on the bank of the *Hiranyavati* river. Duryodhan sends offensive messages to Pandavas and Krishna saying fight if you can.

134. Adhya. 161. Uluka goes with the messages.

135. Adhya. 162—Angry Pandavas send back angry messages. They give order that the war will start tomorrow.

6

Brahmins Versus Kshatriyas

This manuscript consists of 43 foolscap typed pages. All the loose pages are tagged. The original title, 'Brahmins and Kshatriyas and the Counter-Revolution ' has been modified in Dr. Ambedkar's hand-writing as 'Brahmins Versus Kshatriyas ' on the title page. The essay seems to be complete.—Editors.

The sacred literature of the Hindus contains many cases of conflicts between the Brahmins and the Kshatriyas and even of sanguinary wards between the two.

The first case reported was that of the King Vena. Vena was a Kshatriya King. His conflict with the Brahmins has been referred to in various authorities. The following account is taken from the Harivansa.

"There was formerly a Prajapati (lord of creatures), a protector of righteousness, called Anga, of the race of Atrai, and resembling him in power. His son was the Prajapati Vena, who was but indifferently skilled in duty, and was born of Sunitha, the daughter of Mrityu. This son of the daughter of Kala (Death), owing to the taint derived from his maternal grandfather, threw his duties behind his back, and lived in covetousness under the influence of desire. This king established an irreligious system of conduct ; transgressing the ordinances of the Veda, he was devoted to lawlessness. In his reign men lived without study of the sacred books and without the Vashatkara, and the gods had no some-libations to drink at sacrifices."

No sacrifice or oblation shall be offered,—such was the ruthless determination of that Prajapati, as the time of his destruction approached. 'I', he declared, 'am the object, and the performer of sacrifice, and the sacrifice itself; it is to me that sacrifice should be presented, and oblations offered.' This transgressor of the rules of duty, who arrogated to himself what was not his due, was then addressed by all the great Rishis, headed by Marichi : "We are about to consecrate ourselves for a ceremony which shall last for many years; practise not unrighteousness, of Vena ; this is not the eternal rule of duty. Thou art in every deed a Prajapati of Atri's race and thou hast engaged to protect thy subject. `The foolish Vena, ignorant of what was right, laughingly answered those great Rishis who had so addressed him: "Who but myself is the ordainer of duty? or whom ought I to obey? Who on earth equals me in sacred knowledge, in process, in austere fervour, in truth? Ye who are deluded and senseless know not that I am the source of all beings and duties. Hesitate not to believe that I, if I willed, could turn up the earth, or deluge it with water, or close up heaven and earth.' When owing to his delusion and arrogance Vena could not be governed, then the mighty Rishis becoming licensed, seized the vigorous and struggling king, and rubbed his left thigh. From this thigh, so rubbed, was produced a black man, very short in stature, who, being alarmed, stood with joined hands. Seeing that he was agitated, Atri said to him 'Sit down' (Nishida). He became the founder of the race of the Nishadas, and also progenitor of the Dhivaras (Fishermen), who sprang from the corruption of Vena.'

The second case is that of Pururavas. Pururavas is another Kshatriya King, son of Ila and grandson of Manu Vaivasvata. He came in conflict with the Brahmans the following account of which appears in the Adi Parva of the Mahabharata :

"Subsequently the wise Pururavas was born of lla who, as we have heard was both his father and his mother. Ruling over thirteen islands of the ocean, and surrounded by beings who were all superhuman, himself a man of great renown, Pururavas, intoxicated by his prowess, engaged in a conflict with the Brahmans, and robbed them of their jewels, although they loudly remonstrated. Sanatkumara came from Brahma's heaven, and addressed to him an admonition, which however, he did not regard. Being then straightway cursed by the incenses Rishis, he perished, this covetous monarch, who, through piece of power, had lost his understanding." The third and a somewhat serious conflict was that between King Nahusha and the Brahmins. Nahusha is the grandson of Pururavas. The story is told in two places in the Mahabharata once in the Vanaparvan and a second time in the Udyogaparvan. The following account is taken from the Udyogaparvan of the Mahabharata:

"After his slaughter of the demon Vritta, Indra became alarmed at the idea of having taken the life of a Brahman (for Vritta was regarded as such) and hid himself in the waters. In consequence of the disappearance of the king of the gods, all affairs, celestial as well as terrestrial, fell into confusion. The Rishis and gods then applied to Nahusha to be their king. After the first excusing himself on the plea of want of power, Nahusha at length, in compliance with their solicitations, accepted the high function. Upto the period of his elevation he had led a virtuous life, but he now became addicted to amusement and sensual pleasure, and even aspired to the possession of Indrani, Indra's wife, whom he had happened to see. The queen resorted to the Angiras Vrihaspati, the preceptor of the gods, who engaged to protect her. Nahusha was greatly incensed on hearing of this interference ; but the gods endeavoured to pacify him, and pointed out the immorality of appropriating another person's wife. Nahusha, however, would listen to no remonstrance, and insisted that in his adulterous designs he was no worse than Indra himself."

"The renowned Ahalya, a rishi's wife, was formerly corrupted by Indra in her husband's lifetime. Why was he not prevented by you? And many barbarous acts, and unrighteous deeds, and frauds were perpetrated of old by Indra; Why was he not prevented by you?" The gods, urged Nahusha, then went to bring Indrani; but Vrihaspati would not give her up. At his recommendation, however, she solicited Nahusha for some delay, till she should ascertain what had become of her husband. This request was granted." Indrani now went in search of her husband ; and by the help of Upasruti (the goddess of night and revealer of secrets) discovered him existing in a very subtile form in the stem of a lotus growing in a lake situated in a continent within an ocean north of the Himalayas. She made known to him the wicked intentions of Nahusha, and entreated him to exert his power, rescue her from danger, and resume his dominion. Indra declined any immediate interposition on the plea of Nahusha's superior strength ; but suggested to his wife a device by which the usurper might be hurled from his position. She was recommended to say to Nahusha that "if he would visit her on a celestial vehicle borne by Rishis, she would with pleasure submit herself to him."

"I desire for thee, king of the gods, a vehicle hitherto unknown, such as neither Vishnu, nor Rudra, nor the Asuras, nor the Rakshases employ. Let the eminent Rishis, all united, bear thee, lord, in a car: this idea pleases me." Nahusha receives favourably this appeal to his vanity, and in the course of his reply thus gives utterance to his self-congratulation : "He is a personage of no mean prowess who makes the Munis his bearers. I am a fervid devotee of great might, lord of the past, the future, and the present. If I were angry the world would no longer stand ; on me everything depends.......... Wherefore, 0 goddess, I shall, without doubt, carry out what you propose. The seven Rishis, and all the Brahman-rishis, shall carry me. Behold, beautiful goddess, my majesty and my prosperity." The narrative goes on : "Accordingly this wicked being, irreligious, violent, intoxicated by the force of conceit, and arbitrary in his conduct, attached to his car the Rishis who submitted to his command, and compelled them to bear him." Indrani then again resorts to Vrihaspati, who assures her that vengeance will soon overtake Nahusha for his presumption, and promises that he will himself perform a sacrifice with a view to the destruction of the oppressor, and the discovery of Indra's lurking place. Agni is then sent to discover and bring Indra to Vrihaspati ; and the latter, on Indra's arrival, informs him of all that had occurred during his absence. While Indra, with Kuvera, Yama, Soma and Varuna was devising means for the destruction of Nahusha, the sage Agastya came up, congratulated Indra on the fall of his rival, and proceeded to relate how it had occurred :

"Wearied with carrying the sinner Nahusha the eminent divine-rishis, and the spotless Brahman-rishis, asked that divine personage Nahusha (to solve) a difficulty; "Dost thou, O Vasava, most excellent of conquerors, regard as authoritative or not those Brahmana texts which are recited at the immolation of kine? " 'No', replied Nahusha, whose understanding was enveloped in darkness. The Rishis rejoined : 'Engaged in unrighteousness, thou attainest not unto righteousness : these texts, which were formerly uttered by great Rishis, are regarded by us as authoritative.`Then (proceeds Agastya) disputing with the Munis, Nahusha, impelled by unrighteousness, touched me on the head with his foot. In consequence of this the king's glory was smitten and his prosperity departed. When he had instantly become agitated and oppressed with fear, I said to him, 'Since thou, O fool, contemnest that sacred text, always held in honour, which has been composed by former sages, and employed by Brahman-rishis, and has touched my head with thy foot, and employest the Brahma—like the irresistible Rishis as bearers to carry thee,—therefore, shorn of thy lusture, and all thy merit exhausted, sink down, sinner, degraded from heaven to earth. For ten thousand years thou shalt crawl in the form of a huge serpent. When that period is completed, thou shalt again ascend to heaven. `So fell that wicked wretch from the sovereignty of the gods. Happily, 0 Indra, we shall now prosper, for the cnemy of the Brahmans has been smitten. Take possession of the three worlds, and protect their inhabitants, O husband of Sachi (Indrani) subduing thy senses, overcoming thine enemies, and celebrated by the great Rishis."

The fourth case is of King Nimi. Nimi was one of the sons of Ikshvaku. The facts of his conflict with the Brahmans are related in the Vishnu Purrana which says :

"Nimi had requested the Brahman Rishi Vashistha to officiate at a sacrifice, which was to last a thousand years. Vashistha in reply pleaed a pre-engagement to Indra for five hundred years, but promised to return at the end of that period. The king made no remark, and Vashistha went away, supposing that he had assented to his arrangement. On his return, however, the priest discovered that Nimi had retained Gautama (who was, equally with Vashistha, a Brahmin-rishi) and others to perform the sacrifice ; and being incensed at the neglect to give him notice of what was intended, he cursed the king, who was then asleep, to lose his corporeal form. When Nimi awoke and learnt that he had been cursed without any previous warning, he retorted by uttering a similar curse on Vashistha, and then died. Nimi's body was emblamed. At the close of the sacrifice which he had begun, the gods, were willing, on the intercession of the priests, to restore him to life, but he declined the offer; and was placed by the deities, according to his desire, in the eyes of all living creatures. It is in consequence of this that they are always opening and shutting (nimisha means "The twinkling of the eye").

The fifth case relates to the conflict between Vashishtha and Vishvamitra. Vashishtha was a Brahmin priest. Vishavamitra was a Kshatriya. His great ambition was to become a Brahmin. The following episode reported from the Ramayana explains the reasons why he became anxious to become a Brahmin.

"There was formerly, we are told, a king called Kusa, son of Prajapati, who had a son called Kusanabha, who was father of Gadhi, the father of Vishvamitra. The latter ruled the earth for many thousand years. On one occasion, when he was making a circuit of the earth, he came to Vashishtha's hermitage, the pleasant abode of many saints, sages, and holy devotees, where, after all first declining, he allowed himself to be hospitability entertained with his followers by the son of Brahma. Vishvamitra, however, coveting the wonderous cow, which had supplied all the dainties of the feast, first of all asked that she should be given to him in exchange for a hundred thousand common cows, adding that "she was a gem, that gems were the property of the King, and, therefore, the cow owas his by right." On this price being refused, the King advances immensely in his offers, but all without effect. He then proceeds very ungratefully, and tyrannically, it must be allowed—to have the *cow* removed by force, but she breaks away from his attendants, and rushes back to her master, complaining that he was deserting her. He replies that he was not deserting her, but that the king was much more powerful than he. She answers, 'Men do not ascribe strength to a Kshatriya : the Brahmans are stronger. The strength of Brahmins is divine, and superior to that of Kshatriyas. Thy strength is immeasurable. Vishvamitra, though of great vigour, is not more powerful than thou. Thy energy is invincible. Commission me, who have been acquired by thy Brahmanical power, and I will destroy the pride, and force, and attempt of this wicked prince." She accordingly by her bellowing creates hundred of Pahalvas, who destroy the entire host of Vishvamitra, but are slain by him in their turn. Sakas and Yavanas, of great power and valour, and well armed, were then produced, who consumed the king's soldiers, but were routed by him. The cow then calls into existence by her bellowing, and from different parts of her body, other warriors of various tribes, who again destroyed Vishvamitra's entire army, foot soldiers, elephants, horses, chariots, and all. A hundred of the monarch's sons, armed with various weapons, then rushed in great fury on Vashishtha, but were all reduced to ashes in a moment by the blast of that sage's mouth.

Vishvamitra, being thus utterly vanquished and humbled, appointed one of his sons to be regent, and travelled to the Himalaya, where he betook to austerities, and thereby obtained a vision of Mahadeva, who at his desire revealed to him the science of arms in all its branches, and gave him celestial weapons with which, elated and full of price, he consumed the hermitage of Vashishtha, and put its inhabitants to flight.

Vashishtha then threatens Vishvamitra and uplifts his Brahmanical mace. Vishvamitra, too, raises his fiery weapon and calls out to his adversary to stand. Vashishtha bids him to show his strength and boasts that he will soon humble his pride. He asks: "What comparison is there between a Kshatriya's might and the might of a Brahman? Behold, thou contemptible Kshatriya, my divine Brhmanical power.'

The dreadful fiery weapon uplifted by the son of Gadhi was then quenched by the rod of the Brahman, as fire is by water." Many and various other celestial missiles, as the nooses of Brahma, Kala (Time), and Varuna, the discuss of Vishnu, and the trident of Shiva, were hurled by Vishvamitra at his antagonist, but the son of Brahma swallowed them up in his all-devouring mace. Finally, to the intense consternation of all the gods, the warrior shot off the terrific weapon of Brahma ; but this was equally ineffectual against the Brahmanical sage. Vashishtha had now assumed a direful appearance. "Jets of fire mingled with smoke darted from the pores of his body ; the Brahmanical mace blazed in his hand like a smokeless mundane conflagration, or a second sceptre of Yama." Being appeased, however, by the munis, who proclaimed his superiority to his rival, the sage stayed his vengeance ; and Vishvamitra exclaimed with a groan: "Shame on a Kshatriya's strength : the strength of a Brahman's might alone is strength;

by the single Brahmanical mace all my weapons have been destroyed."

No alternative now remains to the humilated monarch, but either to acquiesce in this help less inferiority, or to work out his own elevation to the Brahmanical order. He embraces the latter alternative : " Having pondered well this defeat, I shall betake myself, with composed senses and mind, to strenuous austere fervour, which shall exalt me to the rank of a Brahman."Intensely vexed and mortified, groaning and full of hatred against his enemy, he travelled with his queen to the south, and carried his resolution into effect. At the end of a thousand years Brahma appeared, and announced that he had conquered the heaven of royal sages (rajarshis): and, in consequence of his austere fervour, he was recognised as having attained that rank."

The conflict seems to have begun in the reign of King Sudas who belonged to the line of Ikshavaku. Vashishtha was the hereditary priest of King Sudas. For some reason which is not very clearly stated Sudas appointed Vishvamitra as his family priest. This brought about a conflict between Vishvamitra and Vashishtha. This conflict once started raged on for a long time.

The conflict between the two took a peculiar turn. If Vishvamitra was involved in a dispute Vashishtha came into the fray and sided with his opponent. If Vishvamitra was involved in dispute Vashishtha entered into fray and sided with Vishvamitra as opponent. It was a case of one persecuting the other.

The first such episode is that of Satyavrata otherwise called Trishanku. The story as told in the Harivamsha is as follows:

"Meanwhile Vashishtha, from the relation subsisting between the King (Satyavrata's father) and himself, a disciple and spiritual preceptor, governed the city of Ayodhya, the country, and the interior apartments of the royal palace. But Satyavrata, whether through folly or the force of destiny, cherished constantly an increased indignation against Vashishtha, who for a (proper) reason had not interposed to prevent his exclusion from the royal power by his father. 'The formulas of the marriage ceremonial are only binding,' said Satyavrata, 'when the seventh step has been taken, and this had not been done when I seized the damsel : still Vashishtha, who knows the precepts of the law, does not come to my aid.' Thus Satyavrata was incensed in his mind against Vashishtha, who however, had acted from a sense of what was right. Nor did Satyavrata understand (he propriety of) that silent penance imposed upon him by his father..... When he had supported this arduous rite, (the supposed that) he had redeemed his family position. The venerable muni Vashishtha did not, however, (as has been said) prevent his father from setting him aside, but resolved to install his son as King. When the powerful prince Satyavrata had endured the penance for twelve years, he beheld, when he was without flesh to eat, the milch cow of Vashishtha which yielded all objects of desire ; and under the influence of anger ; delusion, and exhaustion, distressed by hunger, and failing in the ten duties he slew.......... and both partook of her flesh himself, and gave it to Vishvamitra's sons to eat. Vashishtha hearing of this, became incensed against him", and imposed on his the name of Trisanku as he had committed three sins. On his return home, Vishvamitra was gratified by the support which his wife had received, and offered Trisanku the choice of a boon. When this proposal was made, Trisanku chose the boon of ascending bodily to heaven. All apprehension from the twelve year's drought being now at an end, the muni (Vishvamitra) installed Trisanku in his father's kingdom, and offered sacrifice on his behalf. The mighty Kausika then, in spite of the resistance of the gods and of Vashishtha, exalted the king alive to heaven." 2. As stated in the Harivamsa :

"In consequence of the wickedness which had been committed, Indra did not rain for a period of twelve years. At that time Vishvamitra had left his wife and children and gone to practise austerties on the sea-shore. His wife, driven to extremity by want was on the point of selling her second son for a hundred cows, in order to support the others ; but this arrangement was stopped by the interventions of Satyavrata, who liberated the son when bound, and maintained the family by providing them with the flesh of wild animals ; and according to his father's injunction, consecrated himself for the performance of a silent penance for twelve years." The next episode in which they appear on opposite sides is that of Harishchandra the son of Trisanku. The story is told in the

Vishnu Purana and in the Markendeya Purana. This is how the story runs:

"On one occasion, when hunting the king heard a sound of female lamentation which proceeded, it appears, from the sciences who were becoming mastered by the austerely fervid sage Vishvamitra, in a way they had never been before by anyone else ; and were consequently crying out in alarm at his superiority. In fulfilment of his duty as a Kshatriya to defend the weak, and inspired by the god Ganesha, who had entered into him, Harishchandra exclaimed. "What sinner is this who is binding fire in the hem of his garment, while, I, his lord. am present, resplendent with force and fiery vigour?' He shall today enter on his long sleep, pierced in all his limbs by arrows, which, by their discharge from my bow, illuminate all the quarters of the firmament." Vishvamitra was provoked by this address. In consequence of his wrath the Sciences instantly perished, and Harishchandra, trembling like the leaf of an Asvattha tree submissively represented that he had merely done his duty as a king, which he defined as consisting in the bestowl of gifts on eminent Brahmins and other persons of slender means, the protection of the timid, and war against enemies. Vishvamitra hereupon demands a gift as a Brahman intent upon receiving one. The king offers him whatsoever he may ask : Gold, his own son, wife body, like kingdom, good fortune.

The saint first requires the present for the Rajasuya sacrifice. On this being promised, and still more offered, he asks for the empire of the whole earth, including everything but Harishchandra himself, his wife and son and his virtue which follows its posses or wherever he goes." "Harishchandra joyfully agrees. Vishvamitra then requires him to strip off all his ornaments, to clothe himself in the bark of trees, and to quit the kingdom with his wife Saviya (Taramati) and his son. When he is departing the sage stops him and demands payment of his yet unpaid sacrificial fee. The king replies that he has only the persons of his wife his son, and himself left. Vishvamitra insists that he must nevertheless pay: and that "unfulfilled promises of gifts to Brahmans bring destruction." The unfortunate prince, after being threatened with a curse, engages to make the payment in a month ; and commences his journey with a wife unused to such fatigues, amid the universal lamentations of his subjects. While he lingers, listening to their affectionate remonstrances against his desertion of his kingdom, Vishvamitra, comes up and being incensed at the delay and the King's apparent hesitation, strikes the queen with his staff, as she is dragged on by her husband.

Harishchandra then proceeded with his wife and little son to Benares, imagining that this divine city, as the special property of Siva, could not be possessed by any mortal. Here he found the relentless Vishvamitr waiting for him, and ready to press his demand for the payment of his sacrificial gift, even before the expiration of the full period of grace. In this extremity Saivya the queen suggests with a sobbing voice that her husband should sell her. On hearing this proposal Harishchandra swoons, then recovers, utters lamentations, and swoons again, and his wife, seeing his said condition, swoon also.

While they are in a state of unconsciousness, their famished child exclaims in distress, " O father, father, give me bread ; O mother, mother give me food : hunger overpowers me and my tongue is parched." At this moment Vishvamitra returns, and after recalling Harishchandra to consciousness by spinkling water over him, again urges payment of the present. The king again swoons, and is again restored. The sag threatens to curse him if his engagement is not fulfilled by sunset. Being now pressed by his wife, the King agrees to sell her ading, however, "If my voice can utter such a wicked word, I do not what the most inhuman wretches cannot perpetrate."

He then goes into the city and in selfacusing language offers his queen for sale as a slave. A rich old Brahman offers to buy her at a price corresponding to her value, to do his household work. Seeing his mother dragged away, the child ran after her, his eyes dimmed with tears, and crying 'mother'. The Brahman purchaser kicked him when he came *up;* but he would not let his mother go, and continued crying 'mother, mother.' The queen then said to the Brahman, ' Be so kind, my master, as to but also this child, as without him I shall prove to thee but a useless purchase. Be thus merciful to me in my wretchedness, unite me with my son, like a cow to her calf." The Brahman agrees: "Take this money and give me the boy." After the Brahman had gone out of sight with his purchases,

Vishvamitra again appeared and renewed his demands ; and when the afflicted Harishchanda offered him the small sum he had obtained by the sale of his wife and son, he angrily replied, "If, miserable Kshatriya, thou thinkest this a sacrificial gift befitting my deserts, thou shall soon beheld the transcendent power of my ardent austere fervour, of my spotless Brahmanhood of my terrible majesty, and of my holy study. Harishchandra promises an additional gift, and Vishvamitra allows him the remaining quarter of the day for its liquidation. On the terrified and afflicted prince offering himself for sale, in order to gain the mean of meeting this cruel demand, Dharma (Righteousness) appears in the form of a hideous and offensive Chandala, and agrees to buy him at his own price, large or small. Harishchandra declines such a degrading servitude, and declares that he would rather be consumed by the fire of his persecutor's curse than submit to such a fate. Vishvamitra however again comes on The scene, asks why he does not accept the large sum offered by the Chandala ; and, when he pleads in excuse his descent from the solar race, threatens to fulminate a curse against him if he does not accept that method of meeting his liability. Harishchandra implores that he may be spared this extreme of degradation, and offers to become Vishvamitra's slave in payment of the residue of his debt; whereupon the sage rejoins, "If thou art my slave, then I sell thee as such to the Chandala for a hundred millions of money."

"The Chandala, delighted, pays down the money, and carries off Harishchandra, bound beaten, confused and afflicted, to his own place of abode. Harishchandra is sent by the Chandala to steal grave clothes in a cemetary and is told that he will receive two-sixths goind to his masters, and one-sixth to the King. In this horrid spot, and in this degrading occupation, he spent in great misery, twelve months, which seemed to him like a hundred years. He then falls asleep and has a series of dreams suggested by the life he had been leading. After he awoke, his wife came to the cemetary to perform the obsequies of their son, who had died from the bite of a serpent. At first the husband and wife did not recognize each other, from the change in appearance which had been brought upon them by their miseries. Harishchandra however, soon discovered from the tenor of her lamentations that it is his wife, and falls into a swoon; as the queen does also when she recognizes her husband. When consciousness returns, they both break out into lamentations, the father bewailing in a touching strain the loss of his son, and the wife the degradation of the King. She then falls on his neck, embraces him, and asks "whether all this is a dream, or a reality, as she is utterly be wildered ", and adds, that "if it be a reality, then righteousness is unvailing to those who practise it." After hesitating to devote himself to death on his son's funeral pyre without receiving his master's leave, Harishchandra resolves to do so, braving all the consequences, and consoling himself with the hopeful anticipation: "If I have given gifts, and offered sacrifices an gratified my religious teachers, then may I be reunited with my son and with thee (my wife) in another world."

The queen determines to die in the same manner. When Harishchandra., after placing his son's body on the funeral pile, is meditating on the Lord Shri Narayan krishna, the supreme spirit, all the gods arrive, headed by Dharma (righteousness), and accompanied by Vishvamitra. Dharma entreats the king to desist from his rash intention; and Indra announces to him that he, his wife, and son have conquered heaven by their good works. Amrosia, the antidote of death, and flowers are rained by the god from the sky ; and the king's son is restored to life and the bloom of youth. The king, adorend with celestial clothing and garlands, and the queen, embrace their son. Harishchandra, however declares that he cannot go to heaven till he has received his master the Chandala's permission, and has paid him a ransom. Dharma then reveals to the king that it was he himself who had miraculously assumed the form of a Chandala. The king next objects that he cannot depart unless his faithful subjects, who are shares in his merits, are allowed to acompany him to heaven, at least for one day. This request is granted by Indra; and after Vishvamitra has inaugurated Rohitasva the king's son to be his successor, Harishchandra, his friends and followers, all ascend in company to heaven. Even after this great consummation, however, Vashishtha, the family-priest of Harishchandra, hearing, at the end of a twelve years' abode in the waters of the Ganges, an account of all that has occured, becomes vehementaly incensed at the humiliation inflicted on the excellent monarch, whose virtues and devotion to the gods and Brahmans he celebrates, declares that his indignation had not been so great roused even when his own hundred sons had been slain by Vishvamitra, and in the following words dooms the latter to be transformed into crane. Wherefore that wicked man, enemy of the Brhmans, smitten by my curse, shall be expelled from the society of intelligent beings, and losing his understanding shall be transformed into a Vaka." Vishvamitra reciprocates the curse, and changes Vashishtha into a bird of the species called Ari. In their new shapes the two have a furious fight the Ari being of the portentous heiht of two thousand yojanas = 18,000 miles, and the Vaka of 3090 yojanas. The first assail each other with their wings ; then the Vaka smites his antagonist in the same manner, while the Ari strikes with his talons. Falling mountains, overturned by the blasts of wind raised by the flapping of their wings, shake the whole earth, the waters of the ocean overflow, the earth itself, thrown off its perpendicular slopes downwards patala, the lower regions. Many creatures perish by these various convulsions. Attracted by the dire disorder, Brahma arrives, attended by all the gods, on the spot, and command the comptants to desist from their fray. They were too fiercely infuiriated to regard this injunction; but Brahma put an end to the conflict by restoring them to their natural forms, and conselling them to be reconciled.

The next episode in which they came in as opponents is connected with *Ambarish* King of Ayodhya.

The story relates that Ambarisha was engaged in performing a sacrifice, when Indra carried away the victim. The priest said that this ill-omened event had occurred owing to the king's had administration, and would call for a great expiation, unless a human victim could be produced. After a long search the royal rishi (Ambarisha) came upon the Brahman-rishi Richika, a descendent of Bhrigu, and asked him to sell one of his sons for a victim, at the price of a hundred thousand cows. Richika answered that he would not sell his eldest son; and his wife added that she would not sell the youngest: eldest sons" she observed, "being generally the favourites of their fathers, and youngest sons of their mothers." The second son, Sunassena, then said that in that case he regarded himself as the one who was to be sold, and desired the king to remove him. The hundred thousand cows, with ten millions of gold pieces and heaps of jewels, were paid down, and Sunassepa carried away. As they were passing through Pushkara Sunassepa beheld his maternal uncle Vishvamitra who was engaged in austerities there with other rishis, threw himself into his arms, and implored his assistance, urging his orphan friendless, and helpless state, as claims on the sage's benevolence.

"Vishvamitra soothed him: and pressed his own sons to offer themselves as victim in the room of Sunassepa. This proposition met with no favour from Madhushyanda and the other sons of the royal hermit, who answered with haughtiness and derision: "How is that thou sacrificest thine own sons, and seekest to rescue those of others? We look upon this as wrong, and like the eating of one's own flesh." The sage was exceedingly wroth at this disregard of his injunction, and doomed his sons to be born in the most degraded classes, like Vashishtha's sons, and to eat dog's flesh, for a thousand years. He then said to Sunassepa : When thou art bound with hallowed cords, decked with a red garland, and annointed with unguents, and fastened to the sacrificial post of Vishnu, then address thyself to Agni, and sing these two divine verses (gathas), at the sacrifice of Ambarisha ; then shalt thou attain the fulfilment." Being furnished with the two gathas, Sunassepa proposed at once to king Ambarisha that they should set out for their destination. When bound at the stake to be immolated, dressed in a red garment, " he celebrated the two gods, Indra and his younger brother (Vishnu), with the excellent verses. The thousand-eyed (Indra) was pleased with the secret hymn, and bestowed long life on Sunassepa." The last episode recorded in which the two appear as opponents is connected with King *Kalmashapada*. The episode is recorded in the Adi Parva of the Mahabharata.

"Kalmashapada was a King of the race Ikshvaku. Vishvamitra wished to be employed by him as his officiating priest; but the king preferred Vashishtha." It happened, however, that the king went out to hunt, and after having killed a large quantity of game, he became very much fatigued, as well as hungry and thirsty. Meeting Saktri, the eldest of Vashishtha's hundred sons, on the road, he ordered him to get out of his way. The priest civilly replied : "The path is mine, 0 King; this is the immemorial law; in all observances the king must cede the way to the Brahman." Neither party would yield, and the dispute waxing warmer, the king struck the muni with his whip. The muni, resorting to the usual expedient of offended sages, by a curse doomed the king to become a man eater. "It hapened that at that time enmity existed between Vishvamitra and Vashishtha on account of their respective claims to be priest to Kalmashapada."

Vishvamitra had followed the king; and approached while he was disputing with Saktri. Perceiving, however, the son of his rival Vashishtha, Vishvamitra made himself invisible, and passed them, watching his opportunity. The king began to implore Saktri's clemency: but Vishvamitra wishing to prevent their reconciliation, commanded a Rakshasa (a man-devouring demon) to enter into the king. Owing to the conjoint influence of the Brahma-rishi's curse, and Vishvamitra's command, the demon obeyed the injunction. Perceiving that his object was gained, Vishvamitra left things to take their course, and absented himself from the country.

The king having happened to meet a hungry Brahman, and sent him, by the hand of his cook (who could procure nothing else), some human flesh to eat, was cursed by him also to the same effect as by Saktri. The curse, being now augmented in force, took effect, and Saktri himself was the first victim, being eaten up by the King. The sarne fate befell all the other sons of Vashishtha at the instigation of Vishvamitra. Perceiving Saktri to be dead, Vishvamitra again and again incited the Rakshasa against the sons of Vashishtha; and accordingly the furious demon devoursed those of his sons who were younger than Saktri as a lion eats up the small beasts of the forest. On hearing of the destruction of his sons by Vishvamitra, Vashishtha supported his affliction, as the great mountain sustains the earth.

He meditated his own destruction, but never thought of exterminating the Kausikas. This divine sage hurled himself from the summit of Meru, but fell upon the rocks as if on a heap of cotton. Escaping alive from his fall, he entered a glowing fire in the forest; but the fire, though fiercely blazing, not only failed to burn him, but seemed perfectly cool. He next threw himself into the sea with a heavy stone attached to his neck; but was cast up by the waves on the dry land. He then went home to his hermitage; but seeing it empty and desolate, he.

was again overcome by grief and went out; and seeing the river Vipasa which was swolen by the recent rains and sweeping along many trees torn from its banks, he conceived the design of drowning himself into its water, he accordingly tied himself firmly with cords, and threw himself in, but the river severing his bonds, deposited him unbound (vipasa) on dry land; whence the name of the stream, as imposed by the sage. He afterwards saw and threw himself into the dreadful Satadru (Sutlej), which was full of alligators, etc., and derived its name rushing away in a hundred directions on seeing the Brahman brilliant as fire. In consequence of this he was once more stranded; and seeing he could not kill himself, he went back to his hermitage." There are only particular instances of their general enmity towards each other. This general enmity was of a mortal kind so much so that Vishvamitra wanted even to murder Vashishtha. This is related in the Shalyaparva of the Mahabharata. Says the author of the Mahabharata :

"There existed a great enmity, arising from rivalry in their austerities, between Vishvamitra and the Brahman rishi Vashishtha. Vashishtha had an extensive hermitage in Sthanutirtha, to the east of which was Vishvamitra's......... These two great ascetics were every day exhibiting intense emulation in regard to their respective austerities. But Vishvamitra, beholding the might of Vashishtha, was the most chagrined; and fell into deep thought. The idea of this sage, constant in duty(!) was the following: 'This river Sarasvati will speedily bring to me on her current the austere Vashishtha, the most eminent of all mutterers of prayers. When that most excellent Brahman has come, I shall most assuredly kill him.`Having thus determined, the divine sage Vishvamitra, his eyes reddened by anger, called to mind the chief of rivers. She being thus the subject of his thoughts, became very anxious, as she knew him to be very powerful and very irascible. Then trembling palid, and with joined hands, the Sarasvati stood before the chief of munis. Like a woman whose husband has been slain, she was greatly distressed; and said to him, 'What shall I do?' The incensed muni replied, 'Bring Vashishtha hither speedily, that I may slay him. 'The lotus-eyed goddess, join ing her hands trembled in great fear, like a creeping plant agitated by the wind ".......... Vishvamitra, however, although he saw her condition, repeated his command. "The Sarasvati, who knew how sinful was his design, and that the might of Vashishtha was unequalled, went trembling, and in great dread of being cursed by both the sages, to Vashishtha, and told him what his rival had said. Vashishtha seeing her emaciated, pale, and anxious, spoke thus: 'Deliver thyself, O chief of rivers; carry me unhesitatingly to Vishvamitra, lest he curse thee'. Hearing these words of the merciful sage, the Sarasvati considered how she could act most wisely. She reflected, 'Vashishtha has always shown me great kindness; I must seek his welfare.' Then obsering the Kausika sage praying and sacrificing on her brink, she regarded that as a good opportunity, and swept away the bank by the force of her current. In this way the son of Mitra and Varuna (Vashishtha) was carried down; and while he was bieng borne along, he thus celebrated the river: 'Thou, O Sarasvati, issuest from the lake of Brahma, and pervadest the whole world with thy excellent streams. Residing in the sky, thou dischargest water into the colouds. Thou alone art all waters. By these we study.' 'Thou art nourishment, radiance, fame, perfection, intellect, light. Thou art speech; thou art Svaha; this world is subject to thee. Thou, in fourfold form, dwellest in all creatures '..........

Beholding Vashishtha brought near by the Sarasvati, Vishvamitra searched for a weapon with which to make an end of him. Perceiving his anger, and dreading lest Brahmanicide should ensue, the river promptly carried away Vashishtha in an easterly direction; thus fulfilling the commands of both sages, but eluding Vishvamitra. Seeing Vashishtha so carried away, Vishvamitra, impatient, and enraged by vexation, said to her : ' Since thou, O chief of rivers, hast elued me, and hast receded, roll in waves of blood acceptable to the chief of demons," (which are fabled to gloat on blood). "The Sarasvati, being thus cursed, flowed for a year in a stream mingled with blood. . . .. Rakshasas came to the place of pilgrimage, where Vashishtha had been swept away, and revealed in drinking to satiety the bloody stream in security, dancing and laughing, as if they had conquered heaven." Some rishis who arrived at the spot some time after were horrified to see the blood-stained water, and the Rakshasas quaffing it, and "made the most strenuous efforts to rescue the Sarasvati."

The foregoing cases relate to individual conflicts between a particular Brahmin and a particular Kshatriya. The cases which follow are cases of class or communal conflicts between Brahmins on the one hand and the Kshatriyas on the other. They are not mere conflicts. Nor is it correct to say that they were like communal riots. They were class wars undertaken by one community with the avowed intention of exterminating the other root and branch. Two such class wars of extermination have been recorded in the Mahabharat. The first is a war of the Haihaya Kshatriyas on the Bhargava Brahmins. It occurred in the reign of the Haihaya King Kritavirya. The following is the description of this war in the Adiparvan of the Mahabharat.

"There was a king named Kritavirya, by whose liberality the Bhrigu, learned in the Vedas, who officiated as his priest, had been greatly enriched with corn, and money. After he had gone to heaven, his descendants were in want of money, and came to beg for a supply from the Bhrigus, of whose wealth they were aware. Some of the latter hid their money under ground, others bestowed it on Brahmans, being afraid of the Kshatriyas, while others again gave these last what they wanted. It happened, however, that a Kshatriya, while digging the ground, discovered some money buried in the house of a Bhrigu. The Kshatriyas then assembled and saw this treasure, and, being incensed, slew in consequence all the Bhrigus, whom they regarded with contempt, down to the children in the womb. The widows, however, fled to the Himalaya mountains. One of them concealed her unborn child in her thigh. The Kshatriyas, hearing of its existence from a Brahmani informant, sought to kill it; but it issued forth from its mother's thigh with lustre, and blinded the persecutors. After wandering about bewildered among the mountains for a time, they humbly supplicated the mother of the child for the restoration of their sight; but she referred them to her wonderful infant Aurva into whom the whole Veda, with its six Vedangas, had entered, as the person who (in retaliation of the slaughter of his relatives) had robbed them or their eye-sight, and who alone could restore it.

They accordingly had recourse to him, and their eye-sight was restored. Aurva, however, meditated the destruction of all living creatures, in revenge for the slaughter of the Bhrigus, and entered on a course of austerities which alarmed both gods, asuras, and men; but his progenitors (Pitris) themselves appeared, and sought to turn him from his purpose by saying that they had no desire to be revenged on the Kshatriyas : It was not from weakness that the devout Bhrigus overlooked the massacre perpetrated by the murderous Kshatriyas. When we became distressed by old age, we ourselves desired to be slaughtered by them. The money which was buried by someone in a Bhrigu's house was placed there for the purpose of exciting hatred, by those who wished to provoke the Kshatriyas. For what had we, who were desiring heaven, to do with money?" They add that they hit upon this device because they did not wish to be guilty of suicide, and concluded by calling upon Aurva to restrain his wrath; and abstain from the sin he was meditating, "Destroy not the Kshatriyas, O son, nor the seven worlds.

Suppress thy kindled anger which nullifies the power of austere-fervour." Aurva, however, replies that he cannot allow his threat to remain unexecuted. His anger, unless wreaked upon some other object, will, he says, consume himself. And he argues on grounds of justice, expediency, and duty, against the clemency which his progenitors recommend. He is, however, persuaded by the Pitris to throw the fire of his anger into the sea, where they say it will find exercise in assailing the watery element, and in this way his threat will be fulfilled." The second class war and which was also a war of extermination was declared by the Bhargava Brahmins on the Haihaya Kshatriyas. In this the leader of Bhargava Brahmins was one Parashuram. The story of the birth of Parashuram is described in the Vishnu Purana in the following terms:

"Gadhi's daughter Satyavati had been given in marriage to an old Brahman called Richika, of the family of Bhrigu. In order that his wife might bear a son with the qualities of a Brahman, Richika had prepared for her a dish of Charu (rice, barley, and pulse, with butter and milk) for her to eat; and a similar mess for her mother, calculated to make her conceive a son with the character of a warrior. Satyavati's mother, however, persuaded her to exchange messes. She was blamed by her husband on her return home for what she had done. I quote the words of the original:

"Sinful woman, what improper deed is this that thou has done? I beheld thy body of a very terrible appearance. Thou hast certainly eaten the Charu prepared for thy mother. This was wrong. For into that Chari I had infused all the endowments of heriosm, vigour, and roce, whilst into thine I had introduced all these qualities of quietude, knowledge, and patnence which constitute the perfection of a Brahmin. Since thou hast acted in contravention of my design a son shall be born to thee who shall live the dreadful, martial, and murderous life of a Kshatriya and thy mother's offspring shall exhibit the peaceful disposition and conduct of a Brahman." As soon as she had heard this, Satyavati fell down and seized her husband's feet, and said, 'My lord, I have acted from ignorance; show kindness to me, let me not have a son of the sort thou hast described; if thou pleasest, let me have a grandson of that description. `Subsequently she bore Jamadagni, and her mother gave birth to Vishvamitra. Satyavati became the river called Kausiki. Jamadagni wedded Renuka, the daughter of Renu, of the family of Ikshvaku; and on her he begot a son called Parasurama." The following additional details about Parshuram's family history is given in the Venaparvan of the Mahabharata :

"Jamadagni and Satyavati had five sons, the youngest of whom was the repubtable Parasurama. By his father's command he kills his mother (who by the indulgence of impure desire, had fallen from her brevious sanctity), after the four elder sons had refused this matricidal offen, and had in consequence been deprived of reason by their father's curse. At Parasurama's desire however, his mother is restored by his father to life, and his brothers to reason; and he himself is absolved from all the guilt of murder; and obtains the boon of invincibility and long life from his father." This second class war took place in the reign of the Haihaya king Arjuna the son of King Kartavirya. To understand it correctly it is necessary to devide it into two parts for there are two stages in it. The trouble began with the Brahmans claiming certain prerogatives and powers exclusively for themselves and King—Arjuna scouting them in most contemptuous terms. As the Anushasanparvan of the Mahbharata puts it.

"Then ascending his chariot glorious as the resplendent sun, he exclaimed in the intoxication of his prowess, ' Who is like me in fortitude, courage, fame, heriosm, energy, and vigour?' At the end of this speech a bodiless voice on the sky addressed him: 'Thou knowest not, O fool, that a Brahman is better than a Kshatriya. It is with the help of the Brahman that the Kshatriya rules his subjects. Arjuna answers 'If I am pleased, I can create, or, if displeased, annihilate, living beings; and no Brahman is superior to me in act, thought, or word. The first proposition is that the Brahmans are superior; the second that the Kshatriyas are superior: both of these thou hast stated with their ground, but there is a difference between them. The Brahmans are dependent on the Kshatriyas, and not the Kshatriyas on the Brahmans; and the Kshatriyas on the Brahmans; and the Kshatriyas are eaten up by the Brahmans, who wait upon them and only make the Vedas a pretence. Justice the protection of the people, has its seat in the Kshatriyas. From them the Brahmans derive their livelihood: how then can the latter be superior? I always keep in subjection to myself those Brahmans, the chief of all beings, who subsist on alms, and who have a high opinion of themselves. For truth was apoken by that female the Gayatri in the sky. I shall subdue all those unruly Brahmans clad in hides. No one in the three worlds, god or man can hurl me from my royal authority; wherefore I am superior to any Brahman." On hearing this Vayu comes and says to Arjuna :

"Abandon this sinful disposition, and to obeisance to the Brahmans. If thou shalt do them wrong, thy kingdom shall be convulsed. They will subdue thee; those powerful men will humble thee, and expel thee from thy country' The king asks him, 'who art thou? Vayu replies, 'I Vayu, the messenger of the gods, and tell thee what is for thy benefit'. Arjuna rejoins, '*Oh* thou displayest today a great warmth of devotion to the Brahmans. But say that a Brahman is like (any other) earth-born creature. Or say that this most excellent Brahman is something like the wind. But fire is like the waters, or the sun, or the sky.' Vayu then adduces various instances in which the superiority of the Brahmins has been mainfested. Arjuna then drops his hostility against the Brahmins and becomes their friend. In the Anushasanparva he is reported to have said :

"I live altogether and always for the sake of the Brahmans. I am devoted to the Brahmans, and do obeisance to them continually. And it is through the favour of Dattatreya (A Brahman) that I have obtained all this power and high renown, and that I have practised righteousness."

It is in the second stage that Parashuram comes on the scene and extreminates the Kshatriyas. The story is told in the Shantiparvan in the following terms :

"Being of a meek, pious, kind and charitable turn of mind, the valiant Arjuna thought nothing of the curse; but his sons, who were of an arrogant and barbarous disposition, became the cause of its resulting in his death. Without their father's knowledge they took away Jamadagni's calf; and in consequence Parasurama attacked Arjuna and cut off his arms." His son retaliated by killing Jamadagni. Parashurama incensed at the slaughter of his father, having vowed in consequence to sweep away all Kshatriyas from the earth, seized his weapons; and slaying all the sons and grandsons of Arjuna, with thousands of the Haihayas, he turned the earth into a mass of ensanguined mud. Having thus cleared the earth of Kshatriyas, he became penetrated by deep compassion and retired to the forest. After some thousands of years had elapsed, the hero, naturally irascible, was taunted by Paravsu, the son of Raibhya and grandson of Visvamitra, in a public assembly in these words: 'Are not these virtuous men, Pratardana and the others, who are assembled at the sacrifice in the city of Yayati,—are they not Kshatriyas? Thou hast failed to execute thy threat, and vainly boastest in the assembly. Thou has withdrawn to the mountain from fear of those valiant Kshatriyas, while the earth has again become overrrun by hundred of their race. `Hearing these words, Rama seized his weapons. The hundreds of Kshatriyas who had before been spared had now grown powerful kings. These, however, Parasurama now slew with their children, and all the numerous infants then unborn as they came into the world. Some, however, were preserved by their mothers." Those who are curious to know the subsequent history of the Kshatriyas might be interested in the following extract from the Adiparvan.

" Having one and twenty time swept away all the Kshatriyas from the earth, the son of Jamadagni engaged in austerities on Mahendra the most excellent of mountains. After he had cleared the world of Kshatriyas, their widows came to the

Brahmans, praying for offspring. The religious Brahmans, free from any impulse of lust cohabited at the proper seasons with these women, who in consequence became pregnant, and brought forth valiant Kshatriya boys and girls, to continue the Kshatriya stock. Thus was the Kshatriya race virtuously begotten by Brahmans on Kshatriya women, and became multiplied and long-lived, thence arose four castes inferior to the Brahmans." These instances of enmity were accompanied by challenges from one side to the other which shows how high were the tempers running on both sides.

The conduct of king Nimi in yoking the Brahmins to his chariot and making them drag it like horses show how determined the Kshatriyas were to humiliate the Brahmans. The challenges uttered by Arjuna Kartavirya against the Brahmins indicates his determination to level them down. The Brahmins on their side were not slow to take up this challenge and send counter challenges to the kshatriyas not to provoke the Brahmins.

This is very clear from the way Vayu the messenger or Ambassador of the Brahmins talks to Arjuna Kartivirya after he had issued his challenge to the Brahmans. Vayu tells Arjuna how the Brhmans Atri made sea water saltish by urinating in it, how Dandakas were overthrown by the Brahmans, how the Kshatriyas of the Talajaughas were destroyed by a single Brahmin Aurva; The striking power of the Brahmins is not only superior to that of the Kshatriya it is superior to that of the Devas and Vayu proceeds to tell Arjuna some of the victories achieved by the Brahmins over the Devas. He tells him how Varuna ran away with Bhadra the daughter of Soma and the wife of the Brahman Utathya of the race of Angiras how Utathya by his curse caused the earth to be dried up and how Varuna as a consequence submitted to Utathya and returned his wife. He tells him how once the *Devas* were conquered by the Asuras and the Danavas, how deprived of all oblations, and stripped of their dignity they came to the earth went to the Brahmin Agastya and applied to him for protection and how Agastya scorched the Danavas from heaven and earth and made him fly to the South and reinstated the Devas in their dominion. He tells Arjuna how once the Adityas were performing a sacrifice and while engaged in it were attached by Danvas called Khalims, who came in ten in thousands to slay them, how the Adityas went to Indra and how Indra himself attached by the Daityas not being able to render help to the Adityas went to the Brahmin Vashishtha for help and how Vashishtha taking mercy on the Adityas saved them by burning the Danavas alive. He next tells Arjuna how the Danavas once fought with the Devas, how by enveloping them in dreadful darkness the Danavas slaughtered the Devas, how the Devas implored the Brahmin Atri to become the moon and dispell the glown around the sun which Atri did thereby saved the Devas from the Danvas. The last episode of Brahmin prowess which Vayu tells Arjuna is how the Brahmin Chyavana compelled Indra to admit the Ashwins to equal rank and drink Soma with them as a token of equality and how when Indra refused he took away both the earth and heaven from them and how he created a Demon Mada and put the Devas including Indra into his mouth and how he compelled Indra to admit the Ashwins to equal rank and drink Soma with them and how Indra ultimately surrendered to Chyavana.

Vayu did not merely recount these exploits of the Brahmins. He did something more. Every time he gave Arjuna an instance of the power of the Brahmins he ended by asking Arjuna pointed questions such as "Can you tell me of any Kshatriya who was superior to him (i.e. the Brahmins hero of the story) "Declare on your part, any Kshatriya who has been superior to him, "Tell me of any Kshatriya superior to Atri."

This class war between the Brahmins and the Kshatriyas must have gone on for ages. In the light of this the attitude of Manu towards this Class War comes as very strange. Consider the following verses from the Manu Smriti :

IV. 135. "Let him who desires prosperity, indeed, never despise a Kshatriya, a snake, and a learned Brahmana, be they ever so feeble."

IV. 136. "Because these three, when treated with disrespect, may utterly destroy him; hence a wise man must never despite them."

X. 322. "Kshatriyas prosper not without Brahmans, Brahmans prosper not without Kshatriyas; Brahmans and Kshatriyas, being closely united, prosper in this (world) and in the next." Here there is a clear attempt on the part of Manu to close the ranks. Against whom did Manu want the Brahmins and the Kshatriyas to close their ranks? Was this an attempt to forget and forgive or was the motive to combine them in a conspiracy to achieve some unholy purpose. What were the circumstances that forced Manu to advise the Brahmins to forget their age old enmity with Kshatriyas and seek the helping hand? The circumstances, must have been very hard and very pressing. For there was no room left for a reapproachment between the two. The Brahmins had hurled a terrible insult against the Kshatriyas and had wounded their price by saying quite openly that the Kshatriyas were the illegitimate children of Brahmins begotten by them on Kshatriya widows. The next offensive thing that the Brahmins had done to wound the feelings of the Kshatriyas was to extract from the latter a confession that the Brahmins were superior to the Kshatriyas in military prowess and had made Bhishma say :

"'The prowess of the Brahmans can destroy even the gods. Those wise beings beholdall these worlds. To them it is indifferent whether they are perfumed with sandal wood or deformed with mire, whether they eat or fast, whether they are clad in silk, or in sack cloth or skins. They can turn what is not divine into what is divine, and the converse; and can in their anger create other worlds with their guardians. They are the gods of the gods; and the cause of the cause. The ignorant Brahman is a god, whilst a learned Brahman is yet more a god, like the full ocean."

All this makes this sudden climb down by the Brahmins, this stoping down to win over the Kshatriyas very mysterious. What can be the key to this mystery?

7

Shudras and the Counter—Revolution

This is a 21-page foolscap typed manuscript. The cover page is having a title 'Shudras and the Counter-Revolution' and the text on next page starts with the same title. All these pages were loose and tagged together. Unfortunately, only 21 pages are available and the latter pages seem to be lost.— Editors.

The laws of Manu relating to the Status of the Shudra make a very interesting reading for the simple reason that they have moulded thed psychology of the Hindus and determined their attitude towards the Shudras who forms at the present and at-all times the most numerous part of Hindu society. They are set out below under separate heads so that it may be possible for the reader to have a complete idea of the status given by Manu to the Community of Shudras.

Manu asks the householders of the Brahmana, Kshatriya and Vaishya Class :

IV. 61. Let him not dwell in a country where the rulers are Shudra. A Shudra is not to be deemed as a respectable person. For Manu enacts that:

XI. 24. A Brahmin shall never beg from a Shudra property for (performing) a sacrifice i.e. for religious purpose. All marriage ties with the Shudra were proscribed. Marriage with a woman belonging to any of the three other classes was forbidden. A Shudra was not to have any connection with a woman of the higher classes and an act of adultery committed by a Shudra with her was declared by manu to be an offence involving capital punishment.

VIII. 374. A Shudra who has an intercourse with a woman of the higher caste guarded or unguarded, shall be punished in the following manner :

If she was unguarded, he loses the offending part. If she was guarded then he should be put to death and his property confiscated.

As to office Manu prescribes.

VIII. 20. A Brahmana who is only a Brahmana by decent i.e. one who has neither studied nor performed any other act required by the Vedas may, at the king's pleasure, interpret the law to him i.e. act as the Judge, but never a Shudra (however learned he may be).

VIII. 21. The kingdom of that monarch who looks on while a Shudra settles the law will sink low like a cow in a morass.

VIII. 272. If a Shudra arrogantly presumes to preach religion to Brahmins the King shall have poured burning oil in his mouth and oars.

In the matter of acquiring learning the knowledge Manu ordains as follows :

III. 156. He who instructs Shudra pupils and he whose teacher is a Shudra shall become disqualified for being invited to a Shudra.

IV. 99. He must never read the Vedas. . . . . in the presece of the Shudras.

Manu's successors went much beyond him in the cruelty of their punishment of the Shudra for studying the Veda. For instance Katyayana lays down that if a Shudra overheard the Veda or ventured to utter a word of the Veda the King shall cut his tongue in twain and pour hot molten lead in his ears. As to right to property by the Shudra Manu enjoins as follows:

X. 129. No superfluous collection of wealth must be made by a Shudra, even though he has power to make it, since a servile man, who has amassed riches, becomes proud, and, by his insolence or neglect, gives pain to Brahmans.

VIII. 417. A Brahmanas may seize without hesitation if he be in distress for his subsistence, the goods of his Shudra. The Shudra can have only one occupation. This is one of the inexhorable Laws of Manu. Says Manu :

1. 91. One occupation only, the Lord prescribed to the Shudra, to serve meekly these other three castes (namely Brahmin, Kshatriya and Vaishyas).

X. 121. If a Shudra, (unable to subsist by serving Brahmans) seeks a livelihood, he may serve Kshatriyas, or he may also seek to maintain himself by attending on a wealthy Vaisya.

X. 122. But let (Shudra) serve Brahmans, either for the sake of heaven, or with a view to both (this life and the next); for he who is called the servant of a Brahmana thereby gains all his ends.

X. 123. The service of Brahmanas alone is declared (to be) an excellent occupation for a Shudra for whatever else besides this he may perform will bear him no fruit. Service by Shudra is not left by Manu to be regulated as a free contract. If the Shudra refuses to serve there is a provision for conscription which runs as follows :

VIII. 413. A Brahmana may compel a Shudra, whether bought or unbought to do servile work; for he is created by the creator to be the slave of a Brahmana.

X. 124. They must allot to him out of their own family (property) a suitable maintenance, after considering his ability, his industry, and the number of those whom he is bound to suport.

X. 125. The remnants of their food must be given to him, as well as their old household furniture.

A Shudra is required by Manu to be servile in his speech and manner towards the other classes.

VIII. 270. A Shudra who insults a twice-born man with gross invective, shall have his tongue cut out; for he is of low origin.

VIII. 271. If he mentions the names and castes of the (twice-born) with contumely, an iron nail, ten fingers long, shall be thrust red hot into his mouth.

Manu is not satisfied with this. He wants this servile status of the Shudra to be expressed in the names and surnames of persons belonging to that community. Manu says :

II. 31. Let the first part of a Brahman's name denote something auspicious, a Kshatriya's be connected with power and a Vaishya's with wealth, but a Shudra's, express something contemptible.

II. 32. The second part of a Brahman's name shall be a word implying happiness; of a Kshatriya's word implying protection; of a Vaishya's a term expressive of thriving and of a Shudra's an expression denoting services.

What was the position of the Shudra before Manu? Manu treats the Shudra as though he was an alien Non-Aryan not entitled to the social and religious privileges of the Aryan. Unfortunately the view that the Shudra was a Non-Aryan is too readily accepted by the generality of the people. But there can be no doubt that this view has not the slightest foundation in the literature of the ancient Aryans.

Reading the Religious literature of the ancient Aryans one comes across the names of various communities and groups of people. There were first of all the Aryans with their fourfold divisions of Brahmins, Kshatriyas, Vaishyas and Shudras. Besides them and apart from them there were *(i)* Asuras *(ii)* Suras or Devas (iii)Yakshas *(iv)* Gandharvas *(v)* Kinnars *(vi)* Charanas *(vii)* Ashvins and *(viii)* Nishadas. The Nishadas were a jungle people primitive and uncivilized. The Gandharvas, Yakshas, Kinnars, Charanas and Ashvins were professional classes and not communities. The word Asura is generic name given to various tribes known by their tribal names of Daityas, Danavas, Dasyus, Kalananjas, Kaleyyas, Kalins, Nagas, Nivata-Kavachas, Paulomas, Pishachas and Raxasas. We do not know if the Suras and Devas were composed of various tribes as the Asuras were. We only know the leaders of the Deva Community. The well known amongst them were Brahma, Vishnu Rudra, Surya, Indra, Varuna, Soma etc.

Due mostly to the ignorant interpretations of Sayanacharya some very curious beliefs prevail even among the best informed people about these communities namely the Aryans, the Asuras and the Devas and their inter-relation and their consanguinity. It is believed that the Asuras were not a human species at all. They are held to have been ghosts and goblins who plagued the Aryans with their nocturnal visitations. The Suras or Devas are understood to be poetic deifications of nature's forces. With regard to the Aryans the belief is that they were a fair race with sharp nose and had a great deal of colour prejudice. As to the Dasyus it is asserted that a Dasyu is only another name for a Shudra. The Shudras it is said formed the aboriginals of India. They were dark and flat nosed. The Aryans who invaded India conquered them and made them slaves and as a badge of slavery gave them the name Dasyu which it is said comes from the word Das which means a slave.

Every one of these beliefs is unfounded. The Asuras and Suras were communities of human beings as the Aryans were. The Asuras and Suras were descended from a common father Kashapa. The story is that Daksha Prajapati had 60 daughters, of them thirteen were given in marriage to Kashapa. Diti and Aditi were two among the 13 of Kashapa's wives. Those born to Diti were called Asuras and those born to Aditi were called Suras or Devas. The two faught a long and a bloody battle for the soverignty of the world. This no doubt is mythology and mythology though it is history in hyperbole is still history.

The Aryans were not a race. The Aryans were a collection of people. The cement that held them together was their interest in the maintenance of a type of culture called Aryan culture. Any one who accepted the Aryan culture was an Aryan. Not being a race there was no fixed type of colour and physiognomy which could be called Aryan. There was no dark and flat nose people for the Aryans to distinguish themselves from· The whole of this edifice of colour prejudice as being factors for division and antagonism between Aryans and the Dasyus is based upon a wrong meaning given to the two words *Varna* and *Anas* which are used with reference to the Dasyus. The word Varna is taken to mean colour and the word *Anas* is taken to mean without nose. Both these meanings are erroneous. Varna means Caste or group and *Anas* if read as An-As means uncultivated speech. That statement that the Aryans had a colour prejudice which determined their social order is arrant nonsense. If there were any people who were devoid of colour prejudice it is the Aryans and that is because there was no dominant colour to distinguish themselves.

It is wrong to say that the Dasyus were non-Aryans by race. The Dasyus were not a pre-Aryan race of aboriginals of India. The Dasyus were members of the Aryan community who were deprived of the title of Arya for opposing some belief or cult which was an essential part of the Aryan Culture. How this belief that the Dasyus were Non-Aryans by race could have arisen it is difficult to understand. In the Rig Veda (X. 49) Indra says : "I (Indra) have killed with my thuderbolt for the good of the man, known as Kavi. I have protected Kupa by adopting means of protection. I took up the thunderbolt for killing Susna. I *have deprived the Dasyus of the appellation of Arya."*

Nothing can be more positive and definite than this statement of Indra that the Dasyus were Aryans. Further and better proof of this fact can be had in the impeachment of Indra for the various atrocities he had committed. In the list of atrocities for which Indra was impeached there was one charge namely the killing of Vratra. Vratra was the leader of the Dasyus. It is unthinkable that such a charge could be framed against Indra if the Dasyus were not Aryans.

It is erroneous to believe that the Shudras were conquered by the Aryan invaders. In the first place the story that the Aryans came from outside India and invaded the natives has no evidence to support it. There is a large body of evidence that India is the home of the Aryans. In the second place there is no evidence anywhere of any wa.rfare having taken place between Aryans and Dasyus but the Dasyus have nothing to do with the Shudras. In the third place it is difficult to believe that the Aryans were a powerful people capable of much military prowess. Any one who reads the history of the Aryans in India in their relation to the Devas will be reminded of the relationship that subsisted between the Viellens and their lords during the feudal times. The Devas were the feudal lords and the Aryans were the Villens. The innumerable sacrifices which the Aryans performed have the look of fudal dues paid to the Deva. This servility of the Aryans to the Devas was due to the fact that without the help and the protection of the Devas they could not withstand the assualts of the Asuras. It is too much to presume that so effete a people could have conquered the Shudras. Lastly there was no necessity to conquer the Shudra. Thy were Aryans in the only sense in which the word Aryan is used, namely, the upholders of the Aryans Culture. Two things are clear about the Shudras. Nobody has ever contended that they were dark and flat nosed. Nobody has contended that they were defeated or enslaved by the Aryans. It is wrong to treat the Dasyus and Shudras as one and the same. As a people they may be the same. But culturally they were quite different.The Dasyus were Non-Aryans in the sense they had fallen away and rebelled against the Aryan culture. The Shudras on the other hand were Aryans i.e. they were believers in the Aryan way of life. The Shudra was accepted as an Aryan and as late as Kautilya's Artha Shastra was addressed an Arya.

The Shudra was an intergral, natural and valued member of the Aryan Society is proved by a prayer which is found in the Yajur Veda and which is offered by the Sacrificer. It runs as follows : "......... 0 Gods

Give lustre to our holy priests, set lustre in our ruling chiefs, Lustre to Vaisyas, Sudras : Give, through lustre; Lustre unto me." It is a remarkable prayer, remarkable because it shows that the Shudra was a member of the Aryan Community and was also a respected member of it.

That the Shudras were invited to be present at the coronation of the King along with Brahmins, Kshatriyas and Vaishyas is proved by the description given in the Mahabharata of the coronation of Yudhisthira the eldest brother of the Pandavas. Shudra took part in the consecration of the King. According to ancient writer called Nilkantha speaking of the coronation ceremony expressly says : "that the four chief Ministers, Brahmin, Kshatriya, Vaishya and Shudra consecra.ted the new king. Then the leaders of each Varna and by the Castes lower still consecrated him with the holy water. Then followed acclamation by the twice-born. In the post-vedic period preceding Manu there was group of the representatives of the people called the Ratnis. The Ratnis played a significant part in the investiture of the King. The Ratnis were so called because they held the Ratna (jewel) which was a symbol of sovereignty. The king received his sovereignty only when the Ratnis handed over to him the jewel of sovereignty and on receiving his sovereignty the King went to the house of each of the Ratnis and made an offering to him. It is a significant fact that the Shudra was one of the Ratnis.

Shudras were members of the two political Assemblies of ancient times namely the Janapada and Paura and as a member of this he was entitled to special respect even from a Brahmin.

That the Shudra in the Ancient Aryan Society had reached a high political status is indisputable. They could become ministers of State. The Mahabharat bears testimony to this. Enumerating the different classes of ministers within his memory the writer of the Mahabharata mentions a list of 37 Ministers of whom four are Brahmins, eight Kshatriyas, twenty one Vaishyas, three Shudras and one Suta.

Shudras did not stop with being ministers of State. They even became Kings. The story of Shudras which is given in the Rig Veda stands in cruel contrast with the views expressed by Manu regarding the eligibility of the Shudra to be a King. The reign of Sudas if referred to at all is referred only in connection with the terrible contest between Vashishtha and Vishvamitra as to who should become the purohit or Royal priest of King Sudas. The issue involved in the contest was as to the right to officiate as the Purohit or the King. Vashishtha who was a Brahmin and who was already an officiating priest of Sudas claimed that a Brahmin alone could become the Purohit of a King while Vishvamitra who was a Kshatriya contended that a Kshatriya was competent for that office.

Vishvamitra succeeded and in his turn became the Purohit of Sudas. The contest is indeed memorable because the issue involved in it is very crucial although the result has not been a permanent deprivation of the Brahmins. But there can be no doubt the story is probably the best piece of social history that is to be found in the ancient literature. Unfortunately nobody has taken serious notice of it. Nobody has even asked who this King was. Sudas was the son of Paijavana and Paijavana is the son of Devodas who was the King of Kasi i.e. Benares. What was the Varna of Sudas? Few would believe if they were told that King Sudas was a Shudra. But that is a fact and it can be proved by the testimony of the Mahabharata where in the Santipurva a reference is made to this *Paijavana.* It is stated that Paijavana was a Shudra. In the light of this the story of Sudas sheds new light on the status of the Shudra in the Aryan Society. It shows that a Shudra could be a reigning monarch. It also shows that both the Brahmins and the Kshatriyas not only saw no humiliation in serving a Shudra King but they with each other to secure his patronage and were ready to perform vedic ceremonies at his house.

It cannot be said that there were no Shudra Kings in later times. On the contrary history shows that the two dynasties which preceded Manu were dynasties of Shudras Kings. The Nandas who ruled from B.C.413 to B.C. 322were Shudras. The mauryas who succeded the Nandas and who ruled from 322 B.C, to 183 B.C. were also Shudras. What more glaring piece of evidence can there be to show the high dignity enjoyed by the Shudra than to point to the case of Asoka who was not merely the Emperor of India but a Shudra and his Empire was the Empire built by the Shudras.

On the question of the right of the Shudra to study the Vedas a reference may be made to the Chhandogya Upanished (V. 1.2). It relates the story of one Janasruti to whom Veda Vidya was taught by the preceptor Raikva. This Janasruti was a Shudra. This story if it is a genuine story leaves no doubt that there was a time when there was no bar against the Shudra in the matter of studying the Vedas.

Not only was Shudra free to study the Vedas but there were Shudras who had reached the status of Rishis and has been composers of the Hymns of the Vedas. The story of the Rishi Kavasha Aliusha is very illuminating. He was a Rishi and the author of several hymns of the Tenth Book of the Rig-Veda.

On the question of the spiritual eligibility of the Shudra to perform the Vedic ceremonies and sacrifies the following data may be presented. Jaimin the author of the Purva Mimansa mentions an ancient teacher by name Badari—whose work is lost as an exponent of the view that even Shudra could perform Vedic sacrifices. The Bharadvaja Srauta Sutra (v. 28) admits that there exists another school of thought which holds that a Sudra can consecrate the three sacred fires necessary for the performance of a Vedic Sacrifice. Similarly the Commentator of the Katyayana Srauta Sutra (I & 5) admits that there are certain Vedic texts which lead o the inference that the Shudra was eligible to perform Vedic rites. In the Satpath Brahmana (1. 1.4.12) there is enunciated a rule of etiquette which the priest officiating at the performance of a sacrifice is required to observe. It relates to the mode in which the priest should address the Haviskut (the person celebrating the sacrifice) calling upon him to begin the ceremony. The rule says:

"Now there are four different forms of this call, viz. 'Come hither' (Ehi) in the case of a Brahmana; 'approach' (Agahi) and 'hasten hither' (Adarva) in the case of a Vaishya and a member of the Military caste and 'run hither' (Adhava) in that of a Shudra." In the Satpatha Brahman there is evidence to show that the Shudra was eligible to perform the Soma Yaga and to partake of the divine drink Soma. It says that in the Soma Yaga in place of a 'payovrata' (vow to drink milk only) Mastu (whey) is prescirbed for the Shudra. In another place the same Satapatha Brahmana says :

"There are four classes, the Brahmin, Rajanya, Vaishya and Sudra. There is no one of these who dislikes Soma. If any one of them however should do so, let there be an atonment." This means that the drinking of Soma was not only permissible but it was compulsory on all including the Shudra. But in the story of the Ashvins there is definite evidence that the Shudra had a right to the divine drink of Soma. The Ashvins as the story goes once happened to behold Sukanya when she had just bathed and when her person was bare. She was young girl married to a Rishi by name Chyavana who at the time of marriage was so old as to be dying almost any day. The Ashvins were captivated by the beauty of Sukanya and said "accept one of us for your husband, it behoveth thee not to spend thy youth fruitlessly."

She refused saying "I am devoted to my husband." They again spoke to her and this time proposed a bargain—" We two are the celestial physicians of note. We will make thy husband young and graceful. Do thou then select one of us as thy husband." She went to her husband and communicated to him the terms of the bargain. Chyavana said to Sukanya "Do thou so" and the bargain was carried out and Chyavana was made a young man by the Ashwins. Subsequently a question arose whether the Ashwins were entitled to Soma which was the drink of the Gods. Indra objected saying that the Ashwins were Shudras and therefore not entitled to Soma. Chyavana who had received perpetual youth from the Ashwins set aside the contention and compelled Indra to give them Soma.

All these provisions can have no meaning unless the Shudra was in fact performing the Vedic ceremonies to which they relate—there is evidence to show that a Shudra woman took part in the Vedic sacrifice known as the Ashwamedha. With regard to the Upanayana ceremony and the right to wear the sacred thread there is nowhere an express prohibition against the Shudra. On the other hand in the Sansakara Ganapati there is an express provision declaring the Shudra to be eligible for Upanayan. The Shudra though belonging to a lower class was nonetheless a free citizen in days before Manu cannot be gainsaid. Consider the following provisions in Kautilya's Artha Shastra :

"The selling or mortgaging by kinsmen of the life of a Sudra who is not a born slave, and has not attained majority, but is an Arya in birth shall be punished with a fine of 2 panas."

"Deceiving a slave of his money or depriving him of the privileges he can exercise as an Arya (Aryabhava), shall be punished with half the fine (levied for enslaving the life of an Arya)."

"Failure to set a slave at liberty on the receipt of a required amount of ransom shall be punished with a fine of 12 panas; putting a slave under confinement for no reason (samrodhaschakaranat) shall likewise be punished.

"The offspring of a man who has sold himself off as a slave shall be an Arya. A slave shall be entitled without prejudice to his master's work but also the inheritance he has received from his father."

Bibliography

Abbe, D.: *Hindu Manners, Customs and Ceremonies*, AES, New Delhi, 1983.

Ahir, D.C.: *Dr. Ambedkar, Buddhism and Social Change*, BR Publishing, Delhi, 1993.

Anandhi, S.: *Contending Identities: Dalits and Secular Politics in Madras Slums*, Indian Social Institute, New Delhi, 1995.

Asghar Ali.: *Mandal Commission Controversy*, Ajanta Publications, Delhi, 1991.

Bakshi, S. R.: B.R. *Ambedkar: His Political and Social Ideology*. New Delhi: Deep & deep publications, 2000.

Bandyopadhyay, Sekhar: *Caste, Class and Politics in Colonial Bengal: A Case Study of the Namasudra Movement of 1872-1937*, Rawat Publications, New Delhi, 1994.

Barill, C.: *Social and Political Ideas of B.R. Ambedkar*, Aalekh Publishers, Jaipur, 1977.

Benjamin, Joseph: *Scheduled Castes in Indian Politics and Society*, Ess Ess Publications, New Delhi, 1989.

Bhatia, K.L.: *Dr. B.R. Ambedkar: Social Justice and the Indian Constitution,* Deep & Deep, New Delhi, 1994.

Bhatt, V.: *The Harijans of Maharashtra*, All India Harijan Sevak Sangh, Delhi, 1941.

Bose, Sipra: *Social Mobility Among Untouchables,* Cohesion and Conflict in Modern India, New Delhi, 1978.

Carsten, F. L.: *The Rise of Fascism*, Methuen and Co., London, 1967.

Chanchreek, K.L., Prasad, S. & Kumar, R.: *Dr. Ambedkar. Social Justice and Political Safeguards for Depressed Classes,* Shree, New Delhi, 1991.

Chatterjee, Partha: *Caste and Subaltern Consciousness*, Oxford University Press, Delhi, 1994.

Danda, A.K.: *Weaker Sections in Indian Villages*, Inter-India, New Delhi, 1993.

Epstein, T. S.: *Economic Development and Social Change in South India*, Manchester University Press, Manchester, 1962.

Galanter, Marc.: *Competing Inequalities: Law and the Backward Classes in India,* University of California Press, CA, 1984.

Gawali, P.A.: *Society and Social Disabilities under the Peshwas*, National, New Delhi, 1988.

Gore, M.S.: *The Social Context of an Ideology: Ambedkar's Political and Social Thought*, Sage, New Delhi, 1993.

Gorhe, Neelam: *Social Development and Dalit Women*, Gyan Pub. House, New Delhi, 1995.

Gupta, S. K.: *Scheduled Castes in Modern Indian Politics: Their Emergence as a Political Power*, Munshiram Manoharlal Publishers, New Delhi, 1985.

Ishwaran, K.: *Shivpur: A South Indian Village*, Routledge, London, 1968.

Jeevaratanam, A. G.: *Political Implications of Untouchability*, Kondaveedu Press, Hyderabad, 1973.

Jogdan, Prahlad G.: *Dalit Movement in Maharashtra*, Kanak Publications, New Delhi, 1991.

Johnson, S. B.: *Social Mobility Among Untouchables*, Vikas, New Delhi, 1979.

Jose, K.: *Constitutional Provisions for the Scheduled Castes*, Indian Social Institute, New Delhi, 1984.

Joshi, B.R.: *Democracy in Search of Equality: Untouchable Politics and Indian Social Change*, Hindustan Publishing Co., Delhi, 1982.

Joshi, B.R.: *Untouchable! Voices of the Dalit Liberation Movement*, Zed and MRG, London, 1986.

Khare, R. S.: *The Untouchable as Himself: Ideology, Identity and Pragmatism Among the Lucknow Chamars*, Cambridge University Press, London, 1984.

Kshirsagar, R. K.: *Dalit Movement in India and Its Leaders (1857-1956)*, MD Pub. Pvt. Ltd., New Delhi, 1994.

Lal, Shyam: *Caste and Political Mobilisation: The Bhangis*, Panchsheel Prakashan, Jaipur, 1981.

Lynch, Owen M.: *The Politics of Untouchability: Social Mobility and Social Change in a City of India*, Columbia University Press, New York, 1969.

Mahar, Michael J.: *The Untouchables in Contemporary India*, University of Arizona Press, Arizona, 1972.

Majumdar, D. N.: *Caste and Communication in an Indian Village*, Asia Publishing House, Bombay, 1958.

Mann, K.: *Tribal Women in a Changing Society*, Mittal Publications, Delhi, 1987.

Mark J.: *Religion as Social Vision: The Movement Against Untouchability in 20th Century in Punjab*, University of California Press, Berkeley, 1982.

Marriott, Mckim: *Village India: Studies in the Little Community*, The University of Chicago Press, Chicago, 1955.

Michael J.: *The Untouchables in Contemporary India*, University of Arizona Press, Arizona, 1972.

Mohan, P.E.: *Scheduled Castes: History of Elevation, Tamil Nadu, 1900-1955*. New Era Pub., Madras, 1993.

Mumtaz Ali: *Human Rights and the Dalits*, Uppal Publishing House, New Delhi, 1995.

Naidu, Ch. M.: *Salt Satyagraha in the Coastal Andhra*, Mittal Publications, Delhi, 1986.

Nath, Trilok: *Politics of the Depressed Classes*, Deputy Publications, Delhi, 1987.

Nim, H.L.: *Thoughts on Dr. Ambedkar*, Siddhartha Educational and Cultural Society, Agra, 1969.

O'Malley, L. S. S.: *Indian Caste Customs*, Vikas Publishing House, Delhi, 1974.

Omprakash, S.: *Development of the Weaker Section: Problems, Policies and Issues*, Uppal Publishing House, New Delhi, 1989.

Omvedt, G.: *Dalits and the Democratic Revolution: Dr Ambedkar and the Dalit Movement in Colonial India*, Sage, New Delhi, 1994.

Pantavane, G.: *Patrikar Dr. Babasaheb Ambedkar*, Abhijit, Nagpur, 1987.

Parmaji, S.: *Caste Reservations and Performance*, Mamata Publications, Warangal, 1985.

Pradhan, A. C.: *The Emergence of the Depressed Classes*, Bookland International, Bhubaneshwar, 1986.

Prahlad G.: *Dalit Movement in Maharashtra*, Kanak Publications, New Delhi, 1991.

Rajasekharaiah, A.M.: *B.R. Ambedkar: the Politics of Emancipation*, Sindhu Publications, Bombay, 1971.

Raju, G.G.: *The Life of B.R. Ambedkar*, Babasaheb Dr. Ambedkar Memorial Society, Hyderabad, 1979.

Ram, B.: *Educating Harijans*, Academic Press, Haryana, 1981.

Ram, Jagivan: *Caste Challenge in India*, Vision Books, New Delhi, 1980.

Robb, Peter: *Dalit Movements and the Meanings of Labour in India*, Oxford University Press, New Delhi, 1993.

Shabbir, M.: *B.R. Ambedkar. Study in Law & Society,* Rawat, Jaipur, 1997.

Shah, Ghanshyam: *Caste Association and Political Processes in Gujarat*, Popular Prakashan, Bombay, 1975.

Sharma, Kusum: *Ambedkar and Indian Constitution*, New Delhi, Ashish Pub. House, 1992.

Shetty, V. T. Rajshekar: *Dalit Movement in Karnataka*, Christian Literature Society, Madras, 1978.

Shyam, L.: *Caste and Political Mobilisation: The Bhangis*, Panchsheel Prakashan, Jaipur, 1981.

Silverberg, James: *Social Mobility in the Caste System in India*, Mouton Publishers, The Hague, 1968.

Tope, T.K.: *Dr. B.R. Ambedkar, A Symbol of Social Revolt*, Maharashtra Information Centre, New Delhi, 1964.

Varale, B.H.: *Dr. Babasaheb Ambedkarrancha Sangaki*, Shrividya Prakashan, Pune, 1988.

Vasant, D.: *Towards Social Intergration: Problems of Adjustment of SC Elites*, Shubhada- Saraswat, Pune, 1978.

Wolf, G.: *Re-inventing Tradition,* Indian Institute of Advanced Studies, Shimla, 1992.

Index

A

Achievement, 16, 147.
Administering, 14, 16, 39.
Ahicchatra, 4.
Ambalatthika, 28, 50.
Ancient Regime, 3, 7.
Aryan Society, 3, 4, 5, 7, 15, 17, 19, 20, 21, 27, 39, 44, 280.
Aryans, 3, 4, 5, 6, 7, 19, 21, 22, 23, 25, 26, 27, 102, 164, 165, 273, 274, 275, 276.
Aryavarta, 4.
Asura, 1, 2, 4, 19, 27, 247, 249, 263, 264, 266, 267, 273, 274, 275.

B

Badarayana, 80, 81, 82, 91, 92, 93, 95, 96, 211, 216, 217, 229.
Ballads Recitations, 8, 31.
Bhagvat Gita, 71, 205, 206, 208, 209, 210, 211, 212, 213, 214, 215, 216, 217, 218, 219, 220, 221, 222, 224, 225, 226, 227, 228, 229, 230.
Brahaspati, 4, 19.
Brahma, 5, 21, 22, 27, 45, 77, 88, 195, 199, 211, 216, 217, 237, 248, 249, 250, 251, 257, 259, 261, 273.
Brahma Jala Sutta, 27.
Brahmadatta, 28.
Brahmana, 67, 79, 93, 100, 108, 114, 115, 116, 117, 118, 119, 120, 121, 124, 130, 152, 155, 160, 161, 162, 163, 169, 170, 173, 174, 175, 176, 182, 183, 247, 268, 270, 271, 272, 278, 279.
Brahmanism, 64, 66, 67, 68, 71, 101, 102, 103, 104, 105, 106, 111, 112, 114, 117, 119, 122, 123, 126, 127, 128, 129, 131, 132, 133, 134, 141, 144, 145, 147, 148, 149, 155, 159, 164, 169, 170, 171, 172, 175, 176, 217, 218.
Brahmins, 4, 5, 7, 8, 10, 12, 13, 14, 16, 19, 20, 21, 26, 27, 60, 64, 67, 68, 71, 75, 81, 84, 85, 89, 91, 101, 103, 104, 108, 109, 112, 113, 114, 115, 117, 118, 119, 120, 122, 124, 126, 127, 128, 129, 143, 145, 150, 151, 159, 160, 165, 166, 167, 168, 169, 170, 172, 173, 174, 175, 180, 181, 182, 204, 212, 229, 244, 246, 249, 253, 262, 263, 265, 267, 268, 269, 271, 273, 276, 277.

Buddha, 2, 3, 15, 16, 17, 18, 27, 28, 40, 41, 57, 58, 59, 60, 61, 62, 65, 70, 85, 165, 167, 169, 212, 213, 217, 219, 220, 229, 230.
Buddhism, 3, 17, 40, 41, 61, 62, 63, 64, 65, 66, 67, 68, 70, 71, 76, 82, 101, 102, 104, 105, 107, 108, 109, 110, 111, 112, 129, 134, 144, 151, 158, 159, 180, 212, 213, 215, 217, 218, 219, 220, 221, 229, 230.
Buddhist, 2, 5, 17, 18, 21, 26, 40, 63, 64, 65, 67, 68, 69, 70, 71, 75, 82, 85, 90, 104, 105, 106, 107, 108, 109, 110, 111, 112, 129, 133, 134, 151, 154, 157, 159, 165, 166, 167, 180, 181, 212, 217, 218, 219, 220, 224, 226, 229, 230.

C

Chaitya, 75, 85.
Communication, 149.
Community, 2, 3, 15, 18, 124, 127, 146, 147, 166, 179, 181, 223, 262, 270, 272, 273, 274, 276.
Consequences, 3, 19, 24, 128, 173, 175, 256.
Culture, 102, 111, 150, 151, 186, 274, 275, 276.

D

Dasyus, 27, 273, 274, 275, 276.
Debauchery, 3, 18, 27.
Decline, 3, 19, 61, 71, 77, 82, 252, 254, 260.
Development, 16.

E

Ekantalomi, 9, 33.
Essential, 7, 18, 23, 72, 78, 104, 123, 124, 125, 128, 140, 144, 147, 177, 178, 181, 209, 214, 275.
Exhumation, 1, 2.

F

Fall of Buddhism, 61, 62, 68, 71.

G

Gana, 1, 33, 66, 280.
Gandharva, 1, 273.
Geneology of Vyas, 130.
Government, 52, 69, 113, 171.

H

Husband His Varna, 130.

K

Karmakanda, 80, 95, 96.
Katthissam, 9, 33.
Katyayana, 153, 271, 278.
Kaurvas, 232.
Kinnars, 1, 273.
Krishna, 4, 19, 27, 66, 79, 96, 97, 98, 99, 148, 205, 206, 207, 208, 209, 213, 214, 218, 219, 220, 223, 225, 226, 227, 228, 229, 234, 235, 236, 237, 238, 239, 240, 241, 242, 243, 256.
Kshatriyas, 4, 5, 10, 19, 20, 21, 34, 52, 56, 64, 113, 115, 118, 124, 134, 162, 169, 170, 172, 173, 174, 175, 176, 204, 241, 244, 249, 262, 263, 265, 266, 267, 268, 269, 272, 273, 276, 277.
Kutadanta Sutta, 50.

L

Laja Hoame, 6, 23.
Leadership, 63, 91.
Literature, 2, 26, 71, 72, 75, 76, 77, 78, 79, 80, 81, 82, 85, 89, 90, 124, 167, 174, 177, 196, 205, 206, 211, 212, 216, 244, 273, 277.

M

Magadha, 50, 103.
Mahabharat, 1, 3, 4, 19, 67, 71, 73, 74, 75, 76, 79, 83, 84, 85, 86, 91, 96, 97, 221, 222, 223, 224, 225, 228, 245, 246, 258, 260, 262, 264, 276, 277.
Mahabharata, 67, 73, 74, 75, 76, 79, 83, 84, 85, 86, 91, 97, 221, 222, 223, 224, 225, 228, 245, 246, 258, 260, 264, 276, 277.
Management, 159.
Morals, 137, 138, 139, 176, 177, 190, 225.

O

Opportunity, 43, 259, 261.

P

Patika, 9, 33.
Philosophic, 81, 205, 206, 209, 210, 211, 213, 214, 215, 226, 227, 228, 230.
Politics, 74, 83, 111, 176.
Puranas, 71, 76, 86, 87, 88, 89, 90, 91, 125, 202, 224, 225.
Purgatives, 14, 39.
Purva Mimansa, 80, 214, 215, 216, 217, 220, 227, 230, 278.

R

Rajanya, 279.
Ramayana, 1, 71, 75, 76, 85, 86, 249.
Reformers, 15.
Regicide, 101, 104, 112, 113.
Religious, 3, 5, 6, 17, 18, 22, 42, 49, 60, 66, 68, 70, 73, 74, 76, 79, 83, 84, 86, 97, 102, 119, 122, 124, 137, 144, 151, 152, 168, 177, 180. 181, 182, 193, 196, 201, 202, 211, 226, 256, 267, 270, 273.
Revolution, 3, 61, 72, 77, 101, 103, 105, 106, 109, 112, 114, 129, 151, 163, 164, 165, 177, 205, 211, 212, 213, 214, 215, 218, 221, 229, 230, 244, 270.

S

Sacrifice, 11, 14, 20, 24, 25, 26, 35, 39, 41, 42, 43, 44, 45, 46, 47, 48, 49, 50, 51, 52, 53, 54, 55, 56, 57, 58, 60, 91, 92, 94, 95, 99, 108, 109, 119, 124, 125, 133, 163, 175, 198, 213, 214, 215, 216, 219, 222, 224, 225, 226, 229, 235, 244, 251, 274, 277, 278, 280.
Sairandhri, 4, 20.
Sansakara, 280.
Sauttarakkhadam, 9, 33.
Shankaracharya, 71, 72, 73, 81, 82, 208, 209.
Shudra, 4, 19, 20, 21, 63, 75, 85, 101, 112, 124, 126, 129, 130, 131, 148, 151, 152, 153, 154, 155, 157, 159, 160, 161, 162, 163, 170, 171, 172, 175, 176,

193, 194, 196, 203, 212, 214, 220, 237, 270, 271, 272, 273, 274, 275, 276, 277, 278, 279, 280.
Social order, 123, 159, 182, 190, 274.
Social Reform, 15.
Social Structure, 111.
Social System, 101, 102, 112, 129, 131, 162.
Society, 3, 4, 5, 7, 15, 17, 19, 20, 21, 27, 39, 40, 75, 85, 105, 117, 122, 123, 129, 130, 135, 139, 145, 146, 147, 149, 163, 164, 165, 166, 169, 170, 171, 172, 177, 213, 220, 257, 270, 276, 277.
Sunken Priesthood, 7.
Suppiya, 28.
Suta, 58, 89, 233, 277.

T

Their Fate, 15.
Triumph, 73, 83, 91, 101, 104, 111, 112, 123, 129, 134, 151, 159.

U

Uddalomi, 33.
Udyog Parva, 205, 230, 235.
Udyogaparva, 234, 246.
Ultara Mimansa, 80.

V

Vaishya, 4, 5, 19, 20, 21, 25, 73, 113, 117, 118, 124, 152, 154, 155, 160, 162, 163, 170, 171, 172, 175, 176, 270, 272, 273, 276, 277, 279.
Vamdevya vrata, 5, 22.
Varnas, 4, 114, 125, 130, 147, 148, 149, 162, 172, 182, 186, 191, 204, 213.
Vashishtha, 130, 174, 249, 250, 251, 252, 256, 257, 258, 259, 260, 261, 268, 277.
Vedant Sutras, 76, 79.
Vedanta, 71, 80, 81, 82, 91, 92, 93, 95, 96, 98, 206, 227, 228, 229.
Vedanta Sutras, 71, 81, 82, 91.
Vedas, 41, 53, 67, 79, 80, 86, 87, 91, 92, 94, 98, 99, 100, 108, 115, 117, 120, 144, 152, 153, 158, 184, 189, 190, 195, 196, 197, 202, 203, 212, 213, 214, 217, 262, 265, 271, 278.
Vikatika, 9, 33.
Virat Nagari, 231, 232, 234.
Virat Parva, 205, 230, 231.
Vishvamitra, 174, 249, 250, 251, 252, 253, 254, 255, 256, 257, 258, 259, 260, 261, 264, 277.
Vrashalas, 75, 84, 85.
Vyasa, 98, 221, 222, 224, 225.

W

Weapons, 12, 36, 96, 198, 232, 250, 251, 266.
Welfare, 42, 43, 51, 52, 146, 261.
Wisdom, 41, 48, 99.
Wrong Sacrifice, 50.

Y

Yadna, 7, 24, 25, 26, 27, 41, 50, 74.
Yadnya Bhumi, 22.
Yaksha, 1, 98, 273.
Yeduka, 75, 85.

□□□